2010 ■ 65ᵗʰ Edition
COINS

The definitive U.S. coin guide since 1943

Frederick Fell Publishers, Inc
2131 Hollywood Blvd., Suite 305
Hollywood, Fl 33020
www.Fellpub.com
email: Fellpub@aol.com

Frederick Fell Publishers, Inc
2131 Hollywood Blvd., Suite 305
Hollywood, Fl 33020

For information about special discounts for bulk purchases, Please contact Frederick Fell Special Sales at business@fellpublishers.com.

Designed by Elena Solis

Manufactured in the United States of America
10 9 8 7 6 5 4 3 2 1

Library of Congress Cataloging-in-Publication Data

Nolte, Steve.
 Coins 2010 : your absolute, quintessential, all you wanted to know, complete guide / Steve Nolte. -- 65th ed., ISSN: 1541-8022
    p. cm.
"First Frederick Fell trade book edition"--T.p. verso.
ISBN-13: 978-0-88391-174-7 (pbk. : alk. paper)
1. Coins, American--Collectors and collecting--Handbooks, manuals, etc. I. Title.
CJ1832.N638 2008
737.4973--dc22
                    2008035759
                                        ISSN: 1541-8022

ISBN 13 978-0-88391-174-7

2010

65th Edition

COINS

The definitive U.S. coin guide since 1943

Part of the New

Numismatic
Library
Series

STEVE NOLTE
Member of the Numismatic Association

COLLECTORS UPDATE
United States Mint Coinage

The US Mint certainly has an ambitious agenda for 2009 coinage. The 100th Anniversary of the Lincoln Cent and the New Circulating Quarters program will tease the average coin collector with many variations in types minted this year. They are hard to find, slow to be released to banks, and highly in demand. Specially prepared sets should have a strong demand by collectors this year in an effort to go around the circulating shortages. The US Mint Set will contain 48 different P and D mint coins alone - a record number. The US Mint Proof Sets (both the Clad and the Silver) are growing in size too. Silver and Gold Eagles will be minted in various permutations, and with the economy struggling, the coins made available by the US Mint have seen incredible demand. So much so, that the mint has begun producing coins to order, and projecting weeks or months of backorder on its products.

Circulating "Business Strike" Coinage: The 4 different types of Lincoln Cents, with issue dates spaced out over the calendar year have set the tone for strong demand by collectors. Limited mintages of Nickels and Dimes are sure to drive up prices for these low mintage coins. US Mint press releases have announced that the annual production of these two denominations ended early in the year - essentially guaranteeing one of the lowest mintages in recent history. The 6 circulating Washington DC and US Territories Quarters are making their way into the business channels, but their mintages will be much, much lower than those of the previous state quarter circulating commemorative quarters. Kennedy Half dollars are minted in limited quantities and can only be obtained from the mint. Like those of the past 10+ years, there will be few if any placed into circulation. The Sacagawea Dollar coin has a new reverse for 2009 and there are 4 new Presidential Coins offered.

Silver/Gold Eagles and Bullion Coins: 2009 Silver Eagles fly out of the mint as fast as the mint can find planchets. Burnished "W" Mint and Proof versions should be equally in demand. Gold Eagles come only in one ounce versions this year, but are having a banner year for sales also. Of special note is the mints 2009 Ultra High Relief "St. Gaudens $20" retro coin. These are simply gorgeous, expensive, and heavily in demand.

Commemoratives and Spouses: 2009 reveals Proof and Uncirculated versions of the Lincoln and Braille 90% Silver Commemorative Dollars. First Spouse, $10 Gold coins again are offered in relatively low quantity for each of the President's wives (Harrison, Tyler, Polk, and Taylor).

2009 LINCOLN CENTS

While 2009 is the 100th anniversary of the Lincoln Cent, it is also the 200th Anniversary of Abraham Lincoln's birth. 4 different cents are being minted this year and the coins are minted in both zinc composition and their original 1909 composition of 95% copper. Details of the 2009 cents:

Released 2/12/09 to commemorate Lincoln's birth and childhood in Kentucky.

Released 5/14/09 showcasing the formative years in Indiana.

Released 8/13/09 in Illinois as a reminder of Lincoln's professional life in Illinois.

Released 11/12/09 in Washington DC as a commemorative of his Presidency.

Proof Coinage: The 18 coin 2009 Proof Set issued beginning 6/1/2009 includes proof examples of each of the four types of cents — coined in 95% Copper as were the original coins 100 years earlier.

Circulating Coinage: Each of the designs were first released to the public in a special ceremony in the state corresponding to the stage of Lincolns life. These follow the composition of the 2008 cents. The demand for examples of each coin far exceed supply. Immediately following each release date, coins were seen on auction sites at $10.00 or more per roll. Banks around the country have seen few of the coins to put into circulation, so many collectors purchased two roll sets (p and d) directly from the mint at $8.95 per the pair.

US Mint Sets: The Lincoln Cents that arrive in the 48 coin Mint Sets are slated to come out in 95% copper composition.

Special Sets: The US mint is offering special sets of Lincoln Cents that will come out late in 2009 and have both mint and proof coins in both compositions. Details are still forthcoming.

2009 JEFFERSON NICKEL

5 Cent Piece: The 2009 Jefferson Nickel could easily have the lowest mintage of any nickel in over 50 years. The last year that mintages dropped below 70,000,000 coins was 1951. With annual production ceasing in April of 2009, it seems highly likely that the 2009 Nickel will come in under 80,000,000 coins made for the year. With annual mintages of prior year coins in the billions, the availability of circulated coins will be greatly reduced. Early auction sales saw individual coins from the Philadelphia mint selling in the $20 range. Denver mint coins have not shown up yet.

2009 ROOSEVELT DIME

10 Cent Piece: The 2009 Roosevelt Dime mirrors the production woes of the nickel. With annual production ceasing in April of 2009, it seems highly likely that the 2009 Dime will only count up to 146,000,000 pieces. With annual mintages of prior year coins in the billions, the availability of circulated dimes will be greatly reduced like their nickel cousins. Early auction sales saw individual coins selling in the $3-$4 range from Philadelphia. Denver mint coins have not surfaced as of yet.

US Mint Sets: The US Mint Sets coming out in Fall 2009 will have both Philadelphia and Denver mint examples of both Nickels and Dimes in the 48 coin set.

Proof Sets: The US mint Proof Sets will be made with specially prepared San Francisco mint nickels and dimes in 2009.

2009 WASHINGTON DC AND US TERRITORIES QUARTERS

Over 37 Billion State Quarters were minted during the 1999-2008 run from the mint. Each year, 5 states in order, were celebrated on the reverse of the Washington Quarter and circulated throughout the country. The fifty states quarter run ended in 2008, but the idea returns for 2009 in the guise of 6 coins celebrating Washington DC and five US Territories.

During 2009, the coins will be released into circulation about every two months in the following sequence:

1. **The District of Columbia**
2. **The Commonwealth of Puerto Rico**
3. **Guam**
4. **American Samoa**
5. **The United States Virgin Islands**
6. **The Commonwealth of the Northern Mariana Islands**

Like their earlier counterparts, each of the quarters is struck for circulation at both the Philadelphia and the Denver Mints. Proof versions are minted at San Francisco in both Clad versions (the same composition as circulation strikes) as well as in 90% Silver composition. Expect 2009 quarters to have much lower mintages than each of the State Quarter releases. 2009.

QUARTERS CAN BE FOUND IN:

Circulation Quality/Business Strikes:
Coins are being distributed through the Federal Reserve to banks for use in commerce. Coins will be distributed with Philadelphia and Denver mint marks.

US Uncirculated Mint Sets/ Business Strikes:
The US mint will include one of each Philadelphia and Denver mint coin it its 48 coin mint set to be available in the Fall of 2009.

Special DC & US Territory Proof Sets/Proof Strikes:
Both Clad (Cupro-Nickel) and Silver versions of each coin are available in special sets from the US Mint with San Francisco Mint mark designations that contain all 6 of the Quarters.

Regular US Clad and Proof Sets/ Proof Strikes:
Both Clad (Cupro-Nickel) and Silver versions of each coin are available in special sets from the US Mint with San Francisco Mint mark designations that contain all 6 of the Quarters along with all other 2009 Coins.

2009 JOHN F. KENNEDY HALF DOLLARS

2009 US fifty cent coins are minted purely for collectors again this year and are available only through the US Mint. Generally you will not find any in circulation, nor will your bank carry these coins. Only a few million coins are minted each year, spread evenly between the Philadelphia, Denver, and San Francisco mints. The coins minted in San Francisco are all proof coins and are prepared in both the clad and 90% silver compositions.

2009 SACAGAWEA "GOLDEN" DOLLARS

2009 US Sacagawea Dollar coins should be available both through regular circulation channels as well as directly from the mint. Each year, the reverse changes on the Sac Dollars to represent one of the scenes from Indian nations. The 2009 coins may be referred to as the "3 Sisters" variety due to the scene on the reverse of a woman planting Beans, Corn, and Squash. Coins are minted at the Philadelphia, Denver, and San Francisco mints. The coins minted in San Francisco are proof coins. **The Sacagawea Dollar coins are minted in sufficient quantity to meet the needs of the country, at least 20% of the dollar coins minted must be Sacagawea dollars. The US Mint also mints presidential dollar coins during 2009 in similarly color and composition. Four different Presidents will be showcased on 2009 Coinage.**

2009 PRESIDENTIAL DOLLARS

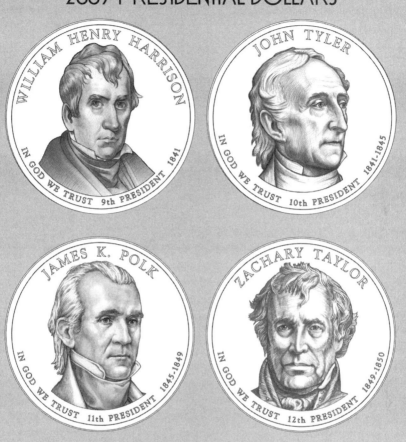

The third year of the Presidential Dollars begins with the ninth president, William Henry Harrison and ends the year with the 12th President, Zachary Taylor. Sandwiched in between are coins to commemorate John Tyler and James Polk. Mintages are lower of the 2009 Presidential Coins than their 2007 and 2008 counterparts echoing a saga of most of the 2009 mint coinage.

Circulation quality Presidential Dollar Coins are circulation quality coins, and minted at Philadelphia and Denver, are issued through the Federal Reserve to Banks. The coins will also be part of the US Mints Uncirculated Mint Set, Proof Sets, and Special Proof edition for just the 4 coins with 2009 dates.

COLLECTORS UPDATE

2009 FIRST SPOUSE COINS

JULIA TYLER

ANNA HARRISON

The US Mint has issues, each year, companion coins to the Presidential Dollars to commemorate each of their Spouses. For 2009, that translates into Anna Harrison, Julia Tyler, Letitia Tylor, Margaret Taylor, and Sarah Polk. The 5 First Spouse Coins for 2009 are a change from past practices, as only 4 Presidents are recognized each year. However a second First Spouse coin is needed in 2009 for John Tyler, as his first wife died while in office and he remarried leading to a second first spouse for his term of office. Each coin is 1/2 ounce of pure gold .9999 minted at West Point in Uncirculated and Proof condition. Coins are available from the US Mint.

MARGARET TAYLOR

SARAH POLK

LETITIA TYLER

2009 AMERICAN EAGLES
GOLD, SILVER & PLATINUM COINS

The Economy may wreak havoc with 2009 Coinage —numbers of coins minted as well as varieties minted by the Mint — especially in relation to Bullion Coinage.

Silver Eagles: The Mint is on pace to have a record year for Silver American Eagle coins. For the latter part of 2008 and the early days of 2009, the mint experienced a shortage of planchets. For 2009, the mint has hinted that no burnished Silver Eagles (Special West Point Mintages) for 2009 as they had in 2006, 2007, and 2008. Expected: 2009 Proof Silver Eagles should be minted late in the year.

Gold Eagles: The US Mint experienced even more trouble obtaining enough gold planchets this year than it did with Silver, and place most of the emphasis on the new High Relief 2009 St. Gaudiens issue. Moreover, in 2009, the US mint may not produce fractional versions of its uncirculated Gold Eagles or Gold Bison coins as it did in past years. 1/10th ounce 1/4 ounce, & 1/2 ounce pieces may not appear at all, or if they do, only in Proof versions —and perhaps only available in the 4 piece proof Gold set.

Platinum. Platinum coins are still on the Mint's agenda, but none have been minted at just past half the year.

Ultra High Relief Gold Coins This fabulous coin is a digitally reproduced version of Saint-Gaudens' original ultra high relief 1907 Double Eagle gold piece, which was never released into circulation. This is a one ounce 24 K version selling for $1289.00

2009 COMMEMORATIVE COINS

ABRAHAM LINCOLN

The 2009 Lincoln Commemorative, sold out early in 2009, was released in both proof and uncirculated versions with a combined authorized mintage of 500,000 coins. The United States Mint released the 2009 Abraham Lincoln Commemorative Silver Dollar on February 12, 2009. This date also marked the 200th anniversary of Lincoln's birth and the release date for the first 2009 Lincoln Cent design.

LOUIS BRAILLE

Congress authorized the U.S. Mint to produce a silver dollar commemorating the 200th anniversary of the birth of Louis Braille, creator of the alphabet for the blind. The second 2009 Commemorative Coin offered by the US Mint became available to purchase from the mint on March 26, 2009. The obverse of the coin bears his portrait and the inscriptions "Louis Braille", "Liberty", "In God We Trust", the dual date "1809 and "2009 and mint mark "P" to represent mintage at the Philadelphia Mint. 400,000 of the coins are to be minted in either Uncirculated or Proof versions. The coins feature Braille's image and raised dots that will spell out "Brl," the contraction for Braille.

2009 US MINT TREATS

PRESIDENTIAL DOLLAR & FIRST SPOUSE MEDAL SET

Sets are offered directly through the mint for a short period of time during the release period for each dollar coin. 4 sets are issued each year for a nominal price ($7.95 - $8.95).

The 2007 Sets are no longer available from the mint (but they can be found in the secondary market, or on Ebay) have steadily risen in value and both the George Washington and Thomas Jefferson sets are selling over $100.00 each at the time of this printing.

2008 Sets are also no longer available from the mint, and like their 2007 counterparts are rising in value. The John Quincy Adams set is currently the highest priced set for 2008, routinely selling for $25 or more.

The sets must be catching on as good value for the price — and with very good upside potential. For 2009, only the William Henry Harrison set has been offered at mid year time, and the sets are always on back order.

WILLIAM HENRY HARRISON MEDAL SET

PREDICTING 2010 US MINT COIN ISSUES

Trend lines will easily show that the number of US Mint Issued Coins is in decline. From nearly 14.44 Billion coins minted in 2007 to 10.14 Billion in 2008 and estimating only 3,000,000,000 coins for 2010, the number of coins with the current year date on them will be greatly reduced for the foreseeable future. The engines of commerce only require so many coins each year, and the Federal Reserve is stockpiled high with many previous year's coins - especially Dollars.

For 2009, this translated into the US Mint ending mintages of circulating nickels and dimes near the first quarter of the year. With mintages approaching 10% of the previous year's numbers, it is becoming harder and harder to find current year dated coins. Due to the recession, depression, and forecasts for the future, 2010 will most likely not show any improvement in the number of newly minted coins available to the coin collector.

So ... here goes one forecast for 2010 US Mint Coinage

ONE CENT

The Circulating Bicentennial Lincoln Cent ends its four coin reign at the end of 2009. There will be a new 2010 design, that is still much up in the air. Below is one artists conception of what it may look like ... but it is only a possibility. The one thing certain is that the reverse will be very much different on the 2010 penny. The obverse will most likely stay the same Abraham Lincoln portrait as on coins since 1959.

2010 LINCOLN CENT

What will mintages look like for 2010? That is anyone's guess. While 2009 saw four different designs, with four different release dates, the combinations made it much harder for collectors to obtain a full set of 2009 pennies. With just one design, the penny should be more available, even if the total mintages stay about the same.

2010 NICKELS

Count on about the same situation in 2010 as in 2009. Low mintages, slow distribution, little ability for collectors to purchase coins in bulk, heavy reliance on more readily available mint and proof sets. Coins will be available with Philadelphia, Denver and San Francisco mint marks as in the past.

2010 DIMES

This may begin to sound like a broken record. I cannot imagine any difference in minting or availability in 2010 as in 2009. Low mintages, slow distribution, little ability for collectors to purchase coins in bulk, heavy reliance on more readily available mint and proof sets. Coins will be available with Philadelphia, Denver and San Francisco mint marks as in the past.

2010 HALVES

John F. Kennedy will once again rule the half dollar market, but only for collectors. The mint will continue to sell the coins in mint sets, proof sets, and silver mint sets, and another million or so in rolls of 20 coin, Philadelphia and Denver rolls, of business strike, uncirculated coins for collectors.

2010 BULLION COINS

Expect more of the same in 2010. Silver Eagles available in mass quantity early in the year, followed by Proof versions later in the year. Gold Eagles sold to collectors and investors looking for a hedge against lower stock and bond earnings. Platinum Eagles too.

NATIONAL PARK QUARTERS

Following on the heels of the very successful 50 State's Quarters program (1999-2008) and the 2009 Washington DC and US Territory Quarters, Congress has authorized a very ambitious 11 year program for circulating commemorative quarters. Over the next 11 years (2010 through 2021) at least 56 individual quarters, at the rate of 5 per year, will be minted to commemorate America's National Monuments or National Parks.

The National Parks Quarter Dollar Coin Act of 1988 requires that one national park in every state or territory be minted with reverse designs emblematic of one national site for each state. There are several hundred parks that are candidates for a quarter design ranging from Abraham Lincoln Birthplace National Historic Site in Hodgenville, Kentucky through Yukon-Charley Rivers National Preserve in Eagle, Alaska. The sites won't be selected till late 2009, so they will not be available till the update of this book is printed in the Spring.

While it is certainly expected that each coin will be minted at the Philadelphia and Denver mint for circulation, as well as at the San Francisco mint for both Clad and Silver Proof strikes, the most innovative part of this legislation is the call for 5 ounce silver, large size duplicates of each of the quarters for sale to the public.

SACAGAWEA DOLLARS

The 2010 Sacagawea dollar once again requires a special one-year reverse design celebrating the important contributions made by Indian Tribes and individual Native Americans to the history and development of the United States. For 2009, it was the "3 Sisters" reverse design. For 2010, the U.S. Commission of Fine Arts recommends a design showing a ceremonial woven wampum belt and five interlocking arrows on the reverse. Sacagawea's rendition remains on the obverse.

2010 PRESIDENTIAL DOLLARS

The Fourth year of the Presidential Dollars begins with the 13th president, Millard Fillmore and ends the 2010 year with the 16th President, Abraham Lincoln. Sandwiched in between are coins to commemorate Franklin Pierce and James Buchanan. The number of coins minted and availability to collectors and the public should generally be about the same as in 2009.

Presidential Dollar Coins are circulation quality coins, and minted at Philadelphia and Denver. These "business strikes" are issued through the Federal Reserve to Banks. The coins will also be part of the US Mints Uncirculated Mint Set, Proof Sets, and Special Proof editions available directly from the US Mint. 2010 Presidents in order of their release include:

- **Milliard Fillmore**
  13th President 1850-1853
- **Franklin Pierce**
  14th President 1853-1857

- **James Buchanan**
  15th President 1857-1861
- **Abraham Lincoln**
  16th President 1861-1865

FILLMORE • PIERCE • BUCHANAN • LINCOLN

2010 FIRST SPOUSE COINS

Again in 2010, the President's Wives (First Spouse) coins will be offered through the mint. First to grace the year is Abigail Fillmore, followed by Jane Pierce, A rendition of "Liberty" since there was no first lady under Buchanan, and rounding out 2010 with Mary Lincoln.

Each "first spouse" will be celebrated on a $10.00 Gold Coin - both in Proof and Uncirculated condition. While the gold coins come with very low mintages, the US Mint also coins Bronze Medals of each first spouse, sold individually through the mint and also included in the Presidential Dollar and First Spouse Medal Set.
2010 Commemorative Coins

Maintaining a tradition of issuing two commemorative coins each calendar year, the US Mint has been authorized to release two new, 2010 coins in commemoration of Disabled Veterans and The Boy Scouts.

DISABLED VETERANS

The US House and Senate unanimously passed a bill in July of 2008 authorizing the Secretary of the Treasury to mint coins in commemoration of veterans who become disabled for life while serving in the Armed Forces of the United States. Revenues will go to help build and maintain the American Veterans Disabled for Live Memorial (AVDLM). Each legal tender, $1 coin, will be made out of 90% silver and 10% copper. The design for the coin will be selected by the Secretary of the Treasury, after consultation with Disabled Veteran's LIFE Memorial Foundation (DVLMF) and the Commission of Fine Arts.

BOY SCOUTS OF AMERICA

The legislation authorizing a Boy Scouts of America commemorative coin was signed into law in October 2008 by President Bush. The 100th anniversary of the Boy Scouts will be celebrated in 2010 and commemorated by up to 350,000 US Commemorative Silver Dollars.

The Boy Scouts of America were founded on February 8, 1910. The legislation states that the design must be emblematic of the 100 years of the largest youth organization in the United States. The coin must also show its designated value, the year 2010, Liberty, In God We Trust, and E Pluribus Unum.

The ultimate design will be selected by the Secretary of the Treasury.

2010 PART II ...

COINS 2010 is a two volume, two release treasury of Numismatic Information. The Spring 2010 edition will bring a complete update to coinage of 2010, as well as a forecast of 2011. Watch for the update in your favorite bookstores in Mid Spring.

TABLE OF CONTENTS

PREFACE

The values of coins showcased in the 2010 edition were complied from personal experience, dealer reports, and the actual prices paid for coins in the United States. Prices represent 10% to 30% above wholesale dealer-to-dealer prices.

As a service to you, I will provide answers to coin-related questions. Should you wish to have a coin identified or need to know where to get an appraisal for a collection, answers may be obtained by sending a self-addressed stamped envelope to me at the following address:

Steve Nolte
P.O. Box 22035
Fort Lauderdale Florida 33335

It is important to give special recognition to the Florida Numismatic Board comprised of leaders from both outstanding and long standing coin clubs in the Greater Fort Lauderdale area in supporting our quest for numismatic leadership.

Steve Nolte

x

ACKNOWLEDGEMENTS

Virtually all the coin photos for this volume were supplied by Numismatic Guaranty Corporation of America (NGC). The offices of NGC are located at Box 4776, Sarasota, Florida 34230. Telephone 941-360-3990 or 800-NGC-COIN. Fax 941-360-2553. Fell recommends the staff at NGC as consummate professionals for any of your coin authentication and certification needs.

The author must also both acknowledge and thank the efforts of Elena Solis for the design work on this book. Her style is inviting, her philosophy is perfection, and her efforts make both the author and Fells shine in ways we both only could ever hope.

INTRODUCTION

This familiar book is written to serve two groups of people. The first is the beginning collector struggling with basic information and financial concerns. This book should assist this type of collector seeking to build a collection that may retain or increase its value.

The middle chapters provide accurate price information on virtually all coins of more than nominal value from half cents to $20 gold pieces.

Chapter 2 is meant to introduce the necessary criteria to determine the worth of a coin. This section contains an initial discussion of what has come to be the most subjective area of the hobby—grading. The recent emergence of a number of grading and authentication services points up the degree to which even an experienced collector is unwilling to rely on his own expertise.

The vast price differences that can now be found, especially between the higher grades of uncirculated coins, has had a chilling effect on potential buyers, to say nothing of the substantial losses suffered by those who have for one reason or another purchased substantially—or even slightly—over graded coins.

Later chapters survey the rudiments of coin collecting. Collecting accessories, where and how to acquire and sell coins, and sources for furthering one's knowledge of numismatics are some of the topics.

The **Centerpiece** to this book is new, and provides a special, set-aside glimpse into the current coin market. It begins with a look back at 2009 US Coin Production as it unfolds throughout the year, and continues with a forecast for 2010 US Coinage. This piece alone is worth the price of admission into COINS 2010. This feature will continue as your annual COINS Publication shifts to a twice a year format in the Spring of 2010. You will find this edition's Centerpiece section following page 138 in the text.

The second group served equally well through the topics contained in this book are non-collectors — those who have come across an occasional coin that looks to be old and valuable. Often it is difficult to get some sense of real value even from friends and relatives who may be to some degree interested in coins. This volume will help non-collectors get a good idea about whether a professional opinion should be sought.

One of the more common challenges that this second group encounters is what to do with a coin collection that is given or passed down to them upon the death of a family member. Who to turn to? It seems unwise to trust blindly in the judgment of anyone until a cursory knowledge of coins and their values is obtained.

One point that applies to readers at any level: It is inadvisable to every clean a coin. The entire numismatic value of a coin can be immediately erased by putting a coin in an acid mix or cleaning solution—or even rubbing a coin with a clean, soft cloth. From a financial standpoint, the more natural state that a coin is kept in, the greater the potential for value.

This volume, therefore, should help prepare the individual with a sense of comfort and confidence about their coins. In doing so, the knowledge obtained through Fells Coins 2010 gives the reader a chance at a level playing field when navigating through the business side of numismatics. For those seeking more basic and in-depth exploration of these topics, please see Fell's latest contribution to its Numismatic Series: ***Collecting US Coins on a Budget*** and ***Collecting Modern Coins***.

COIN MARKET 2009
Generally Speaking

C oin Collectors have found the coin market very, very good to them over the past decade. And although certain cautions and economic realities are present today that have not been so apparent during the past few years, 2010 promises much to the informed coin collector - and to the hobby. All in the numismatic community - buyers, sellers, suppliers, and investors - have seen their coins grow in value and in demand through the first few years of this 21st Century. This continuing upward trend may not play out quite so universally this year. In spite of US and World economies sputtering, receding, or even worse, coin prices have remained very steady. While millions of Americans have found themselves upside down in their mortgages, the same have seen some steadiness and hedge in their coin collections. And as jobs and employment have sputtered and fluttered with double digit unemployment readings, the coin collector has generally been able to bypass calamity and avoid any major type of loss in their coin holdings.

While many segments of the market enjoyed increases in value this past year, there are some areas that may not realize an uptick in values for 2010! What is going up? Values for Early American Coins - Flowing Hair and Bust Type coins minted from 1792-1807 - seem to grow exponentially with every large auction or National Coin Convention. Those owning 1804 Silver Dollars, or 1913 Liberty V. Nickels are in very solid company. Coins dated 1794, 1795 or 1796 seem to show quarterly increases in value - and are predicted to continue their climb. Early American coins from the late 1790's to early 1830s seemed to increase daily. Better date and better grade coins were consistently big winners. Prices of key coins among the Morgan Dollars (especially those from the Carson City Mint, 1893S, and 1894), Standing Liberty Quarters (1916, 1923S), Mercury Dimes (1916D and 1921 P&D), Buffalo (1913D Type 2, 1914D, 1915S, 1931S, 1937D 3-Legged) and Liberty Nickels (1885, 1886, 1912S), Lincoln (1909S VDB, 1914D, 1922 Plain, 1931S) and Indian Cents (1877, 1908S, 1909S), as well as the entire Bust and Liberty Seated series have increased on a monthly basis.

Coins that are dependent on their melt value to buoy their numismatic values continue equally strong. Gold value appears to toy with the $1000 an ounce level, rising and falling from $880 to $980 with daily swings. Silver bullion ranks consistently in the $15 an ounce range, insuring that most silver coins minted before 1964 retain a value of 10 times face. This silver demand has easily sustained the Roosevelt Dime, Washington Quarter and Franklin/Kennedy silver halves at solid levels. In addition, Silver American Eagles and Gold Eagles are incredibly popular. The US Mint has coined more 2009 Eagle coins than any year in the past. Collector and Investors alike are fueling this passion. Overall, Gold coins have risen in price more over the past year than all other coins.

Modern US Coins are slowly becoming a force unto their own. In the past, traditional coin collectors and many coin dealers have generally ignored coins minted after 1964, the benchmark date when silver disappeared from circulating coinage. But numismatic numbers will no longer support this stance. There have easily been more coins minted in the past 50 years than during the previous 160 years of US mint history. Over 37.5 billion State Quarters alone were minted during the past ten years. For 2009, the proof and circulating coinage from the mint will comprise as many as 72 coins - just factoring in the cents, nickels, dimes, quarters, halves and dollars. Adding in the millions of silver and gold eagles, Commemorative Dollars, and special mint issues and you have a virtual modern smorgasbord. The Modern US Coin Collector is challenged with just keeping up with today's releases!

For 2009 and 2010 New and Exciting Mint Issues continue to add to the thrill of collecting. The State Quarter program ending in 2008, is replaced with the District of Columbia and US Territories Coinage (6 vs. 5 coins in 2009). 2010 quarters are replaced with a ten year program of national parks and historical monuments. 55 different clad and silver quarters will be produced during the 2010 to 2020 time frame, with a second ten year round already available.

2009 and 2010 may well become most famous for the Lincoln Cents minted in celebration of the 100th anniversary of Abraham Lincoln's appearance on the Lincoln Cent. For 2009, four reverses depicting stages of Lincoln's life will be produced. The regular released cents will be coined from the current copper-plated zinc composition, while those in the special sets, mint sets, and proof sets will be coined in the original 95% copper alloy. In 2010, the reverse will change again, most likely to the Flag reverse recommended by the Commission of Fine Arts. With the Cents, the variety will not just be limited to variety and composition, but also to finish. Some of the proof coins will be produced with a matte finish as provided by the mint for a small number of 1909 pennies. What a whirlwind!

While the Quarters Program stretches into a one year and ten year addendum, the Presidential Dollar series gears up for its third and fourth years of excitement. The first four presidents were showcased in 2007 (Washington, Adams, Jefferson, and Madison), followed by Monroe, John Quincy Adams, Andrew Jackson, and Martin VanBuren in 2008. During 2009, the next four Presidents will be commemorated on these golden dollar coins - Harrison, Tyler, Polk and Taylor. and 2010 offers the fourth quadrant of presidents The Presidential Wives coin series follows right along with their corresponding spouses. In 2009 and 2010 wives 9-16 will be emblazoned again on the exciting $10 Gold coin minted for this series. The mint is also required to bring out additional dollar coins in the Sacagawea series. Each year, Sacagawea will have a new reverse, emblematic of Indian themes related to the Lewis and Clark expedition.

Bullion coins are also featured in new mint issues. Continued excitement exists with the Burnished "W" American Silver Eagle. These West Point offerings have stirred the numismatic pot since 2006, and interest in these coins continues to grow. Of course the rise of Platinum Eagle program has certainly help fuel the coin world's demand for bullion, and Gold coins - from the Gold Eagles to the Gold Buffalo bullion coins may share the spotlight with a St Gaudien's-like offering in 2009.

Rising Gold, Silver, and Platinum prices. Depending on who you listen to, Gold is regularly predicted to hit $2000 an ounce and silver top $50. In light of the huge influx of US Dollars into the economy as part of President OBama's stimulus programs, the pressure for precious metals to rise is definitely increased. Both benchmarks were stirred in the recent past as Gold rose well over the $1,000 per ounce mark, and Silver topped the charts at $21 an ounce - at least for a short time. Platinum returns to its earlier values, retreating to $1200 per ounce from its 2000+ plateaus. The US Mint is right on board, helping to fuel the frenzy with new and attractive offerings in each of the precious metals. Silver seems to be the metal of choice for the mass of collectors, and at times, the ability to acquire a Silver Eagle has been a major challenge. Gold offerings are more plentiful and varied, but the higher prices deter some from acquiring as much as they might like, **uncirculated platinum coins** are trading reasonably well. First minted in 1997, the Platinum Eagles provide the only means in U.S. coinage to invest in this metal. Total mintage is small by comparison to the gold counterparts. For example, only about 20,000 ½ oz. coins were minted in 1997. Mintages for 1998 to 2004 are tiny. Whether these coins will ever have numismatic value remains to be seen. But the base price of the metal is very strong - well above $1250/ounce, if interest ever surges in the collector market, the meager supply of these issues will quickly disappear, and prices will rise accordingly. Proof platinum pieces have astonishing low mintages. This could make them a very good bet.

Record Setting Auctions. Individual coins are selling at auction for what entire auction catalogs brought in the past. It's rare to see an auction without at least one coin setting a world record. Brasher Doubloons, 1804 Dollars, or a 1913 Nickel are sure to bring four, five, six, or more million at each venture. Early coins - especially Flowing Hair and Bust types are hot! These high grade coins from the late 1700's and early 1800's are chasing bids in the thousands and hundreds of thousands of dollars.

Updates on the Coin Market

As announced earlier, the next generations of commemorative Quarters arrived in 2009. Several of the lower mintage issues in BU are selling well above face. I would never have guessed this at the beginning of the program, given the large quantities minted. In fact, some issues were minted in quantities in excess of 750 million to 1 billion coins for each of the two mint marks (Philadelphia and Denver). The proof versions from San Francisco are found in much smaller quantities, 2-3 million, and are not meant for circulation. A full set of 1999-2007 BU, Proof, and Silver Proof quarters in a Dansco Album now sells for over $800.

Presidential Dollar coins began their run during 2007 and will continue through 2016. These dollar coins, circulating alongside the Sacagawea Dollar, have added an exciting element to the numismatic field. Issued four per year, (one each quarter) the coins feature an obverse portrait of each of our presidents in the order they served in office. 2007 began with George Washington, John Adams, Thomas Jefferson, and James Madison. The reverse of each coin depicts the Statue of Liberty. Most exciting — and controversial — is the way the mint treats the "third edge" of each coin. The date, mint mark, and mottos have been placed on the rim. Some have called "fowl" because of the "In God We Trust" being etched into the edge of the coin rather than on the obverse or reverse. Myriad edge letter errors have been produced fueling the error collector's world. No lettering, weak lettering, dual lettering, and inverted lettering, have been found on the first year's coins.

Type Coins remain in incredible demand. Attractive, problem free circulated examples find a home immediately upon offer. Half cents, large cents, half dimes to half dollars, individual coins representing each of America's denominations and types are leading the coin market. Buyers, it seems, are hungry for nice coins to add to their collection. Circulated coins seem to sell easily as uncirculated pieces — as long as they have nice eye appeal. And the values for type coins are strong in every grade. Common low-grade (good to fine) type coins continue to be in demand. Many new collectors have entered the numismatic, coin collecting hobby as a spin off from collecting the new State Quarters. One of the best places to begin to gain knowledge and explore interests is by putting together a set of each type of American coin minted. Coins of this sort with no defects in G+ condition command the following retail prices: Half-Cents ($35), Large Cents ($15), Indian Head Cents ($1), 2-cent pieces ($10), 3-cent pieces ($10), half-dimes ($10), and 20-cent pieces ($75), Standing Liberty Quarters ($2.50), Bust Halves ($40), and Trade Dollars ($75). Seated and Barber coins are good sellers. G+ (full rims on both sides of the coin and undamaged) coins retail at 12-15 times face. Dealers purchase them at 8-10 times face. In grades of fine (all or almost all of the letters of "Liberty" in the headband on the obverse of the coin) and above, all Barber coins have advanced in price in the last year, some significantly. A nice XF Barber Half, for example, can easily command a price of $150 or more at retail.

Key date coins continue to be much sought after. This is a refrain of many years. Key date coins have been and will continue to be the hot spot in our market. Dealers are happy to pay well for the tough Indian Head Cents (1869-1872, 1877, 1908s and 1909s), Lincolns (1909s, 1909svdb, 1914d, 1922, 1955 double die, 1972 double die), Liberty 5-cent (1885, 1886, 1912s), Buffalo Nickels (1913s and d of both types, 1914d & s, 1921s and virtually all pre-1930 mint marked coins in grades of fine to AU), Barber coins (all low mintage dimes, quarters and halves in fine to AU), Mercury Dimes (1916d, 1921 and 1921d, 1942/1 and 1942/1d), Liberty Standing Quarters (all dates and mints 1916-1924), Washington Quarters (1932, 1932d and s, all mint marked coins 1934-1940 in XF to BU), Walking Liberty Halves (1916pds, 1917ds on obverse, 1919pds, 1921pds and 1938d). And all low-mintage silver dollars, as mentioned earlier, are never found in quantities large enough to fill the demand.

"The times, they are a changing," to quote a popular song phrase. And the coin market is no exception. Your author recognizes these phenomena and in an effort to better meets the coin collectors needs, this publication will begin a journey of twice a year publication. **The fall version of Coins 2010** will focus on the recognized changes to Mint offerings for 2009 with a solid forecast of 2010 offerings and changes. **The Spring version of Coins 2010** will feature an expansion of the mints plans, offerings, mintages, coin availabilities, etc for the 2010 mint year.

COIN QUESTIONS?
Advice, appraisals or offers for selling coins or an entire collection? Write:

Steve Nolte
P.O. Box 22035 - Fort Lauderdale, Florida, 33335
Please enclose a self-addressed stamped envelope.

CHAPTER 1

COIN MINTING AND DESIGN FEATURES
Metal Contents, Weight & Fineness

The color of a coin is as good an indication as any of its composition. U.S. cents have traditionally been made of copper, although the content and amount of the metal has varied considerably over the years. The original large cents 1793-1857 were made entirely of copper and were approximately the size of the half dollar.

Since the end of the large cent era, the one-cent coin has been alloyed from time to time with nickel, zinc and tin. In 1943, due to the need for copper in the war effort, the cent was made of steel with a zinc coating. Since 1982, although the color of the cent does not vary much from previous years since it is still copper coated, the composition was changed to 97.5% zinc and 2.5% copper.

Two other copper coins are the half cent (100%) and the two-cent piece (95%).

All our "nickel" coins, including the "nickel" three-cent piece, are somewhat misnamed as they are 75% copper and only 25% nickel.

The only exception to the above is found in the war years (1942-1945) when the composition of the five-cent piece was changed to 56% copper, 35% silver and 9% manganese. The color of the circulated nickels is a dull gray, albeit a darker cast for the wartime alloys.

Generally, our silver coins have contained 90% of the white metal alloyed with 10% copper. From 1965-1970 the composition of the Kennedy half dollar was changed to 40% silver and 60% copper. This same composition is found in proof dollars (1971-1974) and for some bicentennial quarters, half dollars and dollars.

However, with these exceptions, after 1964 the composition of our coinage changed to a copper-nickel alloy. The nickel is found in the outside layers largely to retain a color similar to the previous silver issues. The layers of these coins become apparent when the coin is turned on edge.

Ninety percent gold and 10% copper is the most often found composition of most U.S. regular issue and commemorative gold coins.

The gold U.S. Eagle bullion coin is composed of 91.67% gold, 3% silver and 5.33% copper. The silver Eagle is 99.93% silver and .07% copper. Each of these coins, however, contains a full ounce of precious metal.

The composition and weight of U.S. coins was, until the 1850s, such that the actual metal content value was virtually identical to and sometimes even greater than the coin's face value.

The effect was to drive out of circulation what few minor coins had not been melted and to give rise to a number of alternative units of exchange—tokens, fractional currency, and the foreign coins from many nations.

In 1853 the problem of a diminished supply of circulating coins was addressed by reducing the weight of the half dime, dime, quarter and half dollar. This weight reduction was evidenced by the addition of arrows at the date and/or rays on the reverse of coins dated 1853-1855.

After the mints had made concerted efforts to provide a large supply of minor coins for exchange purposes, the arrows and rays were removed. At about this time half cents and large cents had finally reached the end of their usefulness. These coins had simply become too cumbersome and costly for continued use in general circulation. Consequently, the size of the cent was greatly reduced, and the copper in its composition has become less and less, so that our most current cents are composed of only 2.5% of the metal.

As confidence was lost in paper currency with the impending Civil War, all types of coins began to quickly disappear from circulation. All manner of ingenious alternatives were substituted. Again tokens, fractional currency, even postage stamps were used in everyday transactions.

By 1873, although fractional coins were now available for circulation, arrows next to the date again became necessary to indicate a slight rise in the weight of dimes, quarter dollars and half dollars.

Also at about this time a special silver dollar sized coin known as a "Trade Dollar" was minted to compete with Mexican and other foreign dollar sized coins in the Orient. To place this coin on a competitive footing, the weight (and thereby amount of silver) was raised by about 2% above the standard silver dollar.

With many minor changes in weights and compositions for individual denominations in the intervening years, the final blow to intrinsic value was struck by the Coinage Act of 1965. This act called for the elimination or reduction of silver from the coins of general circulation and was made necessary by the upward pressure of the free market price of silver. Until the 1960s, the Treasury was willing to sell silver at $1.2929 an ounce. With the depletion of the Treasury's stockpile of silver dollars and bullion, however, by 1967 it became apparent that restrictions on such sales had become necessary. The refusal of the Treasury to continue sales combined with its prohibition on the melting of the hoards of coins withdrawn by the general public further escalated the price rises in the metal.

In a few short years, silver coins had completely disappeared from circulation and Gresham's Law had been obeyed. The government saw the futility of minting additional silver coins.

Coin Dating

Another readily noticeable feature of virtually every United States coin is the date of issue. Usually found on the obverse side of the coin, the date with some exceptions indicates the year in which the coin was minted. In some years, no coins of some denominations were minted at all. In 1815, for example, no half cents, cents, half dimes or dimes were produced by the mint.

Especially in the early days of coinage, it was not uncommon for dies to be re-engraved so that a later date is found engraved over an earlier one. This practice gave rise to many varieties of overdates. Dramatic examples of such superimpositions are found on the 1807 over 6 cent and even on the relatively recent 1942 over one dime. Much research had been conducted as to the circumstances that surrounded overdating techniques and decisions. Collectors have even been known to specialize in the uncovering of new varieties of this sort and to build collections with overdating as the focus.

In a particularly famous exception to dating coins in the year of mintage, silver dollars dated 1804 are generally believed to have been minted in the 1830s, mainly as souvenirs for presentation sets. This date also appears on a number of restrikes struck for collectors as late as 1859.

An even more common practice in the early days of the mint was to use dies until they were no longer serviceable without regard to the actual years in which the coins were being struck. Mintage figures by year for this period are notoriously unreliable.

In 1964, with the drain of silver coins from circulation and consequent shortage, the Treasury sought to respond by doubling the various mints' annual production of coins. Congress aided this effort by permitting the 1964 date on coins regardless of year minted. It was supposed that such high mintage figures would discourage any thought of these coins becoming collectors' items. Intrinsic value of course was soon to defeat this plan for coins struck in silver. However, the initial clad coins (dated 1965-1967) were often struck in a year later than the date found on the coin.

The Cents of 1960 sparked the beginnings of a "small date" craze. That year, two somewhat different sized numerals are found on the Lincoln cent. The smaller of the two dates, especially those from the Philadelphia mint, were initially seen as quite valuable and were much sought after. In retrospect the frenzy seems quite unwarranted. Examples of the "small date" minted in Denver can easily be had for 25 or so cents each. The scarcer one from Philadelphia sells for $2 and demand continues with the renewed interest in the Lincoln Cent series.

Our earliest coinage provides all sorts of varieties of date sizes and numeral styles of interest mainly to specialists.

This is not to say that such considerations as those above have no significant impact on coin prices and overall desirability. Undoubtedly, the 1960 small date cents were not as rare as originally thought. And the value of many "varieties" can be quite ephemeral. I can remember when the price difference between the small and large date variety of the 1857 Large Cent was much more marked. Today the price gap seems to have all but closed.

The price of overdates and other varieties in the date on a coin is much more a function of rarity and popularity than of other components. Even then the scarcity of some items can long go unrecognized or become buried in an unpopular series. Most often relatively small differences in date design are completely ignored.

More will be said about pricing and value considerations in Chapter 2.

Mint Marks

T he mint mark is an important feature in the design of a coin because it shows which mint struck a particular coin and also is quite necessary in determining a coin's value. Since eight different mints have produced coins, small letters are placed on a coin in various locations to indicate the mint of origin.

Philadelphia, Pa.	"P"	1793 - present
Charlotte, N.C.	"C"	1838 - 1861
Dahlonega, Ga.	"D"	1838 -1861
New Orleans, La.	"O"	1838 -1861, 1879 -1909
San Francisco, Ca.	"S"	1854 -1955, 1968 - present
Carson City, Nev.	"CC"	1870 -1893
Denver, Colo.	"D"	1906 - present
West Point, N.Y.	"W"	1984 - present

The location of the mint mark can be either the obverse or reverse of a coin dated before 1968. Since 1968 all mint marks are found on the coin's obverse.

Until recently, with the exception of a few years of wartime nickel production (1942-1945), coins produced at the Philadelphia mint bears no mint mark.

THE FOLLOWING RULES OF THUMB WILL BE HELPFUL IN DETERMINING THE EXISTENCE AND/OR LOCATION OF A MINT MARK ON EACH OF THE VARIOUS DENOMINATIONS:

Half Cents—no mint marks (Philadelphia).

Cents (through 1907)—no mint mark (Philadelphia)

Indian Cents (1908 & 1909)—"S" mint mark on reverse, bottom center.

Lincoln Cents (1909 to present)—"S" or "D" mint marks obverse below date.

Two-Cents—no mint marks (Philadelphia).

Nickel Three-Cents—no mint mark (Philadelphia).

Shield Nickels—no mint mark (Philadelphia).

Liberty Nickels (1912)—"D" or "S" on reverse lower left between "Cents" and "United."
Buffalo Nickel—"D" or "S" on reverse bottom center along rim.

Jefferson Nickel (1939-1964)—"D" or "S" on reverse right center along rim. (1942-1945)—"P," "S," or "D," on reverse large letter above Monticello. (1965-1967)—no mint mark (Philadelphia). (1968 to date)—"P," "D," or "S," on obverse below date along rim.

Silver Three-Cents (In 1851)—"O" on reverse right center at the opening of the design.

Half Dimes (1838-1873)—"O," or "S" on reverse lower center within or outside wreath.

Early Dimes (to 1916)—"O," "CC," "S," or "D" as above on half dimes until Mercury type.

Mercury Dimes (1916-1945)—"D" or "S" on reverse lower left along rim between "One" and "Dime."

Roosevelt Dimes (1946-1964)—"D" or "S" on reverse lower left above "E" in "One." (1965-1967)—no mint mark (Philadelphia). (1968 to date)—"P," "D," or "S" on obverse above date.
Twenty Cents—"CC" on reverse below eagle.

Early Quarters (to 1916)—"O," "S," "CC," or "D" on reverse below eagle.

Standing Liberty Quarters (1916-1930)—"D" or "S" on obverse left of date.

Washington Quarters (1932-1964)—"D" or "S" on reverse below branch. (1965-1967)—no mint mark (Philadelphia). (1968 to date)—"P," "D," or "S" on obverse above date.

Early Halves (1838-1839)—"O" on obverse above date. (1840-1915)—"O," "S," "CC," or "D" on reverse below eagle.

Walking Liberty Halves (1916)—"D" or "S" on obverse below "In God we Trust." (1917)—as above and also on reverse along rim at 7 o'clock. (1918-1947)—"D" or "S" on reverse as above.

Franklin Halves (1948-1963)—"D" or "S" on reverse under "States".

Kennedy Halves (1964)—"D" on reverse below eagle's left claw. (1965-1967)—no mint mark (Philadelphia). (1968 to date)—"P," "D," or "S" on obverse below neck of Kennedy.

Early Dollars (to 1873)—"O," "CC," or "S" on reverse below eagle.

Trade Dollars (1873-1855)—"CC" or "S" on reverse below eagle.

Morgan Dollars (1878-1921)—"O," "CC," "S," or "D" on reverse below wreath.

Peace Dollars (1921-1935)—"D" or "S" on reverse along rim under "One."

Eisenhower Dollars (1971-1978)—"D" or "S" on obverse below neck.

Anthony Dollars (1979-1981)—"P," "D," or "S" on obverse on Anthony's right shoulder.

$1 Gold (1849-1870)—"C," "D," "O," or "S" on reverse under wreath.

$2.50 Gold (1839)—"C," "D," or "O" on obverse above date. (1840-1907)—"C," "D," "O," or "S" on reverse at bottom above "2½" (1908-1929)"D" on reverse lower left along rim.

$3 Gold (1854-1870)—"D" "O," or "S" on reverse below wreath.

$4 Stella—no mint mark (Pattern coins).

$5 Gold (Early issues to 1837)—no mint marks (Philadelphia). (1838-1839)—"C" or "D" on obverse above date. (1840-1907)—"C," "D," "O," "S," or "CC" on reverse at bottom above "Five." (1908-1929)—"D," "S," or "O" on reverse lower left along rim.

$10 Gold (to 1907)—"O," "S," or "CC" on reverse above "Ten." (1907-1933 (Indian))—"D" or "S" on reverses along rim at 7 o'clock.

$20 Gold (Liberty type to 1907)—"O," "S," or "CC" on reverse above "Twenty."

Saint-Gaudens Type (1907-1933)—"D," or "S" on obverse above near date.

Commemorative Coins—various locations. Recent commemoratives have obverse mint marks.

Bullion Coins:
$1 Silver Eagle (1986 to date)—"S" on reverse left of eagle's tail.

$5 1/10 oz. Gold Eagle (1987 to date)—"P" on obverse within lower right   rays (on proofs only).

$10 1/4 oz. Gold Eagle (1987 to date)—"P" on obverse within lower right rays (on proofs only).

$25 1/2 oz. Gold Eagle (1987 to date)—"P" on obverse within lower right rays (on proofs only).

$50 1 oz. Gold Eagle (1986 to date)—"W" on obverse within lower right rays.

Obverse and Reverse

T he obverse, or front, of a coin is the side which presents the most important design features. Generally, a coin series will take on the name of this feature. (There are some exceptions, notably the "Buffalo" nickel.) Most often the obverse is comprised of a bust or head of a famous or fictional person. Heads of presidents, Indians and, of course, The Goddess of Liberty — sitting, standing, walking, head left and head right — have been most popular.

As mentioned before, the date is generally found on the obverse side of a coin.

The reverse or back side of a coin is defined as the side opposite the important design feature. The eagle, in any number of poses, has been selected most often to grace this side of our coinage. Fasces, wreaths, buildings and the Liberty Bell are distant seconds in this competition.

The denomination of most coins and sometimes the mint mark, and assorted inscriptions and mottos is found on the reverse.

A list of mottos, inscriptions and other miscellaneous design features follows:

MOTTOS

E Pluribus Unum—found on the reverse of early coins as part of the Great Seal. Literally, it means "From Many, One" and is undoubtedly a reference to the union of the original and subsequent states. This motto is now a standard feature of all current coins. Its history as a design feature has not been an uninterrupted one. For years it was found absent from our coinage.

In God We Trust—first appearing on two-cent coins in 1864, this motto now appears on all U.S. coins. Briefly, in 1907, there was a flap when, through the effort of President Theodore Roosevelt, the motto was removed from the $10 and $20 gold coin as inconsistent with official church-state separation. As might have been expected, a huge public outcry ensued and the motto was restored in 1908.

INSCRIPTIONS

United States of America—was to be placed on the reverse of all coins under the same law which established the Mint. On many commemorative coins this inscription is found on the obverse.

Liberty—to be placed on the obverse of all coins under the same law that established the Mint. Often found in Liberty's hair and, ironically, one of the first devices to wear away on a circulating coin.

OTHER DEVICES

Designer's Initials—not found on U.S. coins until the 1849 $1 gold coin, the initials of the engraver are often quite inconspicuous and may appear on either the obverse or reverse of a coin. On our most recent coinage these initials can be found as follows:

Cent—V.D.B. (Victor D. Brenner)—on the obverse along the rim under Lincoln's shoulder.

Five-Cent—F.S. (Felix Schlag)—now located on the obverse along the rim under Jefferson's shoulder.

Dime—J.S. (John Sinnock)—found on the obverse under the forward portion of Roosevelt's neck.

Quarter—J.F. (John Flanagan)—located on the obverse at the base of Washington's neck.

Half Dollar—G.R. (Gilroy Roberts)—designed the obverse. His initials are found on the lower portion of the neck of Kennedy's bust.

F.G. (Frank Gasparro)—designed the reverse. His initials are found on the reverse at the right of the eagle's tail.

Anthony Dollar—F.G. (Frank Gasparro)—found on the reverse beneath the eagle.

Major Portraits, Places, & Symbols on U.S. Coinage

T*he Goddess Liberty*—Appears throughout the history of U.S. coinage as a symbol of unextinguished freedom. She is dressed in a war bonnet on the obverse of the $10 gold piece beginning in 1907.

Six Presidents—Lincoln (Cent), Jefferson (Five-Cent), Roosevelt (Dime), Washington (Quarter), Kennedy (Half Dollar), Eisenhower (Dollar).

Benjamin Franklin and Susan B. Anthony—With the exception of the presidents mentioned above, Franklin and Anthony are the only other actual persons to have found their way onto regularly issued coinage. Franklin, of course, holds a special place as a statesman and founder of our country. Anthony was a prominent pioneer of women's rights. Heightened sensitivity to women's issues in the 1970s undoubtedly led to her appearance on the dollar coin. Regrettably, the coin has seen very little circulation.

Buildings—The Lincoln Memorial was placed on the reverse of the Lincoln cent beginning in 1959. Jefferson's home, Monticello, is found on the reverse of the five-cent piece.

The Eagle—the national bird has been the most popular and recurring symbol found on the reverse of our coinage. (It also appears as an obverse device on the cents of 1856-1858 and the Gobrecht Dollar of 1836-1839.) Found even on the very recent bullion silver and gold coins, some particularly majestic examples grace later gold coins and silver dollars. However, the example found on early $5 gold pieces appears extremely scrawny and unattractive.

The Shield—this device is often found on the reverse of our coinage, upon the eagle's breast, or on the obverse resting against the seated Liberty.

Arrows and Olive Branches—usually found in the talons of the full-faced eagle, symbolizing at the same time a readiness for war and a hope for peace.

Indian Princess—found on the one-cent coin of 1859-1909 and the $1 gold coin from 1854 to 1889 among others. The model for these coins is reputed to have been the engravers daughter, Sarah Longacre.

The Indian Chief—the obverse of the five-cent "Buffalo" nickel, as it is sometimes called, is actually a composite portrait of three Indian Chiefs (Iron Tail, Two Moons and John Tree). An unidentified chief sat for the $2.50 and $5 gold coins of 1908-1929.

The Buffalo—"Black Diamond" was the model for the reverse of the five-cent piece of 1913-1938.

The Wreath—Another very popular reverse, especially for our early coinage, the wreath is sometimes found alone as a device, as on the Large cent; at other times it appear with another symbol, as with the shield on the Indian cent of 1860-1909. The wreath most often appears to be composed of oak or laurel branches, but is identified as a composite of tobacco, cotton, wheat and corn on the Flying Eagle cent of 1856-1858.

Fasces—Found on the reverse of the Winged Liberty dime of 1916-1945, the fasces is a bundle of rods encasing an ax with its head protruding meant to symbolize officialdom.

Liberty Bell—Found as the prominent device on the reverse of the Franklin half dollars (1948-1963), and later superimposed upon the moon on the reverse of the Eisenhower dollar commemorating the Bicentennial.

Victory Torch and Branches—this design is presented on the reverse of the Roosevelt dime. The torch symbolizes liberty. The oak branch on the right and the olive branch on the left remind us of strength and peace respectively.

Presidential Coat of Arms—this symbol graces the reverse of the Kennedy half dollar (1964 to present).

MISC. SYMBOLS	WHERE FOUND	SYMBOLIZES
Chain	Large Cents 1793 (Reverse)	Strength of Union
Wheat Ears	Lincoln Cents	Prosperity 1909-1958 (Reverse)
13 Rays	1866 Shield Nickel (Reverse)	13 Original States
13 Stars	Shield Nickels	13 Original States 1866-1883 (Reverse)
Sun	Saint-Gaudens	Exact origin unclear $20 Gold 1907-1933
6 Pointed Star	3-Cent Silver Coins	Exact origins unclear 1851-1864 (Obverse)
5 Pointed Star	$4 Gold (Reverse)	Exact origin unclear

Bicentennial Designs	Denomination
Colonial Drummer	Quarter (Reverse)
Independence Hall	Half Dollar (Reverse)
Liberty Bell and Moon	Dollar (Reverse)

Coin Relief and High Points

Coin relief refers to the relation the features of a coin have to the field. On virtually all U.S. coins minted over the years the design features are raised, sometimes called "bas-relief." They extend above the field and, thereby, these high points of the design show the most wear on a circulated coin.

An extreme example of bas-relief occurred on some 1907 $20 Saint-Gaudens gold coins. The relief was so pronounced that stacking the coins was impractical. A few proofs were minted as pattern pieces with an extremely high relief such that the coin has an almost concave appearance.

The Indian Head $2.50 and $5 gold coins are different from all other U.S. coins in just the opposite way that high relief coins are. They have a recessed or incused design. The design features are below the field.

When grading coins, an absolute necessity is a familiarity with what portions or features of the design experience the inevitable wearing as the coin changes hands in circulation. Even slight wear on the very highest points of the design can make huge differences in grading and price. It is conceivable that simply sliding a high grade uncirculated coin across a table can subtract thousands of dollars from its value to a collector.

Coin Edges and Milling

There is more to a coin than its obverse or reverse. What? Surprisingly, the edges of coins are vastly different. Currently, one-cent and five-cent pieces have plain edges. And generally minor coins, those composed of base metals, have been minted without the reeded edges found on the clad dimes, quarters and halves that circulate today.

Coins minted of precious metals have been known to encourage certain abuses. One obvious one involves scraping small quantities of the metal from the edge of a coin and then passing it along at full face value. The scrapings could then be sold.

To lessen the likelihood of this, practice steps were taken to make tampering of this sort more difficult. Plain edges would not accomplish this. Consequently, U.S. silver and gold coins, almost from the beginning, were minted with small, vertical serrations on the edge, called "reeds."

Notable exceptions are found on 50-cent pieces where stars and lettering along with intermittent reeding can be found, depending on the date of the half dollar, up until 1836. Early silver dollars through 1803 also have lettered edges with decorations attesting to the denomination of the issue. Edge lettering returned to circulated coinage beginning with in 2007 with the Presidential Dollar coin series. On these, the date, mint mark, and mottos are inscribed on the edges.

The very earliest half cents and Large cents have various designs and lettering on the edges. Ten-dollar gold pieces, minted from 1907-1933, can be found with the number of stars corresponding to the states in the Union at the time. The Saint-Gaudens $20 gold pieces of 1907 have the date inscribed on the rim as well as on the obverse. In fact, the rarer variety presents the date in Roman numerals.

One would expect that the reeding, especially on later coins, would be fairly uniform. A small number of studies have shown otherwise. Wide variances in the number of reeds have even been found on the Roosevelt dime.

Coin Manufacturing

The process of minting coins is much like that of any firm that stamps or fashions small parts. The Mint must, of course, proceed with much greater care since its products are legal tender and since "rejects," if security is lax, may well enter the collector market as valuable mint errors.

Simply put, from mine to Federal Reserve Bank, a coin is made through an eight-step process.

1. A mining company extracts the ore (copper, nickel, silver, gold or iron) from the ground.

2. The metal is smelted or refined and the finished product in the form of coils of strip metal or plainchants is shipped to the Mint.

3. The Mint cleans, weighs and then punches the metal into blanks which are slightly larger than the finished coin will be.

4. These blanks are annealed, which is a heating process used to make the metal more receptive to striking and thereby cause less wear and tear on the dies.

5. These blanks then go through a process called "upsetting" which provides the coin with a raised rim. This allows for a more uniform feeding and striking process.

6. These plainchants are fed into a coin press where both the obverse and reverse of the coin are struck from dies. These dies are the products of the original design for the coin and are fashioned in a lengthy process from models to master dies. At the same time the coin is being struck by the obverse and reverse dies, a collar, in effect an "edge die," fashions a smooth or reeded edge on the coin depending on the denomination being struck.

7. The finished products are inspected. All coins must meet specifications with regard to weight, size and fineness. Coins not within certain tolerance limits or coins which are defective in some way due to misstriking are rejected.

8. Finally, acceptable coins are counted and bagged for ultimate shipment to your pocket or purse through the banking system.

A Note on Mintage Figures

A s you can imagine, coins cost the government less to make than their actual value as legal tender. This is especially true now that precious metals have all but disappeared from U.S. coins. The difference in the cost of production and face value of coins is called "seigniorage." It represents the profit the government makes by minting coins.

Sometimes, as has happened several times in the history of U.S. coinage, the intrinsic value or metal worth of coins increases to a level at or above the coin's face value. When this happens the coins quickly disappear from circulation.

Most recently this happened with all our 90% and 40% silver coins. Close calls have come even with pennies of late. The price of copper per pound nearly crept over the point where melting cents would be marginally profitable.

HOW MANY COINS ARE MINTED IN A YEAR?	
Cents	14.26 Billion
Nickels	2.35 Billion
Dimes	3.66 Billion
Quarters	6.47 Billion
Dollars & Gold	1.29 Billion

Recently released figures from the Mint give the totals shown below by denomination for 2000. This total of around 28 billion coins compares with about 21 billion in 1999, 3.3 billion in 1961, and roughly 1.4 billion in 1951. Since the very beginning of official coinage in the U.S., the Mint has produced approximately 350 billion coins.

Estimates have been given that as many as 1/3 of all gold coins minted were melted into bars in 1933-1934. No reliable estimates have ever been produced for the "great silver melt" that began in the middle 1960s and may well continue today since the silver value of many coins is well above their numismatic and face value.

But putting aside any adjustments for the melting of coins which has happened officially and unofficially throughout the history of U.S. coinage, we might still venture estimates for how many coins have been minted per capita.

If we divide the population of the U.S. into a rough estimate of the number of coins "out there," we may be astounded to realize that the mint has produced about 1000 coins for each of us. In fact, each of us should have about 600 cents somewhere in our possession. In 1993 alone, the Mint arranged to supply everyone in the U.S. with 48 pennies. Where have they all gone?

When we realize that 30 years ago we were getting along with cent productions of one-tenth those of today, and that the production itself accumulates, the need for current production levels seems incredible.

One way to account for part of the drain of cents from circulation can be found when we realize that all Lincoln cents through 1958 (the wheat cents) have a slight numismatic value and therefore no longer circulate.

Even then, 192 billion cents have been produced. Are significant numbers lost? Or saved in drawers and piggy banks and seen as not worth carrying around? No one seems to know. As a personal reckoning you might try to count all the pennies you have around the house. Are you above or below the per capita penny wealth level of the U.S.?

Mint Errors

With all the billions of coins produced at the Mint, a few substandard coins escape the inspection process. Sometimes these defective coins are the result of dramatic errors in the production process. Most often they are due to very minor variations in die or striking conditions.

Essentially, there are three types of errors that may occur in the minting process. Coins of course, may be altered or damaged outside the mint; however, we will reserve the term "error" for governmental alteration or damage.

PLANCHANT & BLANKING ERRORS

This sort of error is usually due to a defect in the "raw material" of the minting process. The planchant may be either overweight or underweight, or be the wrong metal for the denomination being struck. With the current clad coinage the planchant may more readily split or flake. Such errors occurred much less frequently with earlier coinage.

STRIKING ERRORS

Coins can be struck off-center when the planchant is not completely lined up with the die.

Double strikes occur when a coin is not expelled from the collar after the initial striking. Should a coin remain stuck in the die, it will produce an incused design on subsequent plainchants that are fed into the press. These are called "capped die strikes."

Another type of doubling can happen if various parts of the production machinery are not tightly fitted so than a "bouncing" of the coin takes place giving the design a blurred appearance in whole or in part.

If two coins enter the collar at the same time, each will be struck on just one side. The remaining side will be blank.

Weak strikes are the result of worn dies or at the end of a striking run when lower coining pressures occur as a result of the presses being turned off.

DIE ERRORS

Due to the extreme pressure needed for the coining process, the coin die experiences a great deal of stress. These stresses result in damage to the die in the form of cracks, chips and scratches. Such damage to the dies is evident on a coin since metal from the planchant will, under pressure; fill any indentations on the die, thus leaving a raised area on the coin.

A "cud" is a die broken to such an extent that a piece of the die actually breaks off. As the planchantis struck metal flows into the empty area and appears as a blob of metal on the resulting coin.

The opposite problem occurs when portions of the die are filled with debris. On coins struck under these circumstances areas of the design will be missing or weak.

When care is not taken in the alignment of the dies, the obverse and reverse side of a coin can be rotated outside the normal 180 degrees alignment called for by mint specifications. This is called a rotated die error.

Changes made to existing dies, while not errors as such, result in coin oddities. Engraved over-dates and mint marks are the most common design feature changes that are made on existing dies, although lettering and portrait changes occur often also.

Most mint errors are surprisingly inexpensive. The existing supply of dramatic errors is quite small. But demand is not great either.

From our proceeding discussion I have listed major types of errors with a range of prices dependent mainly on the denomination and age of the series. Older coins and higher denomination coins are generally more expensive. Prices listed are for coins that otherwise might grade XF or better.

Nickel Struck on a Dime Planchant

Improper Planchant—$25 to $2,000. (Probably the most expensive error. Especially valuable on obsolete and recent $1 coins.)

Split Planchant or Lamination Errors—$1 to $50. (Splitting of planchantmust be considerable.)

Incomplete Planchant—$1 to $100. (Again, missing portion must be considerable.)

Quarter Struck off-Center

Off-Center Strike—$1 to $1,000.

Very dependent on percentage of design missing. The minimum requirement for the value of the error to be significant is 25 to 50%.

Multiple Strike Sacagawea

Double Strike—$10 to $500. (Additional strikes add to the value of the error.)

1979 Lincoln Capped Die Strike

Capped Die Strikes—$25 to $200. (Image of other strikes is clear on most valuable specimens of this error.)

One-Sided Strike—$10 to $500.

Blank Planchant—$1 to $200.

Weak Strikes—usually decreases the value of the coin.

Cuds and Die Breaks—$5 to $250.

Filled Die—$1 to $25. (Certain exceptions exist, for example the 1922 cent, where the mint mark was filled. When errors become recognized and cataloged their prices increase considerably.)

Rotated Dies—$1 to $25.

Re-engravings—Very dependent on date and recognition accorded to the re-engraving.

CHAPTER 2

DETERMINING A COIN'S VALUE

That's it worth? The question seems simple — the answer is not. Let us look at some of the ways the question of worth can be answered and turn to factors that, when taken together, determine value.

CATALOGUE VALUE

This is the price listed in a book like this one. It is an attempt to set out the average price for which a coin retails and is arrived at by comparing the prices at which many sellers are willing to part with a particular coin. It is not; however, an offering price since the author of the catalogue may not even be a dealer and, consequently, have no coins for sale. Further, since catalogues are printed far less frequently than a dealer's price list, it is often the case that a catalogue price can become dated. Also, it is not unusual for a dealer to offer coins at a percentage of catalogue prices. You can see then how unrealistic it would be to think that the price you have found in the catalogue is the one you will eventually or easily receive for your coin. Better to think of this price as a "ballpark" figure from which a deal can be struck.

RETAIL VALUE

This is the price at which a dealer may offer a coin. There may be considerable variance in this price from dealer to dealer. Such a price is dependent on many factors including how much was paid for the coin, when it was purchased, how many of the particular item the dealer may possess, how many coins are being purchased in the deal, how large the overall transaction is, how hard the buyer is willing to bargain to acquire the coin, etc. Further, this is the value that will probably be placed on your coins if you ask for an appraisal or ask to have your collection valued for insurance purposes. Retail price is the closest to the replacement value of a coin.

Wholesale Value

This is the price at which a dealer would expect to purchase a coin from a fellow dealer. The term is also used at times to indicate a quantity price at which a seller or buyer may be willing to exchange a large number of a particular item. Should a dealer make an offer on a coin or collection, it only makes sense that the offer will be somewhat below what he knows he would have to pay a supplier or wholesaler. The reason for this has to do with the fact that when the offer is made to the dealer, it is unlikely that this one coin will be something for which he has an immediate need. Also in buying a collection there will always be particular pieces that the dealer has little interest in buying. His lack of interest will be reflected in the offer he makes.

Buy Price

This is the price that a dealer is most likely to quote you when you persist in asking what your coin or collection is worth. You can see by now that this price will be substantially below what the dealer believes he can ask as a retail price. Most coins will have a buy price of something on the order of 50-75% of the price at which a dealer would retail the coin. If a coin is especially desirable, the offer may be as high as 90% of retail. Many coin publications have a section of want ads, where dealer's nationwide place offers for coins that they especially need. Once you are able to properly identify the coins you have, these ads will give you a good idea of what you can expect to receive for them should you wish to sell.

Factors Determining Value

Essentially, there are four factors that influence or determine the market price of a coin.

Mintage

A common mistake made by the novice collector is to think that "old" means "rare" and, therefore, "valuable." Actually, this is a confusion of categories. Older coins generally have lower mintages, but it is really the number of coins of an issue that were minted (or currently survive, which is also a function of age) that determines a coin's value.

Many Large cents of the early 1800s can be purchased for $10 to $200. Their mintages often run from 6-10 million. The 1857 issue, the last one, has a very low mintage at only one-third of a million. Though a later date, it is considerably scarcer than many earlier dates and commands a retail price of $46 or so in very good condition.

A small number of fairly recent coins are quite valuable because of low mintages. The 1931S Lincoln cent, the 1950D Jefferson nickel, and the 1932D and S Washington quarters are all keys to their series.

Simply by consulting mintage figures one could probably get a fairly good idea as to whether a coin is valuable. There is a confounding variable, however. The surviving number of some issues is considerably less than the quantity originally minted. This is because of melting, loss, or destruction of some other sort. For instance, the mintage of the 1903O Morgan dollar is quite high at 4.5 million. A fine specimen can retail for $200—10 to 15 times the price of silver dollars of far less mintage. Speculation has it that a large portion of this issue was melted under the Pittman Act of 1918. An exact figure on the number of extant 1903O dollars is, of course, not known. But if price is any indication, the number of coins of this issue that survive must be something well below a half million.

During the time around 1980, when silver soared to as high as $50 an ounce, many of the most recent silver coins were sent to the smelters. There has been any number of attempts by those who were buying large quantities of silver coins at that time to give, on the basis of their own sample, an estimate of how the melt might have gone on a date by date basis. It could well turn out that many coins thought to be very common are not so. It is doubtful that any rarities were created, but the unreliability of the mintage figures is nevertheless intriguing.

CONDITION

If the secrets to real estate value are location, location, and location, then the most overlooked factors in coin value are condition, condition, and condition. How well preserved a coin is, how close to its original mint state, how well it was struck, all these greatly affect the value of a coin. For example, a 1921S Walking Liberty half dollar can easily be purchased for $22-$30 in good to very good condition. In mint state 65 (MS-65) you may well have to pay $25,000 for it. So few have survived in such pristine condition that a truly superb specimen can command such a large sum.

To complicate matters, it is difficult, if not impossible for the novice collector to tell the difference between a "super coin" such as the one described above and an MS-60 specimen (the lowest uncirculated grade) which sells for something on the order of $8,000.

Grading differences are found among circulated coins also, although here the price differences are moderate. This entire discussion is meant to drive home the point about how critical it is for the collector to gain experience in learning how to grade coins. This volume can only serve as an introduction to this art/science. Before you purchase or sell your first coin, you should obtain a good book on grading, preferably one with extensive drawings or photos.

The next step is to seek out someone who is knowledgeable about coins, preferably someone who does not desire to buy your coins or sell any to you. A coin club is usually a good place to find such a person. Ask to be shown a coin of the same series in each of the grades that are listed below. Nothing can take the place of this hands-on experience. The point here is to determine what passes for extremely fine condition when a disinterested party grades a coin before you realize the coin you bought actually grades far less. Especially at first, my advice would be to go very slowly, ask a lot of questions, compare the judgments of several people, and then take the plunge with low-priced coins where a mistake will not mean a severe monetary loss.

Grading is a very controversial area. Legitimate differences about how well preserved or worn a coin is can occur. And grading standards have shifted over the years even within the most prestigious grading bodies. The American Numismatic Association Certification Service is far stricter now than it was just a few years ago. Why this happened is anybody's guess, but

I believe in part it was due to more educated buyers entering what had become a buyer's market. The tendency is always there to push the coins one has for sale a grade or two higher. After all, everyone wants to realize the best price they can get. Likewise, when buying, it is not uncommon to talk the coin down. These are some of the things that we come to expect in many of life's transactions. However, once these tendencies are recognized, your strategy should be not to buy or sell unless you and the other person can pretty much agree on the coin's grade. And this means you must do some homework. You must seek to close the advantage in grading knowledge that the other party in the transaction may have.

What follows are generic descriptions of the condition of U.S. coins. Each coin series or type has certain peculiarities regarding high points, etc., by which wear can be detected and calculated.

Fair/Poor (FA)—Most of the design and date of the coin will be obliterated by extreme wear.

About Good (AG)—Rims will be worn into the field of the coin. The date and the design will be partly worn away.

Good (G)—Rims are fully distinct from the field. All of the large design features and dates are intact.

Very Good (VG)—Rims, date and large design features are strong.

Fine (F)—Medium-sized design features specific to the design are clear and distinct. All letters in "Liberty" show on appropriate coins.

Very Fine (VF)—Slight wear apparent on the highest features. All lettering is sharp.

Extremely Fine (XF)—Large and medium design features are sharp. Some mint luster remains.

Almost Uncirculated (AU)—all original design features are sharp. Only slight wear or light rubbing is visible on the highest features. Mint luster is almost completely intact.

Uncirculated (UNC) or (MS60)—No wear or rubbing can be found on the most prominent design features. Luster is intact, although there may be many small marks and scratches evident in the field of the coin.

Choice Uncirculated (CU) or (MS63).

Gem Uncirculated (GU) or (MS65)—a well struck uncirculated coin. Bag marks and other abrasions are minimal. Full mint luster has been retained.

Proof (PR)—a description often included in the grading of coins. However, this description better refers to a special striking process in which care has been taken to bring about an especially well-struck coin, not permitted to come into contact with other coins, and consequently free of all marks and abrasions. Such a coin, of course, can have been mishandled at the mint or afterward (usually referred to as "impaired.") Some have even been known to circulate. Consequently, there can be different grades of proof coins.

THE FOLLOWING PHOTOS SHOW THE WALKING LIBERTY HALF DOLLAR IN EACH OF THE GRADES FROM ABOUT GOOD TO UNCIRCULATED.

ABOUT GOOD

GOOD

VERY GOOD

FINE

VERY FINE

EXTREMELY FINE

ALMOST UNCIRCULATED

UNCIRCULATED

When assessing the condition of a coin there are other important aspects beyond the wear that the coin may have undergone. Below is a handy check list. Listed first are things that detract from a coin's appearance and value.

CLEANED

It is almost never the case that the normal cleaning agents for copper, nickel, silver or gold can be used on coins. If a coin looks cleaned its worth is less. Copper cleaner, for instance, gives copper coins a shiny appearance, but since it is an abrasive, the coin's surface suffers greatly. A silver coin, when dipped in silver cleaners, takes on an unnatural appearance that no experienced collector would mistake for luster. Once a coin is pitted or dark there is not much that can be done about it. Cleaning will only make things worse. Most coins must be dropped a grade or two if cleaning has taken place. It is almost always a good idea to avoid purchasing such coins. Wait for one with no problems to come along. In the long run, it will be much easier to sell.

Scratches, rim nicks, abrasions, dents—all seriously affect a coin's value.

Weak strike—when a great many coins are struck from the same die, the clarity of the impression gradually lessens. Even an uncirculated coin may lack certain high relief features because of this. In extreme cases large elements of the design may be very unclear.

Spots, discolorations, carbon spots—Copper coins especially suffer from exposure to the elements. Corrosion and pitting must be looked for on early copper coins. And, strange as it seems, even very recent coins can be affected. Proof sets, sealed in their original government packaging sometimes develop white spots on the silver coins and carbon spots on the cent.

Holes—when coins have been used as jewelry often a hole has been drilled in them so that they can be worn on a chain. To disguise this, the hole may be filled. However, in every case, the value of the coin is greatly affected.

The absence of all of the previously listed defects combined with some or all of the following features listed usually enhance a coin's value.

Strong strike—early strikes from a die show more of the detail of the design. Coins with evidence of a full strike are much sought after and command considerable premiums. Full steps on the reverse of the Jefferson nickel, a full split band on the reverse of the Mercury dime, a full head on the obverse of the Standing Liberty quarter dollar, full bell lines on the reverse of the Franklin half dollar are all evidence of strong strikes.

Toning—a very small number of mostly uncirculated coins react to the elements such that the surface of the coin takes on a mellow, even quality that at times can even be iridescent. Where the toning is uneven the eye appeal and, thereby, value of the coin is lessened.

POPULARITY

In 1960, when I first began to collect coins, Lincoln pennies were the rage. Everyone, it seemed, wanted to fill the penny boards that provided a hole for each date and mint mark. Since then not only has the lowly Lincoln fallen from favor, but date collecting itself has given way to other styles of collecting. Today silver dollars, gold, and type coins are quite popular. Silver dollars never seem to lose favor with the collecting public. Especially in the uncirculated grades, a silver dollar will often sell for much more than a coin from another series that is of a comparable grade and mintage. For example, one can only imagine how much an 1871 silver three-cent piece would command if the series were as popular as Morgan dollars. The mintage of this coin was only 4,360 and yet it retails for around $750 in the lowest uncirculated grade. Hardly anyone collects this series by date and so the demand for a coin of any particular year is very low. Typically, a collector would want such a coin only as an instance of the type it represents.

Fads come and go in coin collecting as in everything else. Sometimes it pays to stay off the beaten path and simply collect what interests you. Who knows, maybe popularity will eventually coincide with your interests and you will be on the ground floor price-wise.

METAL CONTENT

Every U.S. silver and gold coin has what can be called a "floor" value or "junk" value based on its metal content. Presumably, a coin cannot be worth less than this unless part of it is missing or the coin is so worn that its metal content (by weight or fineness) is not clear. Or, as we shall see directly, the transaction involving it is so inconsequential as not to be worth the time of the buyer.

On the other hand, many silver coins have no significant value over the silver content. Consequently, the junk value and the price at which one would realistically expect to sell that same coin to a dealer (its numismatic value) are the same.

Let us take some examples which will permit us to elaborate on the chart that follows.

CASE NO. 1

We find a badly worn 1934P Walking Liberty half dollar. It is discolored and has some small dents in the rim. In this condition common silver coins have no numismatic value. However, if the spot price of silver for today is $20.00/oz., we can calculate the silver value of the half dollar by multiplying the weight of the coin, 192.9 grains (about .4 oz. since there are 480 grains per ounce) times the fineness (the metal content of the coin is 90% silver) times the going price of silver.

$$.402 \text{ oz.} \times .90 \times \$17 = \$6.15$$

So that ugly half dollar is worth roughly 12 times its face value. Why roughly? Well, we should not lose sight of the fact that this is only one coin. Could we fault a dealer who offered us only $4 or even $5.00 for the coin? I think not. After all, we are still talking about a $1.00

profit for the dealer. Is such a transaction really worth his time? Should we have $100 face of comparable silver coins, it becomes more realistic to expect something very close to $1200—the value of the silver alone in such coins.

Actually, in bag ($1,000 face) quantities, silver coins at times carry a small premium over the silver content, although this has not been true for the last several years. The premium, when there is one, probably derives from the ease with which the bags can be traded, the magic of owning silver pieces that were officially minted and actually circulated, or some such thing. However, there are times when this premium has disappeared and, in fact, as strange as it may sound, there are times when it is very difficult to obtain the full silver-content price for silver coins. Let me explain. The price for silver coin bags might be called somewhat "inelastic" especially when the price of silver rises or falls dramatically. During the phenomenal run-up of the price of silver in 1980, when it peaked at around $50/oz., dealers were quite unwilling to pay much more than 20 to 25 times face. (If we use our chart we can see that even at $40/oz. silver coins should have commanded something like 28 times face—about $14 for a half dollar!)

Dealers claimed they were having difficulty receiving payments on a timely basis from smelters. And, when you think about it, this makes sense. At the time everybody was trying to have their coins melted into bars or other fabricated products, the smelters became backlogged and were unwilling to take the risk that prices would remain high. Dealers likewise began to lay off some of the risk through the lower prices they were willing to pay.

Quick price rises (and in some cases declines) are not necessarily going to be reflected immediately in the coin bag quotes you will receive. When the volatility ends, the bag price once again comes into line. A dealer, especially a small one, is naturally going to minimize his exposure to risk. If one wants better elasticity in price, then one might better hold silver bars, or silver stocks.

Newspapers, both local and national now carry daily spot price information on the price of gold, silver, platinum (and oil!). More and more individuals now access prices on their computers and kitco.com is probably the most visited site. Current values can be found for individual coins, bullion pieces, bars and bags. Most large dealers would normally be willing to sell at these quoted prices and buy at from $200 to $300 less. Bag prices quoted in coin newspaper and magazine dealer ads will typically be several days to several weeks out of date. The price in any actual transaction will almost always have to be negotiated by phone, in person, or on-line that very day. Prices change hourly. So if you have an investment in this area, it is of paramount importance to find some way to keep current on prices.

Also, trading in smaller than bag quantities will mean a wider buy/sell price spread. Increasingly, dealers have sought to make distinctions in types of "junk" silver coins. As you might imagine, a bag of much worn silver coins will contain less silver than a bag containing coins that have seen little circulation. A spot check might be necessary to uncover this. Recently, half dollars, and coins from the earlier series (Mercury dimes and Walking Liberty halves) have become more desirable and command a slight additional premium of about $100 to $300 per bag. Common uncirculated silver coins are traded at a premium of from 5-20% over regular bag prices.

CASE NO.2

Your aunt has given you a 1921 silver dollar. The date is the year of his birth and he had it until he passed away. You don't wish to sell the coin but you do want to know its value so as to make a decision concerning how best to care for it.

The first thing you must do is correctly identify the piece. There were two types of silver dollars issued in 1921. The Peace type, in almost any condition has a numismatic value beyond its silver content. More likely, however, the dollar is of the Morgan type. In this case, unless the coin is in one of the highest grades, its value will be determined largely by the going price of silver. Dollars, because of their extreme popularity, have carried a significant premium above silver content making their price even more inelastic than other silver coins. Dollar bags, for which the 1921 Morgan is a staple, are quoted on the basis of 1,000 piece lots. With silver at $17/oz., bags trade in the $1,400 area. The silver-content value for the bag would be something on the order of $12,500—making dollars a somewhat unsuitable way to invest in silver.

As you can see, your aunt's coin demands no special precautions be taken for its care. You could expect to receive something around $12-18 for it from a dealer, although I am sure your aunt would like you to keep the coin to remember him by. In fact, most people have trouble understanding how a piece they have prized for a lifetime commands such a paltry sum. You could easily buy one like it for around $15, however.

CASE NO.3

A small coin accumulation, assembled by your grandmother has been given to you. Included are three rolls of Kennedy half dollars. They do not look to be silver coins so you decide to spend them. But wait! Even though other denominations ceased being regularly issued in silver after 1964, half dollars were minted for general circulation with a 40% silver content from 1965-70. This part of your inheritance can be calculated as follows:

Weight	Silver Content	Spot Price	Value
.37 oz. x	.40 fine x	$17/oz.	= $2.50

Your rolls ($10 face each) are worth about $50.00 each. Putting them in with your pocket change would certainly have been foolish.

CASE NO.4

One other coin is often traded on the basis of its "junk" silver value. From 1942-45, due to a projected wartime shortage of nickel, the composition of the five-cent piece was changed to include 35% silver. Circulated pieces are identifiable by their darker gray color and the change in the placement and size of the mint mark. Both types of five-cent pieces were minted in 1942. So not every coin with that date will have silver value. In high grades these "silver nickels" have a numismatic value beyond the silver value. The value of low-grade coins can be computed:

Weight	Silver Content	Spot Price	Value
.16 oz. x	.35 fine x	$17 /oz. =	$.95

Quantities of less than a roll are of little interest to a dealer. With silver at $17/oz. expect to sell at about $25 /roll and buy $ 38.00 roll.

CASE NO.5

While remodeling your house, you find a $5 Indian gold piece behind the woodwork. The rim has a number of large dents and the coin has been defaced from what appear to be a number of deep scratches. Should you be tickled with your find?

Well, gold coins, too, have a "junk" value. However, unlike silver coins, very few gold coins fall into this category. A gold coin must either be damaged or very severely worn not to have some numismatic value. Even then, such coins are good candidates for use in jewelry. The purchaser of a ring or pendant is usually not as concerned about a coin's condition since often only one side will show or the rim can be obscured by the setting.

C onsequently, the floor price calculated below and on our chart represents the absolute lowest price an identifiable, complete $5 gold coin can be worth. Your baseboard find is a good one!

Weight	Gold Content		Spot Price	Value
.269 oz. x	.90 fine	x	$875/oz. =	$210

All the above calculations have been based on:

480 grains/troy oz.	1 gram=.0322 troy oz.
31.104 grams/troy oz.	1 gram=15.4342 grains

BULLION VALUE OF SILVER COINS
(Per $1.00 Face Value)

Spot Price	Low Grade/ Circulated 10c, 25c, 50c	40% Silver 50c	Low Grade/ Circulated Silver War 5c	Low Grade/ Damaged Silver $1.00
$ 4.00	$ 2.90	$ 1.18	$4.40	$3.09
$ 5.00	3.60	1.48	5.60	3.87
$ 6.00	4.40	1.78	6.80	4.64
$ 7.00	5.10	2.08	8.00	5.42
$10.00	7.20	2.96	11.20	7.73
$15.00	10.90	4.46	17.00	11.60
$20.00	14.40	5.92	22.40	15.48
$30.00	21.60	8.88	33.60	23.19
$50.00	36.00	14.80	56.00	38.69

Bag Quantities (Wholesale price includes usual premium)

Spot Price	Low Grade/ Circulated 10c, 25c, 50c ($1000 Face)	40% Silver 50c ($1000 Face)	Low Grade/ Circulated Silver War 5c ($1000 Face)	Low Grade/ Damaged Silver $1.00 ($1000 Face)
$4.00	$3000-$3300	$1200-$1300	$3200-$3400	$5300-$5500
$5.00	3700-4000	1500-1600	3800-4200	5400-57500
$6.00	4500-4800	1800-2000	4700- 6000	6500-8000
$8.00	6000-6300	2400-2600	6300-6800	6700-8000
$10.00	7500-7800	3000-3200	7700-8100	8300-8500
$12.00	8900-9200	3600-3800	9100-9500	10000-11000
$14.00	10400-10700	4200-4400	10600-11000	11500-12000
$16.00	12000-12,600	4800-5200	12600-13600	13400-16000
$18.00	13500-14100	5400-5800	14000-14900	15000-16500
$20.00	15000-15600	6000-6400	15400-16200	16600-17000

BULLION VALUE OF GOLD COINS
(Assumes the coin is damaged or otherwise uncollectible)
Denomination

Spot Price	$1.00	$2.50	$5.00	$10.00	$20.00
$ 250.00	12.10	30.25	60.50	121.00	242.00
$ 300.00	14.50	36.25	72.50	145.00	290.00
$ 350.00	17.00	42.50	85.00	170.00	339.00
$ 400.00	19.35	48.00	96.25	193.50	387.00
$ 500.00	24.20	60.50	121.00	242.00	484.00
$ 600.00	29.00	72.50	145.00	290.00	580.00
$ 900.00	43.40	108.50	217.00	434.00	868.00
$1000.00	48.40	121.00	242.00	484.00	968.00

Value as a Function of Time and Knowledge

S ome, I suppose, would argue that in many cases a coin's value is a function of work (time) and knowledge. There is some truth to this—a truth that is often lost on a novice buyer or seller. Let me explain.

With regard to many inexpensive coins, the cost of the time and work involved in identifying, pricing, packaging, marketing, etc., often exceed any intrinsic worth that the coin may have. When one purchases a coin for $2 it may well be that the entire value of the coin can be written off to the costs of selling it. The real value of the coin consequently is derived from getting it to a point where a sale can be made. To speak in terms of resale then is to miss the point. How much is a roll of AU 1950D cents worth beyond its face value? Would it be out of the question for a dealer to charge 25 cents each for such a coin? And what portion of that price might one expect to recover upon a resale? Twenty-five cents does not represent the value of the coin in any sense other than the cost of selling it. One should expect to recover almost nothing with any attempt at resale.

Secondly, and somewhat more controversial, is the part that knowledge should play in the determination of worth. If I were to spend considerable time researching the relative scarcity of various types of early large cents, am I obligated to make that knowledge available to all who request an offer for their collection? Is my knowledge worth something? And is the value of that scarce variety I discover a product of my recognizing it as such?

These questions may well border on the area of business ethics; and therefore may well be outside the scope of this volume. But that is not to say that they will have no bearing on an actual transaction. Rather, I think, the average dealer expects to be compensated for his or her knowledge and experience. How that is to be done often remains fairly unclear to the party in the transaction who lacks the knowledge.

CHAPTER 3

U.S MINOR COINAGE

his chapter attempts to assess the value of U.S. coins composed of base metals (copper and nickel), as opposed to precious metals. Recent clad coinage is discussed in Chapter4, along with the silver coinage these clad coins were meant to replace.

VALUES OF MINOR COINS
HALF CENTS MINTED 1793-1857

LIBERTY CAP TYPE (FLOWING HAIR)　　　　**LIBERTY CAP TYPE**

LIBERTY CAP 1793-1797

	G	VG	F	VF	XF	AU	MS60
1793 Head Left	3000.00	4600.00	7000.00	10400.00	18000.00	28000.00	50000.00
1794 Head Right	360.00	470.00	750.00	1320.00	3200.00	6300.00	12000.00
1795 Lettered Edge, with Pole	360.00	470.00	750.00	1320.00	3000.00	5160.00	7200.00
1795 Lettered Edge, Punct.Date	360.00	470.00	750.00	1320.00	3000.00	6000.00	8640.00
1795 Plain Edge, Punct. Date	360.00	470.00	750.00	1320.00	2880.00	4920.00	7200.00
1795 Plain Edge, No Pole	360.00	470.00	750.00	1320.00	3000.00	6000.00	10200.00
1796 With Pole	16000.00	19000.00	26500.00	47000.00	54000.00	62000.00	128000.00
1796 No Pole	18400.00	24400.00	39350.00	51000.00	66000.00	93600.00	150000.00
1797 Lettered Edge	900.00	1680.00	3360.00	7200.00	21000.00	36000.00	48000.00
1797 Plain Edge	380.00	480.00	780.00	1440.00	2900.00	4920.00	8400.00
1797 Gripped Edge	15600.00	38400.00	48000.00	60000.00	72000.00	90000.00	0.00
1797 1 Above 1, Plain Edge	360.00	470.00	750.00	1320.00	2880.00	4920.00	12600.00

DRAPED BUST TYPE

DRAPED BUST 1800-1808	G	VG	F	VF	XF	AU	MS60
1800	48.00	63.00	84.00	168.00	360.00	600.00	1320.00
1802 2/0 Reverse of 1800	16800.00	22800.00	30000.00	42000.00	72000.00	96000.00	0.00
1802 2/0 2nd Reverse	575.00	1220.00	2830.00	7410.00	16050.00	27600.00	0.00
1803	48.00	63.00	90.00	210.00	720.00	1125.00	2400.00
1804 Plain 4- with Stems	48.00	72.00	120.00	222.00	570.00	1400.00	2500.00
1804 Plain 4-Stemless	48.00	64.00	76.00	120.00	215.00	480.00	900.00
1804 Crosslet 4 w/Stems	48.00	63.00	76.00	120.00	220.00	480.00	910.00
1804 Crosslet 4 - Stemless	48.00	63.00	76.00	120.00	220.00	480.00	910.00
1804 Spiked Chin	48.00	63.00	78.00	120.00	270.00	520.00	1000.00
1805 Medium 5- Stemless	48.00	63.00	78.00	120.00	285.00	550.00	995.00
1805 Small 5 - w/Stems	700.00	1250.00	2775.00	4150.00	7800.00	12000.00	0.00
1805 Large 5 - w/Stems	48.00	63.00	80.00	120.00	285.00	550.00	995.00
1806 Small 6 - w/Stems	162.00	300.00	498.00	900.00	2125.00	4300.00	6960.00
1806 Small 6 - Stemless	48.00	63.00	76.00	120.00	255.00	540.00	940.00
1806 Large 6 - w/Stems	48.00	63.00	78.00	120.00	285.00	575.00	965.00
1807	48.00	63.00	80.00	120.00	380.00	650.00	1350.00
1808 8 over 7	96.00	192.00	420.00	960.00	2820.00	7000.00	11400.00
1808 Normal Date	48.00	63.00	80.00	120.00	275.00	620.00	1320.00

CLASSIC HEAD 1809-1829

	G	VG	F	VF	XF	AU	MS60
1809 Normal Date	44.00	60.00	64.00	68.00	96.00	192.00	360.00
1809 9 over 6	45.00	72.00	78.00	90.00	204.00	540.00	680.00
1809 Circle inside 0	44.00	60.00	68.00	96.00	250.00	378.00	680.00
1810	45.00	65.00	94.00	160.00	370.00	750.00	1150.00
1811	240.00	600.00	1320.00	1680.00	3480.00	5100.00	6600.00

1825	44.00	60.00	64.00	68.00	140.00	320.00	625.00
1826	44.00	60.00	64.00	68.00	102.00	175.00	360.00
1828 13 Stars	44.00	60.00	64.00	68.00	84.00	145.00	225.00
1828 12 Stars	44.00	60.00	65.00	75.00	160.00	268.00	875.00
1829	44.00	60.00	64.00	68.00	108.00	170.00	270.00

CLASSIC HEAD 1831-1836

	G	VG	F	VF	XF	AU	MS60
1831	3600.00	3900.00	4200.00	4800.00	6600.00	9600.00	11400.00
1832	44.00	60.00	64.00	68.00	85.00	137.00	210.00
1833	44.00	60.00	64.00	68.00	85.00	132.00	210.00
1834	44.00	60.00	64.00	68.00	85.00	132.00	210.00
1835	44.00	60.00	64.00	68.00	85.00	132.00	210.00
1836 Proof Only						Proof 63	5000.00

BRAIDED HAIR TYPE

BRAIDED HAIR 1840-1857

1840 Proof Only							
1841 Proof Only							
1842 Proof Only							
1843 Proof On y							
1844 Proof Only							
1845 Proof Only							
1846 Proof On y							
1847 Proof Only							
1848 Proof Only							
1849 Sm Date, Proof Only							
1849 Large Date	44.00	60.00	70.00	75.00	108.00	150.00	240.00
1850	43.00	58.00	68.00	75.00	102.00	145.00	300.00
1851	43.00	58.00	65.00	70.00	81.00	120.00	174.00
1852 Proof Only	(Restrike)					Proof 63	3500.00
1853	43.00	58.00	65.00	70.00	85.00	120.00	175.00

1854	43.00	58.00	65.00	70.00	85.00	120.00	175.00
1855	43.00	58.00	65.00	70.00	85.00	120.00	175.00
1856	43.00	58.00	70.00	75.00	90.00	137.00	210.00
1857	48.00	65.00	96.00	108.00	132.00	187.00	250.00

CENTS MINTED 1793 - DATE
Large Cents Minted 1793 - 1857

CHAIN TYPE

FLOWING HAIR TYPE (CHAIN REVERSE)

	G	VG	F	VF	XF	AU	MS60
1793 "AMERL" In Legend	8700.00	13200.00	18000.00	44000.00	72000.00	125000.00	150000.00
1793 "AMERICA"	6000.00	8400.00	13200.00	29900.00	51000.00	70000.00	105000.00
1793 Periods After "LIBERTY"	7000.00	8800.00	14400.00	31000.00	53000.00	70000.00	110000.00

FLOWING HAIR 1793 WREATH TYPE

FLOWING HAIR TYPE (WREATH REVERSE)

Large Cents-Wreath Type	0.00	0.00	0.00	0.00	0.00	0.00	0.00
1793 Vine/Bars Edge	1750.00	2650.00	4100.00	6300.00	10500.00	19000.00	29000.00
1793 Lettered Edge	1850.00	3100.00	4300.00	6800.00	11500.00	21000.00	31500.00
1793 Strawberry Leaf	125000.00	240000.00	450000.00	0.00	0.00	0.00	0.00

LIBERTY CAP 1793-1796

LIBERTY CAP TYPE

1793 Liberty Cap Type	3400.00	5800.00	11000.00	35000.00	62000.00	101000.00	0.00
1794 Head of 1793	925.00	1440.00	2040.00	5600.00	10200.00	16200.00	0.00
1794 Head of 1794	320.00	420.00	600.00	1275.00	2840.00	4450.00	9000.00
1794 Head of 1795	320.00	420.00	600.00	1275.00	2840.00	4450.00	6200.00

1794 Starred Reverse	9600.00	15000.00	27000.00	42000.00	66000.00	102500.00	
1795 Lettered Edge	320.00	420.00	600.00	1375.00	3250.00	4900.00	6750.00
1795 Plain Edge	320.00	420.00	600.00	1275.00	2600.00	4225.00	4850.00
1795 Reeded Edge	115500.00	165000.00	247500.00	0.00	0.00	0.00	0.00
1795 Jefferson Head	11000.00	18000.00	30000.00	42000.00	84000.00	0.00	0.00
1796	320.00	420.00	745.00	1500.00	3480.00	9100.00	22100.00

LARGE CENTS — DRAPED BUST 1796-1807

	G	VG	F	VF	XF	AU	MS60
1796 Reverse of 1794	120.00	220.00	490.00	1140.00	2360.00	3750.00	0.00
1796 Reverse of 1796	130.00	250.00	480.00	1270.00	2530.00	3860.00	0.00
1796 Reverse of 1797	120.00	210.00	410.00	840.00	1900.00	3220.00	6000.00
1796 "LIHERTY" Error	180.00	550.00	800.00	2100.00	6500.00	16000.00	0.00
1797 Gripped Edge - '96 Rev	120.00	200.00	340.00	510.00	1840.00	3860.00	0.00
1797 Plain Edge -'96 Rev	120.00	200.00	320.00	640.00	2070.00	3920.00	0.00
1797 '97 Rev.- Stems	120.00	200.00	290.00	340.00	950.00	2160.00	3360.00
1797 '97 Rev.-Stemless	130.00	210.00	340.00	750.00	2650.00	4200.00	22800.00
1798 8 over 7	120.00	210.00	310.00	1200.00	3450.00	5200.00	0.00
1798 Reverse of 1796	100.00	170.00	270.00	780.00	2880.00	4500.00	0.00
1798 1st Hair Style	80.00	100.00	180.00	320.00	1270.00	3100.00	4900.00
1798 2nd Hair Style	80.00	100.00	180.00	320.00	1150.00	3010.00	4800.00
1799 9 over 8	2150.00	3750.00	9000.00	22000.00	48000.00	204000.00	0.00
1799	2050.00	3100.00	7450.00	18500.00	41000.00	0.00	0.00
1800 over 1798-Style 1 Hair	65.00	105.00	210.00	610.00	2300.00	4030.00	0.00
1800 80 over 79-Style 2 Hair	65.00	110.00	210.00	400.00	1380.00	2530.00	0.00
1800 Normal Date	65.00	96.00	175.00	340.00	1150.00	2300.00	0.00
1801 Normal Reverse	63.00	93.00	180.00	312.00	840.00	1670.00	2750.00
1801 3 Errors	108.00	168.00	540.00	1240.00	4200.00	7300.00	0.00
1801 Fraction 1/000	66.00	86.00	190.00	320.00	875.00	2050.00	3240.00
1801 1/100 over1/000	66.00	86.00	210.00	440.00	1300.00	2520.00	3960.00
1802 Normal Reverse	54.00	78.00	168.00	300.00	735.00	1250.00	2650.00
1802 Fraction: 1/000	63.00	90.00	204.00	420.00	1420.00	2520.00	4200.00

1802 Stemless	52.00	78.00	168.00	300.00	780.00	1350.00	2100.00
1803SM Date, SM Fraction	52.00	78.00	168.00	300.00	730.00	1250.00	2240.00
1803SM Date, LG Fraction	52.00	78.00	168.00	300.00	750.00	1250.00	2100.00
1803LG Date, SM Fraction	4320.00	6900.00	12600.00	19200.00	0.00	0.00	0.00
1803LG Date, LG Fraction	52.00	84.00	210.00	420.00	1500.00	2840.00	0.00
1803 1/100 over 1/000	60.00	84.00	195.00	380.00	870.00	1560.00	2170.00
1803Stemless Wreath	52.00	78.00	168.00	305.00	780.00	1350.00	2020.00
1804	720.00	1200.00	2100.00	3150.00	6500.00	11300.00	42000.00
1804 Restrike of 1860			420.00	500.00	540.00	570.00	650.00
1805	52.00	78.00	168.00	305.00	750.00	1225.00	2450.00
1806	66.00	90.00	180.00	385.00	1105.00	2450.00	6625.00
1807SM 7 over 6,Blunt 1	1610.00	2725.00	7200.00	10800.00	22000.00	42000.00	0.00
1807 LG 7 over 6	53.00	78.00	168.00	300.00	720.00	1095.00	1980.00
1807 SM Fraction	52.00	78.00	168.00	300.00	720.00	1095.00	1980.00
1807 LG Fraction	52.00	78.00	168.00	300.00	720.00	1095.00	2040.00
1807"Comet" Variety	54.00	80.00	185.00	450.00	1775.00	3630.00	7200.00

Classic Head Type

CLASSIC HEAD 1808-1814

	G	VG	F	VF	XF	AU	MS60
1808	48.00	120.00	195.00	455.00	1050.00	2160.00	3220.00
1809	96.00	204.00	300.00	900.00	2289.00	3960.00	7200.00
1810 10 over 09	44.00	78.00	190.00	490.00	1020.00	2220.00	4200.00
1810 Normal Date	45.00	84.00	190.00	490.00	985.00	1440.00	3220.00
1811 1 over 0	72.00	132.00	380.00	950.00	3280.00	8400.00	12600.00
1811 Normal Date	72.00	132.00	300.00	805.00	1320.00	2340.00	4320.00
1812	44.00	78.00	190.00	440.00	840.00	1825.00	2530.00
1813	44.00	84.00	190.00	490.00	985.00	2125.00	3365.00
1814 Plain 4	44.00	78.00	205.00	420.00	865.00	1970.00	3320.00
1814 Crosslet 4	44.00	78.00	190.00	450.00	920.00	1330.00	2850.00

Coronet Type
[Matron Head 1816 – 1839]
CORONET HEAD 1816-1839

	G	VG	F	VF	XF	AU	MS60
1816	26.00	31.00	38.00	90.00	168.00	283.00	345.00
1817 13 stars	20.00	26.00	33.00	62.00	108.00	209.00	253.00
1817 15 stars	33.00	42.00	53.00	120.00	510.00	850.00	1495.00
1818	20.00	26.00	33.00	62.00	108.00	192.00	247.00
1819 9 over 8	26.00	31.00	38.00	76.00	270.00	385.00	525.00
1819	20.00	26.00	33.00	62.00	102.00	192.00	265.00
1820 20 over 19	30.00	35.00	45.00	84.00	281.00	450.00	635.00
1820	20.00	26.00	33.00	66.00	104.00	197.00	280.00
1821	36.00	57.00	114.00	360.00	780.00	2325.00	5450.00
1822	28.00	34.00	48.00	102.00	186.00	444.00	675.00
1823 3 over 2	50.00	96.00	270.00	480.00	1800.00	3840.00	
1823	60.00	114.00	300.00	600.00	2520.00	7200.00	13750.00
1824 4 over 2	28.00	35.00	72.00	300.00	870.00	1560.00	3350.00
1824	20.00	26.00	33.00	160.00	330.00	480.00	935.00
1825	20.00	26.00	33.00	90.00	270.00	504.00	875.00
1826 6 over 5	22.00	28.00	66.00	180.00	720.00	1320.00	1975.00
1826	20.00	26.00	33.00	75.00	156.00	318.00	720.00
1827	20.00	26.00	33.00	90.00	120.00	228.00	360.00
1828	20.00	26.00	33.00	78.00	150.00	300.00	420.00
1829	20.00	26.00	33.00	90.00	126.00	240.00	380.00
1830	20.00	26.00	33.00	65.00	114.00	228.00	360.00
1831	20.00	26.00	33.00	62.00	96.00	192.00	240.00
1832	20.00	26.00	33.00	63.00	108.00	204.00	360.00
1833	20.00	26.00	33.00	62.00	102.00	198.00	270.00
1834 Lg 8 & Strs,MD Let	65.00	108.00	138.00	228.00	540.00	975.00	
1834	20.00	26.00	33.00	66.00	120.00	198.00	270.00
1835	20.00	26.00	33.00	62.00	84.00	192.00	250.00
1836	20.00	26.00	33.00	62.00	96.00	192.00	250.00
1837	20.00	26.00	33.00	62.00	96.00	192.00	200.00
1838	20.00	26.00	33.00	62.00	96.00	192.00	200.00
1839	20.00	26.00	33.00	62.00	96.00	192.00	270.00

MATURE HEAD

LARGE CENTS — BRAIDED HAIR 1839-1857

	G	VG	F	VF	XF	AU	MS60
1839 Braided Hair	18.50	22.00	25.00	38.00	60.00	180.00	250.00
1840	18.50	22.00	25.00	38.00	58.00	156.00	220.00
1841	18.50	22.00	25.00	38.00	58.00	168.00	230.00
1842	18.50	22.00	25.00	38.00	56.00	130.00	190.00
1843	18.50	22.00	25.00	38.00	56.00	130.00	190.00
1844	18.50	22.00	25.00	38.00	56.00	140.00	190.00
1844 over 81	27.00	33.00	42.00	78.00	120.00	252.00	560.00
1845	18.50	22.00	25.00	38.00	56.00	120.00	150.00
1846	18.50	22.00	25.00	38.00	56.00	120.00	150.00
1847	18.50	22.00	25.00	38.00	56.00	120.00	150.00
1847 7 over SM 7	23.00	28.00	36.00	48.00	114.00	150.00	220.00
1848	18.50	22.00	25.00	38.00	56.00	120.00	150.00
1849	18.50	22.00	25.00	38.00	56.00	126.00	180.00
1850	18.50	22.00	25.00	38.00	56.00	114.00	150.00
1851	18.50	22.00	25.00	38.00	56.00	114.00	150.00
1851 over 81	23.00	29.00	38.00	50.00	144.00	196.00	420.00
1852	18.50	22.00	25.00	38.00	56.00	114.00	150.00
1853	18.50	22.00	25.00	38.00	56.00	114.00	150.00
1854	18.50	22.00	25.00	38.00	56.00	114.00	150.00
1855	18.50	22.00	25.00	38.00	56.00	120.00	150.00
1855 "Knob on Ear"	20.00	24.00	32.00	45.00	90.00	168.00	280.00
1856	18.50	22.00	25.00	38.00	56.00	110.00	150.00
1857	140.00	165.00	195.00	210.00	250.00	300.00	350.00

Flying Eagle Cents Minted 1856 - 1858

FLYING EAGLE CENT

	G	VG	F	VF	XF	AU	MS60
1856	5200.00	6050.00	7900.00	9000.00	10500.00	12500.00	15250.00
1857	25.00	36.00	28.00	38.00	110.00	135.00	265.00
1858 S. Ltrs	24.00	35.00	28.00	38.00	110.00	150.00	265.00
1858 L.Ltrs.	25.00	36.00	32.00	45.00	120.00	175.00	300.00

Indian Head Type Minted 1859 - 1909

INDIAN HEAD CENTS 1859-1909

	G	VG	F	VF	XF	AU	MS60
1859	12.00	16.00	24.00	43.00	98.00	170.00	200.00
1860	11.00	16.00	21.00	30.00	63.00	100.00	190.00
1861	18.00	28.00	38.00	50.00	91.00	160.00	170.00
1862	9.00	12.00	13.00	17.00	33.00	70.00	90.00
1863	9.00	12.00	13.00	14.00	31.00	70.00	80.00
1864	14.00	20.00	31.00	44.00	66.00	95.00	140.00
1864 Bronze	8.00	15.00	22.00	37.00	58.00	80.00	108.00
1864 L Variety	44.00	59.00	109.00	159.00	250.00	300.00	390.00
1865	7.00	13.00	20.00	24.00	38.00	70.00	90.00
1866	36.00	42.00	59.00	89.00	160.00	210.00	245.00
1867	42.00	57.00	76.00	99.00	154.00	210.00	240.00
1868	33.00	38.00	56.00	96.00	143.00	200.00	220.00
1869	67.00	89.00	179.00	279.00	350.00	455.00	495.00
1870	39.00	72.00	174.00	244.00	322.00	420.00	495.00
1871	65.00	84.00	234.00	264.00	360.00	420.00	520.00
1872	77.00	139.00	329.00	364.00	505.00	635.00	680.00
1873	18.00	29.00	52.00	72.00	137.00	185.00	220.00
1874	14.00	22.00	39.00	52.00	91.00	130.00	190.00

	G	VG	F	VF	XF	AU	MS60
1875	14.00	26.00	44.00	54.00	98.00	140.00	195.00
1876	26.00	32.00	54.00	64.00	185.00	240.00	295.00
1877	750.00	830.00	1250.00	1700.00	2200.00	2750.00	3400.00
1878	24.00	33.00	59.00	114.00	190.00	245.00	295.00
1879	8.00	13.00	14.00	31.00	70.00	80.00	90.00
1880	5.00	10.00	11.00	14.00	33.00	61.00	84.00
1881	5.00	9.00	11.00	14.00	29.00	45.00	59.00
1882	5.00	9.00	11.00	14.00	26.00	45.00	59.00
1883	5.00	9.00	11.00	14.00	26.00	45.00	59.00
1884	5.00	9.00	11.00	14.00	33.00	55.00	75.00
1885	8.00	11.00	15.00	27.00	65.00	82.00	105.00
1886	6.00	10.00	21.00	49.00	119.00	145.00	164.00
1887	2.00	2.00	4.00	7.00	16.00	25.00	42.00
1888	2.00	2.00	4.00	6.00	18.00	25.00	41.00
1889	2.00	2.00	4.00	6.00	10.00	23.00	35.00
1890	2.00	2.00	4.00	6.00	10.00	23.00	35.00
1891	2.00	2.00	4.00	6.00	10.00	23.00	34.00
1892	2.00	2.00	4.00	6.00	17.00	23.00	33.00
1893	2.00	2.00	4.00	6.00	10.00	23.00	32.00
1894	5.00	6.00	12.00	18.00	45.00	55.00	75.00
1895	2.00	2.00	4.00	6.00	12.00	18.00	28.00
1896	2.00	2.00	4.00	6.00	10.00	19.00	30.00
1897	2.00	2.00	4.00	6.00	10.00	18.00	27.00
1898	2.00	2.00	4.00	6.00	10.00	17.00	26.00
1899	2.00	2.00	4.00	6.00	10.00	16.00	26.00
1900	2.00	2.00	2.00	3.00	8.00	16.00	26.00
1901	2.00	2.00	2.00	3.00	8.00	16.00	26.00
1902	2.00	2.00	2.00	3.00	8.00	16.00	26.00
1903	2.00	2.00	2.00	3.00	8.00	16.00	26.00
1904	2.00	2.00	2.00	3.00	8.00	16.00	26.00
1905	2.00	2.00	2.00	3.00	8.00	16.00	26.00
1906	2.00	2.00	2.00	3.00	8.00	16.00	26.00
1907	2.00	2.00	2.00	3.00	8.00	16.00	26.00
1908	2.00	2.00	2.00	3.00	9.00	19.00	25.00
1908S	76.00	84.00	95.00	100.00	175.00	250.00	275.00

1909	15.00	16.00	17.00	18.00	20.00	28.00	35.00
1909S	475.00	500.00	530.00	550.00	650.00	700.00	800.00

INDIAN HEAD TYPE MINTED 1909 - 1958

LINCOLN CENT TYPE (WHEAT REVERSE - 1958)

The designer's intials (Victor D. Brenner are found at the bottom inside the rim on the reverse in 1909. They were discontinued from 1909-1917 and replaced below Lincoln's shoulder from 1918 to date.

	G	VG	F	VF	XF	AU	MS60
1909	12.00	13.00	14.00	15.00	16.00	17.00	20.00
1909VDB	6.00	6.50	7.00	7.25	7.50	11.00	14.00
1909S	160.00	105.00	170.00	210.00	275.00	290.00	400.00
1909SVDB	800.00	900.00	1050.00	1200.00	1350.00	1500.00	1700.00
1910	0.25	0.30	0.40	0.60	3.00	10.00	18.00
1910S	16.00	19.00	22.00	25.00	45.00	75.00	100.00
1911	0.30	0.40	1.40	2.20	3.25	7.00	17.00
1911D	5.00	6.00	9.00	24.00	50.00	70.00	90.00
1911S	55.00	60.00	65.00	70.00	80.00	105.00	195.00
1912	1.10	1.25	1.80	4.60	9.25	16.75	28.00
1912D	6.00	9.00	12.00	25.00	70.00	98.00	165.00
1912S	23.00	26.00	29.00	40.00	75.00	115.00	170.00
1913	0.60	0.65	1.40	2.75	11.50	17.00	28.00
1913D	2.50	2.80	3.30	8.80	24.20	48.00	77.00
1913S	13.00	16.00	21.00	30.00	55.00	105.00	195.00
1914	0.40	0.70	1.75	4.50	11.00	29.00	44.00
1914D	210.00	250.00	375.00	450.00	900.00	1450.00	2000.00
1914S	24.00	27.00	30.00	38.00	88.00	190.00	305.00
1915	1.15	1.50	2.90	10.50	33.00	56.00	76.00
1915D	1.40	1.50	2.80	5.30	16.00	35.00	66.00
1915S	20.00	22.00	25.00	30.00	75.00	90.00	190.00
1916	0.20	0.25	0.75	1.85	4.20	8.30	14.00
1916D	1.10	1.70	2.80	5.50	16.00	35.00	75.00

	G	VG	F	VF	XF	AU	MS60
1916S	1.40	2.60	3.65	8.50	25.00	46.00	98.00
1917	0.20	0.30	0.40	1.70	3.30	7.80	13.50
1917D	0.80	1.00	2.00	4.50	35.00	42.00	70.00
1917S	0.50	0.70	1.00	1.80	8.00	18.00	46.00
1918	0.20	0.25	0.30	0.60	4.00	8.00	11.00
1918D	0.90	1.20	2.20	4.40	14.00	32.00	70.00
1918S	0.30	0.75	1.25	2.90	10.00	30.00	65.00
1919	0.20	0.25	0.30	0.50	1.20	4.00	6.60
1919D	0.70	0.90	1.10	3.40	12.00	33.00	58.00
1919S	0.20	0.30	1.30	2.10	6.00	16.00	36.00
1920	0.20	0.25	0.30	0.80	2.25	7.00	14.00
1920D	0.75	1.00	2.00	5.00	18.00	35.00	70.00
1920S	0.50	0.55	1.25	2.25	15.00	35.00	99.00
1921	0.30	0.50	0.75	2.00	10.00	20.00	40.00
1921S	1.25	1.75	2.40	4.60	32.00	62.00	92.00
1922 No "D" Faulty Die	675.00	750.00	1200.00	1435.00	2900.00	5750.00	9500.00
1922D	17.00	18.00	22.00	25.00	35.00	75.00	92.00
1923	0.30	0.35	0.50	0.80	5.00	9.00	11.00
1923S	2.75	3.50	5.50	9.25	35.00	82.00	175.00
1924	0.20	0.30	0.40	0.50	5.00	9.00	11.00
1924D	36.00	45.00	50.00	60.00	120.00	165.00	250.00
1924S	1.00	1.35	2.20	5.00	30.00	65.00	105.00
1925	0.20	0.25	0.30	0.40	2.20	5.00	8.80
1925D	0.90	1.05	1.80	3.60	13.00	27.00	57.00
1925S	0.75	0.70	1.30	1.80	11.00	28.00	80.00
1926	0.15	0.20	0.25	0.40	1.10	4.00	7.00
1926D	1.10	0.90	1.65	2.80	13.00	29.00	75.00
1926S	8.00	9.00	11.00	15.50	33.00	65.00	130.00
1927	0.10	0.15	0.20	0.40	1.10	3.00	7.00
1927D	1.00	1.50	2.00	2.50	7.00	23.00	55.00
1927S	1.10	1.60	2.10	4.00	14.00	38.00	60.00
1928	0.10	0.15	0.20	0.35	1.00	2,6	7.00
1928D	0.70	1.00	1.80	3.00	6.00	18.00	30.00
1928S	0.75	1.25	2.10	3.50	8.00	28.00	65.00
1929	0.10	0.15	0.20	0.40	2.25	4.50	6.00

	G	VG	F	VF	XF	AU	MS60
1929D	0.40	0.70	1.00	1.80	6.00	12.00	23.00
1929S	0.45	0.75	1.30	1.80	6.50	13.00	17.75
1930	0.10	0.15	0.20	0.40	1.40	2.20	4.00
1930D	0.20	0.30	0.40	0.50	1.70	4.40	11.00
1930S	0.15	0.20	0.25	0.40	1.00	5.50	8.00
1931	0.40	0.45	0.75	1.55	3.00	9.25	18.00
1931D	5.00	5.50	6.00	7.00	12.00	32.00	45.00
1931S	120.00	125.00	130.00	135.00	140.00	145.00	150.00
1932	1.25	1.50	2.00	3.00	6.00	12.00	18.00
1932D	1.05	1.55	1.95	2.40	3.30	7.70	14.00
1933	1.05	1.40	2.00	2.40	6.00	11.50	23.00
1933D	3.10	3.25	5.00	7.00	12.00	18.00	24.00
1934	0.05	0.10	0.15	0.20	0.70	2.00	4.00
1934D	0.05	0.10	0.20	0.35	1.70	5.50	8.00
1935	0.05	0.10	0.15	0.20	0.70	1.10	2.00
1935D	0.05	0.10	0.20	0.35	0.70	3.30	4.00
1935S	0.05	0.10	0.20	0.35	1.70	4.40	7.70
1936	0.05	0.10	0.15	0.20	0.70	1.10	2.00
1936D	0.05	0.10	0.20	0.35	0.70	1.10	2.00
1936S	0.05	0.10	0.20	0.35	0.70	1.10	2.50
1937	0.05	0.10	0.15	0.20	0.70	1.10	2.00
1937D	0.05	0.10	0.20	0.35	0.70	1.10	2.25
1937S	0.05	0.10	0.20	0.35	0.70	1.10	2.00
1938	0.05	0.10	0.15	0.20	0.70	1.10	2.00
1938D	0.05	0.10	0.20	0.35	0.70	1.10	2.00
1938S	0.05	0.10	0.20	0.35	0.70	1.10	2.00
1939	0.05	0.10	0.15	0.20	0.30	0.40	1.50
1939D	0.05	0.10	0.20	0.35	0.70	1.40	2.25
1939S	0.05	0.10	0.20	0.35	0.70	1.10	2.00
1940	0.05	0.10	0.15	0.20	0.30	0.40	1.25
1940D	0.05	0.10	0.20	0.35	0.30	0.40	1.25
1940S	0.05	0.10	0.20	0.35	0.30	0.40	1.25
1941	0.05	0.10	0.15	0.20	0.20	0.30	1.25
1941D	0.05	0.10	0.20	0.35	0.20	0.90	1.70
1941S	0.05	0.10	0.20	0.35	0.20	1.70	2.20

	G	VG	F	VF	XF	AU	MS60
1942	0.05	0.10	0.15	0.20	0.20	0.30	1.25
1942D	0.05	0.10	0.20	0.35	0.20	0.30	1.00
1942S	0.05	0.10	0.20	0.35	0.20	1.10	3.30
1943	0.10	0.15	0.20	0.25	0.20	0.50	1.00
1943D	0.10	0.15	0.20	0.25	0.20	0.60	1.00
1943S	0.10	0.15	0.20	0.25	0.30	0.60	1.10
1944	0.05	0.05	0.05	0.05	0.05	0.10	0.75
1944D	0.05	0.05	0.05	0.05	0.05	0.10	0.75
1944S	0.05	0.05	0.05	0.05	0.05	0.10	0.75
1945	0.05	0.05	0.05	0.05	0.05	0.10	0.75
1945D	0.05	0.05	0.05	0.05	0.05	0.10	0.75
1945S	0.05	0.05	0.05	0.05	0.05	0.10	0.75
1946	0.05	0.05	0.05	0.05	0.05	0.10	0.75
1946D	0.05	0.05	0.05	0.05	0.05	0.10	0.75
1946S	0.05	0.05	0.05	0.05	0.05	0.10	0.75
1947	0.05	0.05	0.05	0.05	0.05	0.10	0.75
1947D	0.05	0.05	0.05	0.05	0.05	0.10	0.75
1947S	0.05	0.05	0.05	0.05	0.05	0.10	0.75
1948	0.05	0.05	0.05	0.05	0.05	0.10	0.75
1948D	0.05	0.05	0.05	0.05	0.05	0.10	0.75
1948S	0.05	0.05	0.05	0.05	0.05	0.10	0.75
1949	0.05	0.05	0.05	0.05	0.05	0.10	0.75
1949D	0.05	0.05	0.05	0.05	0.05	0.10	0.75
1949S	0.05	0.05	0.05	0.05	0.05	0.10	0.75
1950	0.05	0.05	0.05	0.05	0.05	0.10	0.75
1950D	0.05	0.05	0.05	0.05	0.05	0.10	0.75
1950S	0.05	0.05	0.05	0.05	0.05	0.10	0.75
1951	0.05	0.05	0.05	0.05	0.05	0.10	0.75
1951D	0.05	0.05	0.05	0.05	0.05	0.10	0.75
1951S	0.05	0.05	0.05	0.05	0.05	0.10	0.75
1952	0.05	0.05	0.05	0.05	0.05	0.10	0.75
1952D	0.05	0.05	0.05	0.05	0.05	0.10	0.75
1952S	0.05	0.05	0.05	0.05	0.05	0.10	0.75
1953	0.05	0.05	0.05	0.05	0.05	0.10	0.75
1953D	0.05	0.05	0.05	0.05	0.05	0.10	0.75

	G	VG	F	VF	XF	AU	MS60
1953S	0.05	0.05	0.05	0.05	0.05	0.10	0.75
1954	0.05	0.05	0.05	0.05	0.05	0.10	0.75
1954D	0.05	0.05	0.05	0.05	0.05	0.10	0.75
1954S	0.05	0.05	0.05	0.05	0.05	0.10	0.75
1955	0.05	0.05	0.05	0.05	0.05	0.10	0.75
1955 Double DieObverse	850.00	1050.00	1250.00	1400.00	1550.00	1700.00	1975.00
1955D	0.05	0.05	0.05	0.05	0.05	0.10	0.50
1955S	0.05	0.05	0.05	0.05	0.05	0.10	0.50
1956	0.05	0.05	0.05	0.05	0.05	0.10	0.50
1956D	0.05	0.05	0.05	0.05	0.05	0.10	0.50
1957	0.05	0.05	0.05	0.05	0.05	0.10	0.50
1957D	0.05	0.05	0.05	0.05	0.05	0.10	0.50
1958	0.05	0.05	0.05	0.05	0.05	0.10	0.50
1958D	0.05	0.05	0.05	0.05	0.05	0.10	0.50

Lincoln Cent Type (Memorial Reverse 1958 - Date)

MEMORIAL REVERSE

	G	VG	F	VF	XF	AU	MS60
1959	0.01	0.01	0.01	0.01	0.01	0.01	0.05
1959D	0.01	0.01	0.01	0.01	0.01	0.01	0.05
1960	0.01	0.01	0.01	0.01	0.01	0.01	0.05
1960 Sm. Date	0.50	0.60	0.70	0.80	0.90	1.75	3.00
1960D Sm. Date	0.10	0.15	0.15	0.15	0.20	0.25	0.40
1960D	0.01	0.01	0.01	0.01	0.01	0.01	0.20
1961	0.01	0.01	0.01	0.01	0.01	0.01	0.05
1961D	0.01	0.01	0.01	0.01	0.01	0.01	0.05
1962	0.01	0.01	0.01	0.01	0.01	0.01	0.05
1962D	0.01	0.01	0.01	0.01	0.01	0.01	0.05
1963	0.01	0.01	0.01	0.01	0.01	0.01	0.05
1963D	0.01	0.01	0.01	0.01	0.01	0.01	0.05
1964	0.01	0.01	0.01	0.01	0.01	0.01	0.05
1964D	0.01	0.01	0.01	0.01	0.01	0.01	0.05
1972 Double Die	185.00	195.00	210.00	225.00	245.00	350.00	400.00

DATES AND MINT MARKS AFTER 1964 TO DATE (EXCEPT FOR S-MINT COINS FROM PROOF SETS) HAVE ONLY NOMINAL VALUE.

LINCOLN ONE CENT – PROOF COINS

Proof Coins	Proof 64	Proof Coins	Proof 64
1968S	1.50	1989S	6.50
1969S	1.50	1990S	4.00
1970S	1.50	1991S	13.00
1971S	1.50	1992S	2.00
1972S	1.50	1993S	3.50
1973S	1.50	1994S	4.00
1974S	1.50	1995S	4.50
1975S	4.25	1996S	3.50
1976S	3.25	1997S	6.50
1977S	3.00	1998S	5.50
1978S	3.00	1999S	6.75
1979S	3.25	2000S	3.50
1980S	2.00	2001S	4.25
1981S	2.25	2002S	3.50
1982S	2.75	2003S	3.50
1983S	3.00	2004S	5.00
1984S	3.75	2005S	3.50
1985S	4.00	2006S	3.5
1986S	5.50	2007	4.5
1987S	3.25	2008	5.5
1988S	4.50	2009	

1943 the alloy of the Lincoln cent was changed to zinc-coated steel. These coins are easily recognized by their color, ranging from bright steel to dark steel gray. In 1959 the Lincoln Memorial was placed on the reverse side of the cent to commemorate the 150th anniversary of Lincoln's birth. The coin has undergone further minor modifications since that time. Many other varieties exist due to differing mint mark sizes and metal alloys used. Since 1975, cents minted at San Francisco were produced for proof sets only.

Dates and mint marks after 1964 to date (except for S-mint coins from proof sets) have only nominal value.

Two Cent Pieces Minted 1864 – 1873

TWO-CENT PIECES

	G	VG	F	VF	XF	AU	MS60
1864SM Motto	116.00	170.00	220.00	320.00	470.00	520.00	670.00
1864LG Motto	13.00	14.00	18.00	24.00	31.00	60.00	80.00
1865	13.00	14.00	18.00	24.00	31.00	60.00	80.00
1866	13.00	14.00	18.00	24.00	31.00	60.00	80.00
1867	13.00	14.00	18.00	33.00	39.00	80.00	100.00
1868	13.00	14.00	18.00	33.00	42.00	80.00	110.00
1869	13.00	14.00	24.00	33.00	49.00	90.00	130.00
1870	13.00	14.00	29.00	40.00	72.00	110.00	190.00
1871	18.00	22.00	33.00	50.00	88.00	140.00	200.00
1872	260.00	300.00	355.00	505.00	625.00	685.00	955.00
1873 Proof Only			Impaired		1225.00	1300.00	

Nickel Three-Cent Coins Minted 1865 – 1889

NICKEL THREE-CENT PIECES

	G	VG	F	VF	XF	AU	MS60
1865	13.00	14.00	15.00	20.00	34.00	54.00	90.00
1866	13.00	14.00	15.00	20.00	34.00	54.00	90.00
1867	13.00	14.00	15.00	20.00	34.00	54.00	90.00
1868	13.00	14.00	15.00	20.00	34.00	54.00	90.00
1869	14.00	15.00	16.00	21.00	34.00	56.00	95.00
1870	14.00	15.00	19.00	24.00	34.00	54.00	110.00
1871	14.00	16.00	20.00	25.00	35.00	55.00	120.00
1872	16.00	18.00	20.00	26.00	35.00	65.00	135.00
1873 Close 3	14.00	16.00	20.00	25.00	35.00	55.00	120.00
1873 Open 3	14.00	16.00	20.00	25.00	35.00	55.00	120.00
1874	15.00	17.00	20.00	25.00	35.00	60.00	130.00
1875	16.00	18.00	21.00	27.00	40.00	75.00	160.00

1876	17.00	20.00	24.00	32.00	45.00	85.00	175.00
1877ProofOnly				Impaired	Proof	1050.00	1400.00
1878ProofOnly				Impaired	Proof	675.00	750.00
1879	58.00	65.00	82.00	90.00	98.00	150.00	255.00
1880	85.00	95.00	105.00	125.00	150.00	190.00	325.00
1881	13.00	14.00	15.00	20.00	34.00	54.00	90.00
1882	100.00	110.00	125.00	140.00	160.00	175.00	260.00
1883	160.00	175.00	215.00	240.00	275.00	310.00	395.00
1884	325.00	345.00	465.00	485.00	505.00	575.00	675.00
1885	375.00	410.00	545.00	555.00	600.00	645.00	725.00
1886 ProofOnly				Impaired	Proof	340.00	350.00
1887/6 ProofOnly				Impaired	Proof	420.00	440.00
1887	250.00	300.00	325.00	375.00	400.00	425.00	475.00
1888	43.00	51.00	60.00	67.00	82.00	116.00	195.00
1889	72.00	94.00	118.00	150.00	145.00	165.00	245.00

Nickel Five-Cent Coins Minted 1866 - Date

SHIELD NICKELS

	G	VG	F	VF	XF	AU	MS60
1866	25.00	31.00	45.00	66.00	140.00	210.00	260.00
1867 w/Rays	33.00	32.00	46.00	67.00	141.00	211.00	261.00
1867 w/O rays	16.00	33.00	47.00	68.00	142.00	212.00	262.00
1868	16.00	34.00	48.00	69.00	143.00	213.00	263.00
1869	16.00	35.00	49.00	70.00	144.00	214.00	264.00
1870	25.00	36.00	50.00	71.00	145.00	215.00	265.00
1871	58.00	37.00	51.00	72.00	146.00	216.00	266.00
1872	30.00	38.00	52.00	73.00	147.00	217.00	267.00
1873	26.00	39.00	53.00	74.00	148.00	218.00	268.00
1874	27.00	40.00	54.00	75.00	149.00	219.00	269.00
1875	34.00	41.00	55.00	76.00	150.00	220.00	270.00
1876	34.00	42.00	56.00	77.00	151.00	221.00	271.00
1877 Proof Only		Impaired		1430.00	1490.00	1600.00	0.00
1878 Proof Only		Impaired		660.00	730.00	800.00	0.00

1879	333.00	52.00	56.00	77.00	151.00	221.00	271.00
1880	413.00	600.00	604.00	731.00	1060.00	1470.00	2800.00
1881	218.00	355.00	359.00	406.00	490.00	605.00	690.00
1882	16.00	20.00	24.00	32.00	51.00	90.00	155.00
1883	16.00	22.00	26.00	36.00	51.00	90.00	155.00
1883/2	173.00	310.00	314.00	366.00	610.00	820.00	1050.00

LIBERTY TYPE MINTED 1883-1913

LIBERTY FIVE-CENT PIECE

	G	VG	F	VF	XF	AU	MS60
1883 NoCents	6.00	7.00	8.00	9.00	10.00	11.00	25.00
1883 w/Cents	16.00	25.00	34.00	48.00	75.00	100.00	135.00
1884	17.50	30.00	35.00	50.00	85.00	110.00	170.00
1885	550.00	575.00	750.00	900.00	1150.00	1400.00	1700.00
1886	275.00	290.00	330.00	425.00	595.00	700.00	850.00
1887	12.00	21.00	26.00	36.00	66.00	90.00	120.00
1888	25.00	35.00	55.00	110.00	155.00	200.00	250.00
1889	12.00	18.00	26.00	44.00	66.00	100.00	135.00
1890	8.00	18.00	22.00	33.00	55.00	95.00	135.00
1891	5.00	10.00	18.00	31.00	50.00	90.00	130.00
1892	6.00	10.00	19.00	33.00	56.00	100.00	135.00
1893	5.50	10.00	20.00	31.00	50.00	95.00	125.00
1894	14.00	26.00	85.00	135.00	190.00	250.00	290.00
1895	5.00	7.00	20.00	38.00	57.00	90.00	120.00
1896	8.00	17.00	34.00	55.00	82.00	125.00	170.00
1897	3.00	4.00	10.00	22.00	38.00	58.00	82.00
1898	2.25	4.00	10.00	10.00	33.00	57.00	115.00
1899	1.50	2.00	7.50	17.00	27.00	52.00	77.00
1900	1.50	2.00	7.50	17.00	27.00	52.00	77.00
1901	1.50	2.25	6.50	13.00	26.00	55.00	75.00
1902	1.50	2.25	3.50	13.00	24.00	47.00	65.00
1903	1.50	2.20	4.40	13.00	24.00	47.00	65.00
1904	1.50	1.70	4.40	9.00	22.00	47.00	65.00

	G	VG	F	VF	XF	AU	MS60
1905	1.50	2.00	4.40	9.00	22.00	47.00	65.00
1906	1.60	1.90	3.50	9.00	22.00	47.00	65.00
1907	1.60	1.90	3.50	9.00	22.00	47.00	65.00
1908	1.60	1.90	3.50	9.00	22.00	47.00	65.00
1909	1.60	1.90	3.50	10.00	24.00	58.00	70.00
1910	1.60	1.90	3.50	9.00	22.00	42.00	55.00
1911	1.60	1.90	3.50	9.00	22.00	42.00	55.00
1912	1.60	1.90	3.50	9.00	22.00	42.00	55.00
1912D	2.25	3.25	9.00	31.00	60.00	135.00	230.00
1912S	150.00	200.00	225.00	425.00	700.00	1100.00	1250.00
1913	Only 5 known to exist. Est. $4,000,000+.						

Buffalo Type Minted 1913–1938

BUFFALO FIVE-CENT PIECES

BUFFALO NICKELS

	G	VG	F	VF	XF	AU	MS60
1913 On Mound (T1)	7.00	14.00	15.00	16.00	18.00	22.00	28.00
1913D On Mound (T1)	14.00	17.00	20.00	25.00	30.00	50.00	55.00
1913s On Mound (T1)	38.00	40.00	45.00	55.00	65.00	85.00	125.00
1913 No Mound (T2)	7.00	9.00	9.50	13.00	20.00	22.00	30.00
1913D No Mound (T2)	110.00	140.00	150.00	160.00	195.00	225.00	275.00
1913s No Mound (T2)	310.00	370.00	390.00	400.00	525.00	600.00	800.00
1914	16.00	18.00	20.00	21.00	22.00	30.00	37.00
1914D	80.00	120.00	150.00	180.00	280.00	350.00	395.00
1914S	22.00	32.00	38.00	50.00	75.00	120.00	125.00
1915	5.00	6.00	7.00	9.00	18.00	33.00	45.00
1915D	18.00	27.00	35.00	53.00	105.00	145.00	225.00
1915S	44.00	65.00	100.00	150.00	295.00	450.00	600.00
1916	5.00	5.50	6.00	6.50	12.00	20.00	38.00
1916D	14.00	23.00	26.00	31.00	75.00	100.00	140.00
1916S	9.00	12.00	19.00	28.00	65.00	115.00	175.00
1917	5.00	6.00	6.50	8.00	13.00	25.00	50.00
1917D	17.00	28.00	50.00	75.00	125.00	225.00	320.00

	G	VG	F	VF	XF	AU	MS60
1917S	19.00	40.00	75.00	100.00	175.00	250.00	375.00
1918	4.00	5.00	6.00	12.00	25.00	39.00	82.00
1918D	19.00	33.00	60.00	120.00	200.00	325.00	400.00
1918/17D	950.00	1350.00	2400.00	5000.00	8000.00	9500.00	23000.00
1918S	11.00	22.00	38.00	82.00	150.00	260.00	425.00
1919	2.00	3.00	3.50	5.50	12.00	24.00	50.00
1919D	14.00	27.00	65.00	120.00	210.00	300.00	525.00
1919S	9.00	17.00	45.00	90.00	200.00	330.00	500.00
1920	1.25	2.00	2.75	6.00	12.00	25.00	50.00
1920D	7.00	17.00	28.00	105.00	240.00	325.00	550.00
1920S	4.00	12.00	24.00	90.00	200.00	290.00	450.00
1921	3.00	5.00	7.00	20.00	43.00	70.00	100.00
1921S	55.00	100.00	170.00	440.00	750.00	1000.00	1400.00
1923	1.50	2.75	3.50	8.00	16.00	35.00	50.00
1923S	6.00	8.50	25.00	100.00	210.00	300.00	550.00
1924	1.00	2.00	3.50	7.75	15.50	35.00	60.00
1924D	6.00	9.00	24.00	70.00	195.00	275.00	350.00
1924S	13.00	26.00	77.00	385.00	1000.00	1650.00	2250.00
1925	2.00	205.00	3.00	7.00	14.00	24.00	35.00
1925D	8.00	18.00	30.00	66.00	145.00	225.00	340.00
1925S	4.00	7.50	15.00	62.00	155.00	220.00	350.00
1926	1.00	1.50	2.50	5.00	9.50	16.50	24.00
1926D	8.50	16.00	25.00	84.00	150.00	275.00	300.00
1926S	18.00	37.00	85.00	370.00	775.00	2250.00	4200.00
1927	1.00	1.25	1.75	3.30	10.00	16.50	26.00
1927D	1.75	3.30	5.00	22.00	61.00	88.00	130.00
1927S	1.00	2.00	3.50	25.30	66.00	132.00	400.00
1928	1.00	1.25	1.75	3.30	10.00	16.50	26.00
1928D	1.00	2.00	3.00	12.00	32.00	36.00	40.00
1928S	1.25	1.50	2.00	9.00	22.00	77.00	175.00
1929	1.00	1.25	2.00	3.30	10.00	16.50	28.00
1929D	1.00	1.25	2.00	5.50	26.00	34.00	52.00
1929S	1.00	1.25	2.00	1.25	10.00	20.00	42.00
1930	1.25	1.50	2.00	3.30	10.00	18.00	26.00
1930S	1.25	1.50	2.50	3.50	12.00	32.00	55.00

1931S	14.00	15.00	16.00	18.00	29.00	42.00	52.00
1934	1.25	1.50	2.00	3.30	10.00	16.50	26.00
1934D	1.50	2.25	3.50	7.00	16.50	40.00	66.00
1935	1.00	1.25	1.50	3.30	10.00	16.50	26.00
1935D	1.25	1.75	2.50	6.00	15.50	36.00	55.00
1935S	1.00	1.25	1.50	1.75	2.45	13.00	40.00
1936	1.00	1.25	1.50	1.75	2.00	6.00	12.00
1936D	1.00	1.25	1.50	1.75	3.00	9.00	28.00
1936S	1.00	1.25	1.50	1.75	2.00	8.00	28.00
1937	1.00	1.25	1.50	1.75	2.00	6.00	12.00
1937D	1.00	1.25	1.50	1.75	2.00	7.00	22.00
1937D 3-Legged	475.00	550.00	775.00	975.00	1100.00	1250.00	2300.00
1937S	1.00	1.25	1.50	1.75	2.00	6.50	22.00
1938D	3.75	5.00	7.00	10.00	15.00	26.00	40.00

JEFFERSON TYPE MINTED 1938 - 1942

JEFFERSON FIVE-CENT PIECE

	G	VG	F	VF	XF	AU	MS60
1938	0.30	0.40	0.50	0.80	1.00	2.00	3.00
1938D	0.50	0.75	0.90	1.00	1.50	3.00	8.00
1938S	1.00	1.25	1.50	1.75	2.50	5.00	10.00
1939	0.00	0.10	0.10	0.20	0.25	1.00	1.50
1939D	5.00	8.00	11.00	15.00	22.00	30.00	50.00
1939S	0.25	0.40	0.50	1.00	4.00	7.00	13.00
1940					0.25	0.50	0.75
1940D	PIECES NOT PRICED GENERALLY SELL AT OR CLOSE TO FACE VALUE.				0.25	1.00	2.00
1940S					0.25	1.00	2.00
1941					0.25	0.40	0.60
1941D					0.25	1.00	2.00
1941S					0.25	2.00	3.00
1942					0.25	1.00	1.00
1942D					1.00	5.00	15.00

WAR ISSUES 1942 -1945

35% SILVER CONTENT
1942-1945S

	G	VG	F	VF	XF	AU	MS60
1942P	0.95	0.95	0.95	0.95	1.25	4.00	15.00
1942S	0.95	0.95	0.95	0.95	1.25	3.00	11.00
1943P	0.95	0.95	0.95	0.95	1.25	2.00	9.00
1943D	0.95	0.95	0.95	0.95	1.25	2.00	12.00
1943S	0.95	0.95	0.95	0.95	1.25	2.00	9.00
1944P	0.95	0.95	0.95	0.95	1.25	2.00	12.00
1944D	0.95	0.95	0.95	0.95	1.25	3.00	10.00
1944S	0.95	0.95	0.95	0.95	1.25	3.00	12.00
1945P	0.95	0.95	0.95	0.95	1.25	2.00	12.00
1945D	0.95	0.95	0.95	0.95	1.25	2.25	12.00
1945S	0.95	0.95	0.95	0.95	1.25	2.00	12.00

JEFFERSON HEAD NICKELS (RESUMED) 1946-PRESENT

	G	VG	F	VF	XF	AU	MS60
1946					0.00	0.00	0.50
1946D					0.00	0.00	0.50
1946S					0.00	0.00	0.50
1947					0.00	0.00	0.50
1947D					0.00	0.00	0.50
1947S					0.00	0.00	0.50
1948					0.00	0.00	0.50
1948D					0.00	0.00	0.75
1948S					0.00	0.00	0.75
1949					0.00	0.00	1.50
1949D					0.00	0.00	1.00
1949S					0.00	1.00	2.00
1950					0.00	1.00	2.00
1950D	4.00	5.00	5.25	5.50	11.00	13.00	25.00
1951					0.00	0.00	1.00

PIECES NOT PRICED GENERALLY SELL AT OR CLOSE TO FACE VALUE.

1951D	PIECES NOT PRICED GENERALLY SELL AT OR CLOSE TO FACE VALUE.	0.00	0.00	1.00
1951S		0.00	0.00	1.00
1952		0.00	0.00	0.30
1952D		0.00	0.00	1.00
1952S		0.00	0.00	1.00
1953		0.00	0.00	0.30
1953D		0.00	0.00	0.30
1953S		0.00	0.00	0.30
1954		0.00	0.00	0.20
1954D		0.00	0.00	0.20
1954S		0.00	0.00	0.20
1955		0.00	0.00	0.20
1955D		0.00	0.00	0.20

PROOF JEFFERSON NICKELS 1968S – PRESENT

Proof Coins	Proof Coins	Proof Coins	Proof Coins
1968S	1.50	1985S	1.75
1969S	1.50	1986S	5.25
1970S	1.50	1987S	1.75
1971S	1.50	1988S	4.25
1972S	1.50	1989S	3.00
1973S	1.50	1990S	1.75
1974S	1.50	1991S	3.00
1975S	1.50	1992S	1.75
1976S	1.50	1993S	2.00
1977S	1.50	1994S	1.75
1978S	1.50	1995S	2.50
1979S	1.50	1996S	2.00
1980S	1.50	1997S	4.00
1981S	1.50	1998S	3.50
1982S	1.75	1999S	4.50
1983S	2.25	2000S	2.50
1984S	3.25	2001S	3.50

2002S	2.50	2005S Ocean	8.00
2003S	2.50	2006S	3.00
2004S Peace	12.00	2007s	3.00
2004S Keelboat	12.00	2008s	3.00
2005S Buffalo	8.00	2009s	

Westward Journey Five Cent (Nickel) Series

Beginning in 2004, as part of the Bicentennial Celebration of the Lewis And Clark Expedition, the US Mint coined a series of special five cent coins known as the Westward Journey Series. Most notably were the dual issues of 5 cent pieces in both 2004 and 2005. The 2004 Nickels, using the traditional Jefferson obverse, sported two unique reverses — The earl part of the year by the "Peace" medal type, and the latter part of 2004 with the "keelboat" type. Two reverses were used again in 2005 — The "Buffalo" in the first half of the year, followed by the "Ocean in View" type at the end of 2005. 2006 was marked by the "Return to Monticello" nickel which continues through the present.

CHAPTER 4

SILVER & CLAD COINS

I n 1966 (coins dated 1965); the United States began minting clad coinage to replace the silver dimes, quarters and half dollars that had circulated for more than 150 years. The effect was immediate, although not noticed by the general public at first. For various reasons many people began looking through their change, taking out the silver coins and putting them away. Some felt that the silver coins would become collector's items, others feared the end to "hard cash," still others speculated that the rising price of silver would inevitably push up the value of these 90% silver coins. To some extent everybody was right. As silver zoomed to $50/oz. by 1980, tons of coins came out from hiding and headed to the smelter.

Most of the best, however, have been saved for collectors. This chapter offers some assessments of the value of silver coins and the subsequent clad coins that replaced them. Such evaluations are especially tentative given that increases and decreases in the price of silver can affect values so easily. Minimum prices given are predicated on current wholesale silver coin prices—about 3-4 times face value. Chapter 2 gives a reasonably complete explanation concerning the refiguring of prices based on changes in the price of silver.

VALUES OF SILVER AND CLAD COINS
SILVER THREE-CENT COINS

MINTED 1851-1873

SILVER THREE-CENT PIECES 1851-1873

	G	VG	F	VF	XF	AU	MS60
1851	21.00	40.00	42.00	45.00	53.00	140.00	150.00
1851O	32.00	44.00	48.00	82.00	130.00	200.00	290.00
1852	20.00	40.00	42.00	45.00	53.00	140.00	150.00
1853	20.00	40.00	42.00	45.00	53.00	140.00	150.00
1854	21.00	40.00	42.00	45.00	86.00	210.00	320.00
1855	35.00	47.00	60.00	100.00	175.00	275.00	480.00
1856	25.00	41.00	48.00	53.00	100.00	180.00	250.00
1857	24.00	40.00	43.00	52.00	110.00	220.00	280.00
1858	23.00	40.00	42.00	48.00	90.00	180.00	220.00
1859	25.00	40.00	42.00	48.00	65.00	140.00	150.00
1860	25.00	40.00	42.00	52.00	68.00	140.00	150.00
1861	25.00	40.00	42.00	48.00	65.00	140.00	150.00
1862/1	30.00	42.00	45.00	55.00	70.00	150.00	175.00
1862	31.00	45.00	48.00	2.25	3.00	3.00	185.00
1863/2 Proof Only				Impaired	Proof	550.00	575.00
1863						440.00	610.00
1864						440.00	610.00
1865						440.00	610.00
1866						440.00	610.00
1867						440.00	610.00
1868						440.00	610.00
1869						440.00	610.00
1870						440.00	610.00
1871						550.00	610.00
1872						770.00	610.00
1873 Proof Only				Impaired	Proof	770.00	0.00

HALF DIMES
MINTED 1794-1795

HALF DIMES — FLOWING HAIR 1794-1795

	G	VG	F	VF	XF	AU	MS60
1794	1100.00	1250.00	1750.00	2800.00	5800.00	8500.00	13500.00
1795	875.00	1050.00	1500.00	2400.00	4500.00	7500.00	10800.00

DRAPE BUST TYPE — DRAPED BUST TYPE 1796-1805

	G	VG	F	VF	XF	AU	MS60
1796 6 over 5	1200.00	1275.00	2500.00	3600.00	7400.00	11800.00	23000.00
1796	1100.00	1200.00	2400.00	3450.00	7300.00	10200.00	16300.00
1796 "LIKERTY"	1125.00	1225.00	2400.00	3500.00	7400.00	10100.00	16900.00
1797 15 Stars	1075.00	1150.00	2320.00	3475.00	7400.00	9500.00	15000.00
1797 16 Stars	1150.00	1325.00	2400.00	3500.00	7600.00	9400.00	15250.00
1797 13 Stars	1850.00	2250.00	3200.00	4725.00	9700.00	17000.00	27500.00

DRAPE BUST TYPE — EAGLE & SHIELD REVERSE — HERALD EAGLE REVERSE

		G	VG	F	VF	XF	AU	MS60
1800		800.00	975.00	1450.00	1800.00	5600.00	8200.00	10750.00
1800		800.00	975.00	1450.00	1800.00	5600.00	8200.00	10750.00
1801		925.00	1050.00	1650.00	2200.00	6300.00	9500.00	15000.00
1802		19000.00	24400.00	35400.00	67500.00	150000.00	300000.00	350000.00
1803	LG8	900.00	1050.00	1450.00	1800.00	5750.00	8250.00	10800.00
1803	SM8	1050.00	1250.00	1650.00	2500.00	6250.00	8750.00	12000.00
1805		900.00	1150.00	1550.00	1400.00	6800.00	14000.00	37500.00

CAPPED BUST TYPE — 1829-1837

	G	VG	F	VF	XF	AU	MS60
1829	52.00	62.00	66.00	105.00	165.00	225.00	325.00
1830	50.00	55.00	58.00	88.00	130.00	190.00	285.00
1831	50.00	55.00	58.00	88.00	130.00	190.00	285.00
1832	50.00	55.00	58.00	88.00	130.00	190.00	285.00
1833	50.00	55.00	58.00	88.00	130.00	190.00	285.00
1834	50.00	55.00	58.00	88.00	130.00	190.00	285.00
1835	50.00	55.00	58.00	88.00	130.00	190.00	285.00
1836	50.00	55.00	58.00	88.00	130.00	190.00	285.00
1837 SM50	54.00	62.00	72.00	135.00	190.00	340.00	800.00
1837 LG50	52.00	58.00	66.00	105.00	150.00	200.00	300.00

LIBERTY SEATED TYPE MINTED
1837-1873

LIBERTY SEATED HALF DIME — NO STARS

	G	VG	F	VF	XF	AU	MS60
1837 SM DATE	27.00	36.00	55.00	104.00	180.00	460.00	800.00
1837 LG DATE	30.00	40.00	65.00	104.00	180.00	350.00	610.00
1838 O	74.00	104.00	171.00	336.00	610.00	920.00	1470.00

Stars with No Drapery

	G	VG	F	VF	XF	AU	MS60
1838	14.00	16.00	20.00	27.00	55.00	130.00	240.00
1838 SM Stars	16.00	24.00	37.00	80.00	150.00	300.00	540.00
1839	14.00	16.00	20.00	27.00	60.00	130.00	240.00
1839 O	16.00	20.00	25.00	33.00	75.00	150.00	520.00
1840	14.00	16.00	20.00	27.00	60.00	130.00	240.00
1840 O	14.00	17.00	20.00	30.00	60.00	210.00	610.00

Stars on Reverse

	G	VG	F	VF	XF	AU	MS60
1840 Drapery	19.00	27.00	45.00	86.00	165.00	300.00	380.00
1840 O Drapery	25.00	43.00	86.00	141.00	354.00	860.00	2750.00
1841	14.00	16.00	20.00	27.00	43.00	110.00	150.00
1841 O	15.00	17.00	20.00	37.00	92.00	250.00	600.00
1842	14.00	16.00	20.00	27.00	43.00	110.00	150.00
1842 O	21.00	30.00	47.00	130.00	440.00	710.00	920.00
1843	14.00	16.00	20.00	27.00	43.00	105.00	150.00
1844	15.00	16.00	20.00	27.00	43.00	110.00	160.00
1844 O	70.00	90.00	150.00	410.00	920.00	2100.00	4880.00
1845	14.00	16.00	20.00	27.00	43.00	110.00	150.00
1846	190.00	295.00	510.00	695.00	1850.00	3845.00	9900.00
1847	14.00	16.00	20.00	27.00	43.00	110.00	160.00
1848 Md.Date	15.00	17.00	20.00	27.00	46.00	110.00	210.00
1848 LG Date	20.00	22.00	30.00	43.00	110.00	240.00	450.00
1848 O	16.00	17.00	20.00	40.00	86.00	220.00	340.00
1849 9 OV. 6	16.00	21.00	24.00	35.00	90.00	190.00	370.00
1849 9 Ov. 8	24.00	30.00	38.00	46.00	100.00	220.00	370.00
1849	14.00	16.00	20.00	27.00	55.00	110.00	150.00
1849 O	20.00	29.00	61.00	171.00	366.00	750.00	1830.00
1850	14.00	16.00	20.00	27.00	48.00	110.00	150.00
1850 O	17.00	19.00	25.00	47.00	100.00	250.00	650.00

	G	VG	F	VF	XF	AU	MS60
1851	14.00	16.00	20.00	27.00	45.00	110.00	150.00
1851 O	15.00	16.00	20.00	35.00	92.00	190.00	460.00
1852	14.00	16.00	20.00	27.00	43.00	110.00	150.00
1852 O	24.00	27.00	58.00	110.00	214.00	430.00	740.00
1853 No arrows	28.00	35.00	58.00	110.00	200.00	330.00	630.00
1853 O No arrows	140.00	200.00	290.00	460.00	1100.00	2290.00	4520.00

Arrows at Date

	G	VG	F	VF	XF	AU	MS60
1853	14.00	16.00	20.00	27.00	50.00	120.00	190.00
1853 O	15.00	20.00	25.00	33.00	60.00	125.00	240.00
1854	12.00	15.00	20.00	27.00	48.00	120.00	190.00
1854 O	14.00	16.00	20.00	27.00	61.00	130.00	220.00
1855	13.00	15.00	20.00	27.00	45.00	120.00	190.00
1855 O	16.00	18.00	25.00	43.00	110.00	190.00	540.00

Stars on Reverse

	G	VG	F	VF	XF	AU	MS60
1856	13.00	15.00	16.00	24.00	43.00	110.00	150.00
1856 O	16.00	18.00	20.00	42.00	80.00	250.00	490.00
1857	13.00	15.00	16.00	24.00	43.00	110.00	150.00
1857 O	13.00	15.00	16.00	24.00	49.00	180.00	300.00
1858	13.00	15.00	16.00	24.00	43.00	110.00	150.00
1858 over inverted date	25.00	37.00	50.00	74.00	165.00	250.00	610.00
1858 O	14.00	16.00	20.00	35.00	61.00	120.00	230.00
1859	14.00	16.00	20.00	31.00	61.00	120.00	200.00
1859 O	14.00	18.00	25.00	35.00	98.00	190.00	250.00

Legend on Reverse

	G	VG	F	VF	XF	AU	MS60
1860	13.00	15.00	16.00	21.00	37.00	70.00	130.00
1860 O	13.00	15.00	16.00	21.00	37.00	70.00	130.00

	G	VG	F	VF	XF	AU	MS60
1861	13.00	15.00	16.00	21.00	37.00	70.00	130.00
1861 1 over 0	22.00	27.00	49.00	110.00	232.00	370.00	490.00
1862	18.00	20.00	27.00	35.00	44.00	80.00	150.00
1863	122.00	153.00	190.00	257.00	391.00	460.00	580.00
1863 S	20.00	28.00	38.00	55.00	130.00	260.00	680.00
1864	255.00	354.00	427.00	580.00	732.00	860.00	980.00
1864 S	40.00	50.00	80.00	110.00	214.00	370.00	580.00
1865	225.00	280.00	345.00	427.00	549.00	590.00	760.00
1865 S	20.00	29.00	38.00	55.00	135.00	430.00	860.00
1866	214.00	254.00	342.00	397.00	519.00	580.00	690.00
1866 S	20.00	30.00	40.00	50.00	125.00	280.00	370.00
1867	354.00	397.00	488.00	580.00	671.00	740.00	890.00
1867 S	18.00	22.00	29.00	53.00	116.00	250.00	490.00
1868	41.00	49.00	86.00	141.00	244.00	380.00	600.00
1868 S	13.00	15.00	20.00	25.00	37.00	100.00	280.00
1869	13.00	15.00	21.00	24.00	40.00	110.00	200.00
1869 S	13.00	15.00	20.00	26.00	40.00	100.00	280.00
1870	13.00	15.00	16.00	21.00	37.00	70.00	130.00
1870 S uniques	0.00	0.00	0.00	0.00	0.00	0.00	366000.00
1871	13.00	15.00	16.00	21.00	37.00	64.00	122.00
1871 S	15.00	19.00	25.00	48.00	61.00	153.00	232.00
1872	13.00	15.00	16.00	21.00	37.00	64.00	122.00
1872 S, S above Bow	13.00	15.00	16.00	21.00	37.00	64.00	122.00
1872 S S below Bow	13.00	15.00	16.00	21.00	37.00	64.00	122.00
1873	13.00	15.00	16.00	21.00	37.00	64.00	122.00
1873 S	13.00	15.00	16.00	21.00	37.00	64.00	122.00

Dimes Minted 1796 - Date

EARLY TYPES MINTED 1796-1837

DRAPED BUST TYPE 1796-1807

	G	VG	F	VF	XF	AU	MS60
1796	2300.00	2700.00	4150.00	5800.00	9300.00	14300.00	23000.00
1797-16 ★	2400.00	2850.00	4300.00	6000.00	10000.00	14800.00	28000.00
1797-13 ★	2500.00	2900.00	4500.00	6200.00	10500.00	15400.00	60000.00

Draped Bust Type

EAGLE & SHIELD REVERSE HERALDIC EAGLE

	G	VG	F	VF	XF	AU	MS60
1798-16rev ★	600.00	800.00	1070.00	1500.00	2800.00	4200.00	6500.00
1798/97 13	1000.00	1600.00	2300.00	3660.00	5100.00	7800.00	60000.00
1798 Rev ★	600.00	800.00	1050.00	1500.00	2700.00	3800.00	6000.00
1798 sm 8	620.00	975.00	1350.00	2250.00	4400.00	7400.00	48000.00
1800	540.00	780.00	1050.00	1500.00	3000.00	4800.00	27000.00
1801	535.00	760.00	1250.00	2600.00	4900.00	8600.00	42000.00
1802	800.00	1300.00	2300.00	3300.00	5700.00	9300.00	46000.00
1803	540.00	760.00	1050.00	1400.00	3600.00	7400.00	43000.00
1804	1040.00	1290.00	2320.00	3540.00	10680.00	24400.00	80000.00
1805	480.00	745.00	925.00	1110.00	2110.00	3500.00	5600.00
1807	470.00	735.00	920.00	1075.00	2090.00	3500.00	5500.00

Capped Bust Type

CAPPED BUST 1809-1837

	G	VG	F	VF	XF	AU	MS60
1809	120.00	160.00	305.00	540.00	1150.00	1725.00	3100.00
1811 over 9	65.00	92.00	245.00	450.00	1050.00	1550.00	2950.00
1814 SM Date	50.00	60.00	90.00	200.00	510.00	885.00	1500.00
1814 LG Date	38.00	34.00	46.00	104.00	315.00	520.00	830.00
1820 LG 0	36.00	34.00	40.00	92.00	300.00	520.00	830.00
1820 SM 0	36.00	34.00	40.00	92.00	320.00	520.00	880.00
1821 SM Date	36.00	34.00	44.00	104.00	350.00	710.00	1040.00
1821 LG Date	36.00	34.00	40.00	92.00	310.00	520.00	830.00
1822	330.00	550.00	895.00	1250.00	2200.00	4600.00	8850.00
1823 3 over 2	38.00	34.00	40.00	83.00	320.00	520.00	980.00
1824 4 over 2	36.00	35.00	74.00	269.00	520.00	1020.00	1470.00
1825	36.00	34.00	40.00	83.00	310.00	510.00	830.00
1827	36.00	34.00	40.00	83.00	310.00	510.00	830.00
1828 LG Date, curl 2	43.00	49.00	98.00	196.00	490.00	800.00	1710.00

Capped Bust Reduced

	G	VG	F	VF	XF	AU	MS60
1828	28.00	37.00	68.00	116.00	320.00	490.00	950.00
1829	26.00	32.00	35.00	66.00	240.00	320.00	680.00
1830 30 over 29	29.00	42.00	86.00	153.00	340.00	520.00	950.00
1830	26.00	32.00	35.00	61.00	225.00	310.00	630.00
1831	26.00	32.00	35.00	61.00	225.00	310.00	630.00
1832	26.00	32.00	35.00	61.00	225.00	310.00	630.00
1833	26.00	32.00	35.00	61.00	230.00	320.00	630.00
1834	26.00	32.00	35.00	61.00	225.00	310.00	630.00
1835	26.00	32.00	35.00	61.00	225.00	310.00	630.00
1836	26.00	32.00	35.00	61.00	225.00	310.00	630.00
1837	26.00	32.00	35.00	61.00	235.00	335.00	680.00

Liberty Seated Minted 1837-1891

LIBERTY SEATED TEN-CENT PIECE
LIBERTY SEATED 1837-1891

	G	VG	F	VF	XF	AU	MS60
1837 LG Date	30.00	40.00	75.00	220.00	470.00	680.00	950.00
1837 SM Date	38.00	45.00	85.00	230.00	470.00	680.00	950.00
1838 O	38.00	60.00	110.00	340.00	680.00	1100.00	2570.00

Stars on Obverse with No Drapery

	G	VG	F	VF	XF	AU	MS60
1838 SM Stars	20.00	30.00	45.00	74.00	153.00	350.00	580.00
1838 LG Stars	16.00	18.00	25.00	31.00	98.00	210.00	280.00
1839	15.00	18.00	22.00	31.00	98.00	200.00	280.00
1839 O	19.00	24.00	30.00	35.00	120.00	210.00	360.00
1840	15.00	18.00	24.00	30.00	98.00	200.00	280.00
1840 O	19.00	22.00	29.00	48.00	115.00	250.00	900.00

Stars on Obverse with Drapery

	G	VG	F	VF	XF	AU	MS60
1840	27.00	43.00	76.00	141.00	226.00	330.00	790.00
1841	16.00	18.00	25.00	26.00	41.00	110.00	260.00
1841 O	20.00	22.00	31.00	39.00	73.00	190.00	680.00
1842	15.00	17.00	21.00	26.00	37.00	110.00	240.00
1842 O	21.00	23.00	31.00	56.00	183.00	1100.00	2200.00
1843	15.00	17.00	21.00	25.00	37.00	110.00	240.00
1843 O	24.00	42.00	90.00	200.00	520.00	1800.00	3000.00
1844	180.00	280.00	435.00	650.00	980.00	1470.00	3500.00
1845	16.00	18.00	21.00	26.00	37.00	110.00	240.00
1845 O	27.00	35.00	63.00	155.00	427.00	860.00	2140.00
1846	62.00	95.00	145.00	305.00	793.00	1960.00	4400.00
1847	16.00	20.00	31.00	50.00	98.00	310.00	860.00
1848	18.00	20.00	22.00	39.00	66.00	130.00	490.00
1849	17.00	19.00	21.00	26.00	45.00	110.00	240.00

	G	VG	F	VF	XF	AU	MS60
1849 O	22.00	29.00	42.00	98.00	250.00	650.00	2080.00
1850	17.00	19.00	21.00	26.00	41.00	110.00	240.00
1850 O	20.00	25.00	32.00	44.00	76.00	180.00	860.00
1851	17.00	18.00	21.00	28.00	38.00	110.00	310.00
1851 O	22.00	26.00	34.00	60.00	128.00	400.00	1830.00
1852	15.00	17.00	21.00	27.00	37.00	110.00	240.00
1852 O	24.00	25.00	40.00	108.00	214.00	310.00	1220.00
1853 No Arrows	55.00	95.00	130.00	210.00	275.00	370.00	650.00

Arrows at Date

	G	VG	F	VF	XF	AU	MS60
1853	13.00	15.00	16.00	22.00	42.00	130.00	260.00
1853 O	15.00	16.00	17.00	35.00	74.00	240.00	860.00
1854	13.00	15.00	16.00	22.00	42.00	130.00	260.00
1854 O	13.00	15.00	16.00	22.00	42.00	150.00	260.00
1855	13.00	15.00	16.00	22.00	42.00	140.00	310.00

Stars on Reverse

	G	VG	F	VF	XF	AU	MS60
1856 LG Date	15.00	16.00	17.00	22.00	42.00	130.00	240.00
1856 SM Date	12.00	14.00	16.00	20.00	40.00	110.00	240.00
1856 O	15.00	17.00	18.00	22.00	49.00	210.00	610.00
1856 S	80.00	135.00	290.00	490.00	770.00	1100.00	2750.00
1857	13.00	14.00	15.00	22.00	38.00	110.00	240.00
1857 O	13.00	15.00	16.00	24.00	42.00	180.00	370.00
1858	13.00	14.00	15.00	22.00	38.00	110.00	240.00
1858 O	14.00	18.00	32.00	68.00	110.00	280.00	520.00
1858 S	75.00	115.00	155.00	300.00	675.00	1200.00	2755.00
1859	14.00	16.00	18.00	24.00	42.00	110.00	240.00
1859 O	16.00	19.00	27.00	32.00	70.00	190.00	330.00
1859 S	57.00	80.00	177.00	354.00	671.00	890.00	6660.00
1860 S	26.00	32.00	50.00	129.00	295.00	520.00	1650.00

LIBERTY SEATED 1837 -1891 — LEGEND ON REVERSE

	G	VG	F	VF	XF	AU	MS60
1860	14.00	15.00	16.00	27.00	31.00	80.00	200.00
1860 O	280.00	460.00	740.00	1530.00	3180.00	4850.00	8540.00
1861	12.00	13.00	14.00	16.00	25.00	70.00	140.00
1861 S	28.00	42.00	95.00	141.00	305.00	410.00	1260.00
1862	15.00	16.00	17.00	21.00	32.00	70.00	160.00
1862 S	33.00	40.00	61.00	131.00	240.00	360.00	980.00
1863	250.00	400.00	470.00	600.00	725.00	775.00	950.00
1863 S	31.00	42.00	50.00	90.00	141.00	310.00	920.00
1864	180.00	250.00	360.00	470.00	755.00	865.00	890.00
1864 S	25.00	30.00	40.00	77.50	125.00	260.00	800.00
1865	200.00	290.00	470.00	630.00	720.00	860.00	980.00
1865 S	25.00	30.00	51.00	115.00	183.00	550.00	1830.00
1866	245.00	330.00	490.00	660.00	740.00	950.00	1100.00
1866 S	35.00	44.00	61.00	98.00	171.00	240.00	920.00
1867	340.00	520.00	710.00	860.00	980.00	1100.00	1220.00
1867 S	25.00	34.00	61.00	105.00	183.00	460.00	950.00

DIMES — LIBERTY SEATED 1837 -1891

	G	VG	F	VF	XF	AU	MS60
1868	16.00	18.00	26.00	36.00	56.00	125.00	250.00
1868 S	17.00	21.00	30.00	70.00	92.00	160.00	320.00
1869	18.00	22.00	32.00	75.00	100.00	150.00	360.00
1869 S	15.00	18.00	26.00	29.00	55.00	140.00	350.00
1870	13.00	14.00	15.00	17.00	43.00	110.00	180.00
1870 S	200.00	240.00	310.00	370.00	480.00	770.00	1160.00
1871	13.00	14.00	15.00	16.00	37.00	140.00	250.00
1871 CC	975.00	1450.00	2550.00	5000.00	7500.00	13500.00	36000.00
1871 S	20.00	31.00	48.00	72.00	110.00	210.00	460.00
1872	13.00	14.00	15.00	16.00	21.00	70.00	130.00
1872 CC	330.00	530.00	1280.00	2625.00	5600.00	16000.00	39500.00
1872 S	19.00	22.00	72.00	105.00	165.00	320.00	1100.00
1873 Closed 3	13.00	14.00	15.00	16.00	25.00	80.00	130.00
1873 Open 3	16.00	25.00	50.00	55.00	98.00	180.00	520.00
1873 CC Unique							

Arrows on Date

1873	14.00	18.00	22.00	49.00	116.00	260.00	430.00
1873 CC	1100.00	2200.00	3300.00	800.00	1800.00	38000.00	48000.00
1873 S	14.00	19.00	27.00	49.00	147.00	350.00	830.00
1874	13.00	18.00	22.00	37.00	110.00	270.00	430.00
1874 CC	1250.00	3500.00	7800.00	16000.00	26000.00	35000.00	45000.00
1874 S	19.00	33.00	59.00	92.00	202.00	440.00	800.00

Legend on Obverse

1875	12.00	13.00	14.00	15.00	25.00	70.00	130.00
1875 CC Below Bow	25.00	26.00	27.00	47.00	70.00	110.00	210.00
1875 CC Above Bow	25.00	26.00	27.00	46.00	62.00	98.00	190.00
1875 S Below Bow	12.00	13.00	14.00	17.00	25.00	65.00	130.00
1875 S Above Bow	13.00	14.00	15.00	18.00	29.00	70.00	130.00
1876	12.00	13.00	14.00	17.00	25.00	65.00	130.00
1876 CC	25.00	26.00	27.00	44.00	58.00	98.00	180.00
1876 S	12.00	13.00	14.00	17.00	31.00	65.00	130.00
1877	12.00	13.00	14.00	17.00	25.00	70.00	130.00
1877 CC	25.00	26.00	27.00	45.00	61.00	95.00	180.00
1877 S	12.00	13.00	14.00	20.00	36.00	70.00	130.00
1878	12.00	13.00	14.00	17.00	25.00	70.00	130.00
1878 CC	50.00	70.00	125.00	160.00	310.00	430.00	970.00
1879	150.00	190.00	220.00	310.00	370.00	400.00	420.00
1880	120.00	170.00	230.00	250.00	310.00	400.00	520.00
1881	125.00	175.00	245.00	260.00	320.00	420.00	450.00
1882	12.00	13.00	15.00	17.00	25.00	70.00	130.00
1883	12.00	13.00	15.00	17.00	25.00	70.00	130.00
1884	12.00	13.00	15.00	17.00	25.00	70.00	130.00
1884 S	17.00	18.00	24.00	41.00	80.00	270.00	650.00
1885	12.00	13.00	15.00	17.00	25.00	70.00	130.00
1885 S	340.00	490.00	680.00	1290.00	2050.00	3540.00	5010.00
1886	12.00	13.00	15.00	17.00	25.00	70.00	130.00
1886 S	19.00	31.00	37.00	68.00	86.00	160.00	490.00
1887	12.00	13.00	15.00	17.00	25.00	70.00	130.00
1887 S	12.00	13.00	15.00	17.00	25.00	70.00	130.00
1888	12.00	13.00	15.00	17.00	25.00	70.00	130.00

	G	VG	F	VF	XF	AU	MS60
1888 S	12.00	13.00	15.00	17.00	25.00	90.00	190.00
1889	12.00	13.00	15.00	17.00	25.00	70.00	130.00
1889 S	14.00	14.00	19.00	33.00	55.00	140.00	340.00
1890	12.00	13.00	15.00	17.00	25.00	70.00	130.00
1890 S	14.00	14.00	20.00	37.00	61.00	140.00	300.00
1891	12.00	13.00	15.00	17.00	25.00	70.00	130.00
1891 O	12.00	13.00	15.00	17.00	25.00	70.00	140.00
1891 S	14.00	14.00	15.00	17.00	25.00	70.00	130.00

LIBERTY HEAD TYPE MINTED 1892 – 1916

LIBERTY TEN CENT PIECE(BARBER DIME)

BARBER DIMES

	G	VG	F	VF	XF	AU	MS60
1892	7.00	8.00	15.00	20.00	22.00	60.00	90.00
1892O	10.00	12.00	30.00	50.00	65.00	80.00	140.00
1892S	55.00	95.00	175.00	220.00	250.00	280.00	350.00
1893	7.50	10.00	16.00	25.00	38.00	68.00	140.00
1893O	25.00	37.00	110.00	150.00	170.00	200.00	275.00
1893S	12.00	22.00	35.00	45.00	75.00	125.00	260.00
1894	20.00	37.00	110.00	150.00	160.00	200.00	250.00
1894O	60.00	85.00	172.00	225.00	252.00	570.00	1380.00
1894S MS64	$250,000.00						
1895	75.00	150.00	325.00	425.00	475.00	550.00	650.00
1895O	315.00	465.00	775.00	1100.00	2000.00	3120.00	5280.00
1895S	37.00	50.00	120.00	175.00	205.00	275.00	420.00
1896	10.00	20.00	50.00	70.00	85.00	98.00	140.00
1896O	66.00	125.00	270.00	325.00	390.00	590.00	900.00
1896S	70.00	120.00	275.00	310.00	340.00	440.00	660.00
1897	3.00	4.00	7.00	13.00	27.00	60.00	110.00
1897O	58.00	98.00	260.00	350.00	400.00	480.00	840.00

	G	VG	F	VF	XF	AU	MS60
1897S	20.00	30.00	85.00	120.00	165.00	225.00	360.00
1898	2.50	3.00	6.50	11.00	22.00	60.00	95.00
1898O	10.50	22.00	78.00	125.00	175.00	250.00	390.00
1898S	6.25	12.00	24.00	32.00	53.00	110.00	300.00
1899	2.00	3.00	6.00	10.00	22.00	60.00	90.00
1899O	8.00	18.00	65.00	95.00	125.00	180.00	330.00
1899S	7.00	13.00	28.00	30.00	38.00	80.00	270.00
1900	3.00	3.50	6.00	9.00	20.00	60.00	90.00
1900O	16.00	32.00	98.00	145.00	185.00	300.00	510.00
1900S	4.50	6.00	10.00	17.00	26.00	70.00	140.00
1901	3.00	4.00	9.00	11.00	22.00	60.00	90.00
1901O	4.00	5.00	14.00	25.00	55.00	110.00	390.00
1901S	66.00	125.00	320.00	330.00	420.00	540.00	870.00
1902	3.00	4.00	5.00	7.00	20.00	60.00	90.00
1902O	3.00	5.00	13.00	27.00	60.00	125.00	340.00
1902S	7.00	17.00	50.00	75.00	120.00	175.00	340.00
1903	3.00	4.00	5.00	7.00	22.00	60.00	90.00
1903O	3.00	5.00	12.00	20.00	44.00	90.00	220.00
1903S	68.00	108.00	305.00	440.00	620.00	750.00	1020.00
1904	3.00	4.00	5.00	8.00	20.00	60.00	100.00
1904S	36.00	60.00	140.00	210.00	280.00	385.00	660.00
1905	3.00	4.00	5.00	7.00	20.00	60.00	90.00
1905O	4.00	9.00	32.00	48.00	80.00	135.00	260.00
1905S	3.00	4.00	8.00	16.00	40.00	70.00	200.00
1906	2.00	3.00	3.25	6.00	18.00	60.00	90.00
1906D	2.25	3.50	6.00	13.00	30.00	70.00	150.00
1906O	4.50	12.00	43.00	68.00	85.00	120.00	180.00
1906S	2.75	5.00	11.00	20.00	40.00	90.00	210.00
1907	2.00	2.50	4.00	6.00	18.00	60.00	90.00
1907D	2.25	3.50	8.00	15.00	36.00	95.00	240.00
1907O	3.00	6.00	28.00	43.00	52.00	90.00	190.00
1907S	3.00	5.00	14.00	23.00	55.00	125.00	350.00
1908	2.00	2.50	3.00	6.00	18.00	60.00	90.00
1908D	2.00	2.50	5.00	8.00	24.00	60.00	120.00

	G	VG	F	VF	XF	AU	MS60
1908O	4.50	9.00	40.00	56.00	80.00	120.00	270.00
1908S	3.00	5.00	10.00	18.00	30.00	140.00	290.00
1909	2.00	2.50	3.00	6.00	18.00	60.00	90.00
1909D	6.00	16.00	53.00	86.00	110.00	180.00	440.00
1909O	3.50	6.00	10.00	18.00	42.00	90.00	170.00
1909S	7.50	17.00	72.00	115.00	160.00	270.00	470.00
1910	2.00	2.50	3.00	8.00	19.00	60.00	90.00
1910D	2.00	4.00	7.00	16.00	40.00	90.00	200.00
1910S	4.50	8.00	46.00	76.00	101.00	200.00	450.00
1911	2.00	2.50	3.00	6.00	18.00	60.00	90.00
1911D	2.00	2.50	3.00	6.00	20.00	60.00	90.00
1911S	2.25	3.00	8.00	16.00	33.00	80.00	180.00
1912	2.00	2.50	3.00	6.00	18.00	60.00	90.00
1912D	2.00	2.50	3.00	6.00	18.00	60.00	90.00
1912S	2.00	3.00	5.00	11.00	28.00	80.00	140.00
1913	2.00	2.50	3.00	6.00	18.00	60.00	90.00
1913S	25.00	42.00	90.00	150.00	194.00	275.00	440.00
1914	2.00	2.50	3.00	6.00	18.00	60.00	90.00
1914D	2.00	2.50	3.00	6.00	18.00	60.00	90.00
1914S	2.00	2.50	7.00	15.00	35.00	70.00	140.00
1915	2.00	2.50	3.00	6.00	18.00	60.00	90.00
1915S	6.00	9.00	28.00	43.00	55.00	120.00	220.00
1916	2.00	2.50	3.00	7.00	18.00	60.00	90.00
1916S	2.00	2.50	4.00	7.00	20.00	60.00	90.00

MERCURY HEAD TYPE MINTED 1916-1945

MERCURY DIMES

	G	VG	F	VF	XF	AU	MS60
1916	3.00	4.00	6.00	8.00	9.00	20.00	30.00
1916D	900.00	1400.00	2250.00	3300.00	5200.00	8080.00	10000.00
1916S	3.75	4.00	8.00	12.00	20.00	26.00	41.00
1917	1.75	2.00	3.00	6.00	9.00	16.00	33.00
1917D	4.00	5.00	9.00	17.00	45.00	76.00	140.00
1917S	1.75	2.00	5.00	8.00	12.00	29.00	58.00
1918	2.00	3.00	6.00	14.00	29.00	42.00	81.00
1918D	2.25	3.00	6.00	11.00	23.00	45.00	114.00
1918S	2.00	3.00	5.00	8.00	16.00	36.00	95.00
1919	1.75	2.00	5.00	6.00	10.00	23.00	39.00
1919D	3.00	6.00	8.00	16.00	39.00	76.00	159.00
1919S	2.75	3.00	6.00	15.00	33.00	76.00	190.00
1920	1.75	2.00	3.00	6.00	8.00	16.00	33.00
1920D	2.00	2.50	4.00	9.00	17.00	39.00	114.00
1920S	2.00	2.50	6.00	8.00	15.00	35.00	76.00
1921	55.00	65.00	110.00	230.00	450.00	720.00	900.00
1921D	68.00	110.00	180.00	330.00	550.00	960.00	960.00
1923	1.75	2.00	3.00	4.00	6.00	13.00	29.00
1923S	2.00	3.00	7.00	17.00	64.00	85.00	159.00
1924	1.75	2.00	2.25	4.00	12.00	21.00	45.00
1924D	2.50	3.50	8.00	21.00	60.00	92.00	165.00
1924S	2.50	3.00	4.00	10.00	50.00	92.00	165.00
1925	2.00	2.25	2.50	3.50	9.00	20.00	33.00
1925D	4.00	4.25	11.00	45.00	120.00	230.00	330.00
1925S	2.50	3.00	6.00	14.00	180.00	110.00	170.00
1926	1.75	2.00	2.25	2.50	5.00	14.00	33.00
1926D	2.50	3.50	4.00	11.00	27.00	39.00	76.00
1926S	11.00	12.00	26.00	60.00	250.00	420.00	780.00

	G	VG	F	VF	XF	AU	MS60
1927	1.75	2.00	2.25	3.00	6.00	10.00	26.00
1927D	2.50	5.00	7.00	22.00	80.00	85.00	190.00
1927S	2.00	3.00	5.00	10.00	27.00	45.00	140.00
1928	1.75	2.00	2.25	3.00	4.00	14.00	26.00
1928D	3.00	4.00	9.00	25.00	55.00	89.00	152.00
1928S	1.75	2.00	3.00	6.00	18.00	33.00	76.00
1929	1.75	2.00	2.25	3.00	4.00	11.00	23.00
1929D	1.75	3.00	4.00	6.00	15.00	22.00	29.00
1929S	1.75	2.00	2.25	4.00	7.00	17.00	39.00
1930	1.75	2.00	2.25	3.00	8.00	17.00	26.00
1930S	2.00	3.00	4.00	6.00	15.00	45.00	76.00
1931	1.75	3.00	5.00	6.00	11.00	23.00	39.00
1931D	7.00	9.00	11.00	17.00	43.00	56.00	89.00
1931S	1.75	3.00	6.00	9.00	15.00	39.00	76.00
1934	1.75	1.75	1.75	4.00	6.00	11.00	17.00
1934D	1.75	1.75	1.75	4.00	10.00	20.00	36.00
1935	1.75	1.75	1.75	4.00	6.00	9.00	11.00
1935D	1.75	1.75	1.75	4.00	12.00	20.00	36.00
1935S	1.75	1.75	1.75	4.00	8.00	16.00	26.00
1936	1.75	1.75	1.75	4.00	5.00	8.00	10.00
1936D	1.75	1.75	1.75	4.00	9.00	17.00	24.00
1936S	1.75	1.75	1.75	4.00	6.00	8.00	18.00
1937	1.75	1.75	1.75	4.00	5.00	8.00	12.00
1937D	1.75	1.75	1.75	4.00	6.00	11.00	23.00
1937S	1.75	1.75	1.75	4.00	6.00	9.00	21.00
1938	1.75	1.75	1.75	4.00	5.00	6.00	16.00
1938D	1.75	1.75	1.75	4.00	8.00	11.00	17.00
1938S	1.75	1.75	1.75	4.00	5.00	10.00	17.00
1939	1.75	1.75	1.75	4.00	4.00	6.00	11.00
1939D	1.75	1.75	1.75	4.00	5.00	8.00	11.00
1939S	1.75	1.75	1.75	4.00	5.00	10.00	26.00
1940	1.75	1.75	1.75	1.00	3.00	4.00	9.00
1940D	1.75	1.75	1.75	1.75	3.00	4.00	10.00
1940S	1.75	1.75	1.75	1.75	3.00	4.00	10.00
1941	1.75	1.75	1.75	1.75	3.00	4.00	8.00
1941D	1.75	1.75	1.75	1.75	3.00	4.00	10.00

1941S	1.75	1.75	1.75	1.75	3.00	4.00	12.00
1942	1.75	1.75	1.75	1.75	3.00	4.00	8.00
1942/1	440.00	510.00	560.00	600.00	670.00	1325.00	1680.00
1942D	1.75	1.75	1.75	1.75	3.00	4.00	8.00
1942 D 41D	420.00	475.00	575.00	675.00	725.00	1150.00	1680.00
1942S	1.75	1.75	1.75	1.75	3.00	4.00	8.00
1943	1.75	1.75	1.75	1.75	3.00	4.00	9.00
1943D	1.75	1.75	1.75	1.75	3.00	4.00	10.00
1943S	1.75	1.75	1.75	1.75	3.00	4.00	12.00
1944	1.75	1.75	1.75	1.75	3.00	4.00	8.00
1944D	1.75	1.75	1.75	1.75	3.00	4.00	10.00
1944S	1.75	1.75	1.75	1.75	3.00	4.00	11.00
1945	1.75	1.75	1.75	1.75	3.00	4.00	8.00
1945D	1.75	1.75	1.75	1.75	3.00	4.00	10.00
1945S	1.75	1.75	1.75	1.75	3.00	4.00	10.00
1945S Micro S"	3.00	3.00	3.00	4.00	5.00	8.00	18.00

Roosevelt Type Minted 1946 - Date

ROOSEVELT DIMES

BV=Bullion	G	VG	F	VF	XF	AU	MS60
1946	BV	BV	BV	BV	BV	1.75	2.00
1946D	BV	BV	BV	BV	BV	1.75	1.50
1946S	BV	BV	BV	BV	BV	1.75	1.50
1947	BV	BV	BV	BV	BV	1.75	1.50
1947D	BV	BV	BV	BV	BV	1.75	2.50
1947S	2.00	2.00	2.25	2.25	3.00	3.00	5.00
1948	2.00	2.00	2.25	2.25	3.00	3.00	5.00
1948D	2.00	2.00	2.25	2.25	3.00	3.00	5.00
1948S	2.00	2.00	2.25	2.25	3.50	4.00	6.00
1949	3.00	3.25	3.50	3.75	4.00	5.00	10.00
1949D	2.00	2.00	2.25	2.25	3.00	3.00	4.00
1949S	4.00	4.50	5.00	6.00	7.00	8.00	28.00

	G	VG	F	VF	XF	AU	MS60
1950	BV	BV	BV	BV	BV	1.75	2.00
1950D	BV	BV	BV	BV	BV	1.75	3.00
1950S	2.00	2.00	2.25	2.25	3.00	3.00	8.00
1951	BV	BV	BV	BV	BV	1.75	2.50
1951D	BV	BV	BV	BV	BV	1.75	2.50
1951S	2.00	3.00	4.00	4.50	5.00	7.00	19.00
1952	BV	BV	BV	BV	BV	1.75	2.50
1952D	BV	BV	BV	BV	BV	1.75	2.50
1952S	2.00	2.00	2.25	2.25	3.00	3.00	4.00
1953	BV	BV	BV	BV	BV	1.75	2.50
1953D	BV	BV	BV	BV	BV	1.75	2.50
1953S	BV	BV	BV	BV	BV	1.75	2.50
1954	BV	BV	BV	BV	BV	1.75	2.50
1954D	BV	BV	BV	BV	BV	1.75	2.50
1954S	BV	BV	BV	BV	BV	1.75	2.50
1955	1.75	1.75	1.75	1.75	1.75	1.75	2.50
1955D	1.75	1.75	1.75	1.75	1.75	1.75	2.50
1955S	1.75	1.75	1.75	1.75	1.75	1.75	2.50
1956	BV	BV	BV	BV	BV	1.75	2.50
1956D	BV	BV	BV	BV	BV	1.75	2.50
1957	BV	BV	BV	BV	BV	1.75	2.50
1957D	BV	BV	BV	BV	BV	1.75	2.50
1958	BV	BV	BV	BV	BV	1.75	2.50
1958D	BV	BV	BV	BV	BV	1.75	2.50
1959	BV	BV	BV	BV	BV	1.75	2.50
1959D	BV	BV	BV	BV	BV	1.75	2.50
1960	BV	BV	BV	BV	BV	1.75	2.50
1960D	BV	BV	BV	BV	BV	1.75	2.50
1961	BV	BV	BV	BV	BV	1.75	2.50
1961D	BV	BV	BV	BV	BV	1.75	2.50
1962	BV	BV	BV	BV	BV	1.75	2.50
1962D	BV	BV	BV	BV	BV	1.75	2.50
1963	BV	BV	BV	BV	BV	1.75	2.50
1963D	BV	BV	BV	BV	BV	1.75	2.50
1964	BV	BV	BV	BV	BV	1.75	2.50
1964D	BV	BV	BV	BV	BV	1.75	2.50

BV = bullion value

Only circulated pieces after 1964 have any value over face. And these are generally solf for 20-30 cents each.

Proof Coins		Proof Coins	
1968S	2.00	1995S Clad	18.00
1969S	2.00	1995S Silver	20.00
1970S	2.00	1996S Clad	3.00
1971S	2.00	1996S Silver	6.00
1972S	2.00	1997S Clad	13.00
1973S	2.00	1997S Silver	20.00
1974S	2.00	1998S Clad	4.00
1975S	2.00	1998S Silver	7.00
1976S	2.00	1999S Clad	8.00
1977S	2.00	1999S Silver	18.00
1978S	2.00	2000S Clad	2.00
1979S	2.00	2000S Silver	4.00
1980S	2.00	2001S Clad	7.00
1981S	2.00	2001S Silver	11.00
1982S	2.00	2002S Clad	3.00
1983S	2.00	2002S Silver	5.00
1984S	2.00	2003S Clad	2.00
1985S	2.00	2003S Silver	4.00
1986S	3.00	2004S Clad	10.00
1987S	2.00	2004S Silver	6.00
1988S	3.00	2005S Clad	3.00
1989S	2.00	2005S Silver	4.00
1990S	2.00	2006S Clad	3.00
1991S	3.00	2006S Silver	5.00
1992S Clad	3.00	2007s	3.00
1992S Silver	4.00	2007s Silver	5.00
1993S Clad	5.00	2008s Clad	6.00
1993S Silver	6.00	2008s Silver	6.00
1994S Clad	5.00	2009s Clad	10.00
1994S Silver	6.00	2009s Silver	10.00

Twenty-Cent Coins Minted 1875-1878

LIBERTY SEATED 1875-1978

		G	VG	F	VF	XF	AU	MS60
1875		185.00	230.00	275.00	350.00	430.00	575.00	775.00
1875	CC	325.00	350.00	450.00	575.00	925.00	1350.00	1800.00
1875 S		85.00	95.00	120.00	165.00	200.00	300.00	450.00
1876		190.00	220.00	285.00	350.00	430.00	550.00	775.00
1876	CC	32000.00	40000.00	50000.00	62000.00	72000.00	82000.00	92500.00
1877		1900.00	2200.00	2700.00	3000.00	3300.00	3600.00	
1878		1500.00	1600.00	1900.00	2100.00	2450.00	2750.00	

Quarter Dollars Minted 1796 - Date

TWENTY-FIVE CENT PIECES

DRAPED BUST 1796-1807

	SM	G	VG	F	VF	XF	AU	MS60
1796	eagle	1000.00	15000.00	25000.00	33000.00	45000.00	50000.00	65000.00

HERALDIC EAGLE TYPE

		G	VG	F	VF	XF	AU	MS60
1804		4000.00	5550.00	7600.00	13600.00	25000.00	46500.00	80000.00
1805		375.00	475.00	625.00	1100.00	3000.00	5100.00	9400.00
1806	6 over 5	425.00	520.00	730.00	1500.00	3800.00	5700.00	10000.00
1806		375.00	450.00	610.00	1075.00	2900.00	4900.00	8500.00
1807		375.00	450.00	610.00	1075.00	2900.00	4900.00	8600.00

CAPPED BUST 1815-1838

	G	VG	F	VF	XF	AU	MS60
1815 8/5¢	77.00	95.00	140.00	320.00	1200.00	1250.00	2450.00
1818	70.00	90.00	135.00	320.00	1175.00	1200.00	2350.00
1818	68.00	85.00	125.00	285.00	1075.00	1080.00	2220.00
1819	68.00	85.00	125.00	290.00	1075.00	1050.00	2220.00
1820	68.00	85.00	125.00	290.00	1075.00	1050.00	2220.00
1821	70.00	90.00	130.00	290.00	1125.00	1050.00	2220.00
1822	80.00	95.00	135.00	320.00	1100.00	1900.00	3030.00
1822 25/50¢	975.00	2260.00	3400.00	4600.00	9550.00	17400.00	0.00
1823 3/2	26500.00	32000.00	39000.00	46000.00	52000.00	44400.00	0.00
1824 4/2	135.00	185.00	255.00	700.00	2550.00	3600.00	7200.00
1825 5 /2	85.00	105.00	150.00	325.00	1100.00	1320.00	2460.00
1825 5 /3	70.00	105.00	135.00	290.00	1080.00	1050.00	2000.00
1825 5/4	70.00	100.00	135.00	290.00	1080.00	1050.00	2000.00
1827 Original Proof Only				50000.00	55000.00	60000.00	65000.00
1827 Restrike, Proof Only							
1828	65.00	85.00	125.00	280.00	1075.00	1500.00	2600.00
1828 25/50¢	98.00	190.00	375.00	800.00	1750.00	2900.00	7200.00

REDUCED SIZE BUST

1831	55.00	80.00	85.00	115.00	310.00	575.00	850.00
1832	55.00	80.00	85.00	115.00	310.00	575.00	850.00
1833	60.00	80.00	90.00	135.00	340.00	690.00	1140.00
1834	55.00	80.00	85.00	115.00	310.00	575.00	850.00
1835	55.00	80.00	85.00	115.00	310.00	575.00	850.00
1836	55.00	80.00	85.00	115.00	310.00	575.00	850.00
1837	55.00	80.00	85.00	115.00	310.00	575.00	850.00
1838	55.00	80.00	85.00	115.00	310.00	575.00	850.00

LIBERTY SEATED TYPE MINTED 1838 – 1891

TWENTY-FIVE CENT PIECES

NO DRAPERY — NO MOTTO

	G	VG	F	VF	XF	AU	MS60
1838	27.00	29.00	43.00	75.00	330.00	510.00	1080.00
1839	24.00	26.00	39.00	66.00	330.00	510.00	1080.00
1840 O	30.00	32.00	55.00	96.00	390.00	540.00	1140.00

WITH DRAPERY — NO MOTTO

	G	VG	F	VF	XF	AU	MS60
1840	22.00	28.00	48.00	84.00	160.00	270.00	830.00
1840 O	25.00	32.00	60.00	90.00	180.00	420.00	960.00
1841	42.00	60.00	78.00	114.00	210.00	270.00	720.00
1841 O	23.00	24.00	45.00	60.00	150.00	270.00	660.00
1842 Sm Date/Proof Only							N/A
1842 LG Date	57.00	78.00	126.00	210.00	300.00	600.00	1200.00
1842 O SM Date	240.00	420.00	600.00	1200.00	1980.00	5040.00	6600.00
1842 O LG Date	22.00	26.00	35.00	46.00	110.00	240.00	840.00
1843	20.00	23.00	28.00	37.00	60.00	150.00	390.00
1843 O	24.00	24.00	38.00	84.00	200.00	600.00	1440.00
1844	20.00	23.00	30.00	40.00	60.00	150.00	440.00
1844 O	24.00	26.00	32.00	60.00	110.00	240.00	900.00
1845	20.00	23.00	30.00	39.00	60.00	150.00	450.00
1846	24.00	23.00	30.00	39.00	60.00	150.00	450.00
1847	20.00	23.00	30.00	39.00	60.00	150.00	440.00
1847 O	26.00	33.00	55.00	100.00	188.00	540.00	1740.00
1848	20.00	32.00	66.00	96.00	170.00	270.00	900.00
1849	20.00	23.00	30.00	63.00	110.00	230.00	690.00
1849 O	330.00	440.00	750.00	1320.00	2400.00	4500.00	7500.00
1850	21.00	39.00	54.00	72.00	110.00	200.00	690.00
1850 O	20.00	24.00	42.00	75.00	120.00	380.00	1200.00
1851	30.00	51.00	72.00	96.00	150.00	260.00	720.00

	G	VG	F	VF	XF	AU	MS60
1851 O	120.00	185.00	360.00	560.00	930.00	1830.00	4600.00
1852	36.00	51.00	72.00	108.00	170.00	240.00	450.00
1852 O	130.00	180.00	320.00	600.00	1400.00	3300.00	7200.00
1853 Recut Date	230.00	320.00	480.00	600.00	1020.00	1600.00	2280.00

ARROWS & RAYS

	G	VG	F	VF	XF	AU	MS60
1853	20.00	23.00	30.00	42.00	120.00	260.00	870.00
1853 3 over 4	36.00	66.00	96.00	180.00	270.00	590.00	1680.00
1853 O	20.00	23.00	30.00	54.00	200.00	960.00	2640.00

ARROWS AT DATE

	G	VG	F	VF	XF	AU	MS60
1854	20.00	23.00	30.00	39.00	80.00	210.00	420.00
1854 O	20.00	23.00	30.00	39.00	80.00	210.00	660.00
1854 O Huge O	700.00	1125.00	2350.00	3875.00	6100.00	10000.00	15000.00
1855	20.00	23.00	30.00	39.00	70.00	210.00	420.00
1855 O	32.00	48.00	82.00	174.00	290.00	690.00	2160.00
1855 5	38.00	50.00	72.00	120.00	270.00	650.00	1680.00

NO MOTTO

	G	VG	F	VF	XF	AU	MS60
1856	20.00	23.00	30.00	39.00	55.00	150.00	270.00
1856 O	20.00	23.00	33.00	42.00	55.00	200.00	900.00
1856 S	35.00	39.00	66.00	150.00	275.00	660.00	1680.00
1856 S over S	41.00	62.00	114.00	234.00	410.00	750.00	1920.00
1857	20.00	23.00	30.00	39.00	50.00	150.00	270.00
1857 O	20.00	23.00	30.00	39.00	80.00	240.00	840.00
1857 S	44.00	78.00	144.00	300.00	540.00	900.00	2100.00
1858	20.00	23.00	30.00	39.00	50.00	150.00	270.00
1858 O	20.00	23.00	30.00	44.00	80.00	320.00	1200.00
1858 S	35.00	48.00	108.00	222.00	390.00	960.00	5040.00
1859	20.00	23.00	30.00	39.00	50.00	150.00	320.00
1859 O	20.00	23.00	32.00	54.00	100.00	340.00	990.00
1859 S	70.00	110.00	150.00	275.00	975.00	7200.00	12000.00
1860	20.00	23.00	30.00	39.00	60.00	150.00	360.00

		G	VG	F	VF	XF	AU	MS60
1860 O		25.00	30.00	38.00	45.00	70.00	320.00	930.00
1860 S		120.00	186.00	350.00	690.00	1380.00	3600.00	16000.00
1861		20.00	23.00	30.00	35.00	60.00	150.00	270.00
1861 S		42.00	66.00	144.00	264.00	720.00	1560.00	4200.00
1862		22.00	25.00	35.00	42.00	70.00	150.00	270.00
1862 S		40.00	63.00	84.00	192.00	440.00	750.00	1800.00
1863		32.00	40.00	50.00	94.00	145.00	235.00	450.00
1864		56.00	65.00	90.00	120.00	190.00	330.00	530.00
1864 S		230.00	360.00	510.00	750.00	1500.00	3240.00	5400.00
1865		57.00	65.00	92.00	120.00	160.00	270.00	600.00
1865 S		65.00	72.00	120.00	282.00	480.00	960.00	1860.00

1866 Proof Only (1 Known)

WITH MOTTO

		G	VG	F	VF	XF	AU	MS60
1866		290.00	420.00	510.00	720.00	1020.00	1140.00	1560.00
1866 S		150.00	230.00	450.00	780.00	1080.00	1750.00	2650.00
1867		155.00	230.00	320.00	420.00	540.00	660.00	720.00
1867 S		105.00	198.00	318.00	420.00	540.00	830.00	1800.00
1868		84.00	102.00	156.00	204.00	270.00	390.00	600.00
1868 S		56.00	72.00	110.00	198.00	450.00	720.00	1980.00
1869		192.00	240.00	342.00	450.00	540.00	720.00	1140.00
1869 S		65.00	96.00	150.00	252.00	470.00	1050.00	2200.00
1870		39.00	50.00	90.00	138.00	200.00	300.00	690.00
1870	CC	6500.00	8000.00	10000.00	15000.00	24000.00	38000.00	48000.00
1871		26.00	34.00	48.00	90.00	120.00	240.00	450.00
1871	CC	1550.00	3000.00	5000.00	13000.00	21800.00	31000.00	36000.00
1871 S		210.00	330.00	402.00	600.00	930.00	1500.00	2400.00
1872		22.00	28.00	57.00	84.00	110.00	190.00	410.00
1872	CC	455.00	755.00	1325.00	2400.00	5000.00	8000.00	35000.00
1872 S		600.00	780.00	840.00	1200.00	2100.00	3300.00	5700.00
1873 Closed 3		72.00	144.00	204.00	390.00	480.00	780.00	1650.00
1873 Open 3		25.00	36.00	52.00	75.00	110.00	170.00	330.00
1873 5 known						70000.00	80000.00	90000.00

Arrows at Date

1873		18.00	22.00	33.00	53.00	180.00	390.00	720.00
1873	CC	1200.00	1740.00	4440.00	6840.00	16000.00	22200.00	36000.00
1873 S		26.00	30.00	44.00	78.00	210.00	440.00	1040.00
1874		18.00	22.00	28.00	53.00	180.00	390.00	720.00
1874 S		24.00	28.00	46.00	78.00	200.00	410.00	780.00

With Motto

		G	VG	F	VF	XF	AU	MS60
1875		20.00	24.00	29.00	36.00	60.00	140.00	220.00
1875	CC	52.00	90.00	150.00	240.00	480.00	630.00	1500.00
1875 S		25.00	35.00	58.00	96.00	180.00	270.00	570.00
1876		20.00	24.00	26.00	30.00	50.00	140.00	220.00
1876	CC	32.00	35.00	40.00	53.00	90.00	170.00	310.00
1876 S		20.00	24.00	26.00	28.00	50.00	140.00	220.00
1877		20.00	24.00	26.00	30.00	50.00	140.00	220.00
1877	CC	32.00	35.00	40.00	55.00	90.00	170.00	350.00
1877 S		20.00	24.00	26.00	30.00	60.00	140.00	220.00
1877 S over horizontal S		23.00	37.00	66.00	126.00	210.00	320.00	570.00
1878		20.00	24.00	29.00	36.00	60.00	140.00	220.00
1878	CC	35.00	40.00	54.00	96.00	120.00	180.00	480.00
1878 S		78.00	138.00	204.00	258.00	440.00	600.00	1020.00
1879		90.00	120.00	174.00	198.00	270.00	350.00	450.00
1880		90.00	126.00	174.00	204.00	270.00	350.00	470.00
1881		115.00	150.00	228.00	246.00	290.00	380.00	510.00
1882		105.00	138.00	186.00	246.00	310.00	400.00	510.00
1883		100.00	132.00	204.00	240.00	300.00	370.00	480.00
1884		180.00	240.00	324.00	360.00	420.00	480.00	540.00
1885		110.00	126.00	204.00	234.00	290.00	350.00	500.00
1886		225.00	330.00	444.00	468.00	600.00	660.00	750.00
1887		150.00	222.00	300.00	378.00	440.00	500.00	590.00
1888		145.00	216.00	276.00	360.00	420.00	480.00	570.00
1888 S		22.00	25.00	28.00	35.00	60.00	140.00	220.00
1889		132.00	150.00	186.00	234.00	300.00	380.00	480.00
1890		46.00	51.00	84.00	102.00	160.00	250.00	410.00
1891		20.00	23.00	28.00	34.00	60.00	140.00	220.00
1891 O		120.00	156.00	264.00	360.00	630.00	900.00	2400.00
1891 S		20.00	23.00	28.00	34.00	60.00	140.00	220.00

LIBERTY HEAD TYPE MINTED 1892 -1916

TWENTY-FIVE CENT PIECES

BARBER QUATERS

	G	VG	F	VF	XF	AU	MS60
1892	7.00	8.00	22.00	40.00	65.00	95.00	205.00
1892O	14.00	19.00	39.00	55.00	90.00	130.00	280.00
1892S	32.00	52.00	85.00	130.00	180.00	275.00	410.00
1893	6.00	8.00	22.00	35.00	65.00	100.00	195.00
1893O	8.00	14.00	28.00	52.00	110.00	155.00	245.00
1893S	18.00	33.00	61.00	112.00	170.00	295.00	400.00
1894	5.00	7.00	27.00	42.00	78.00	130.00	225.00
1894O	8.50	17.00	40.00	75.00	125.00	180.00	325.00
1894S	7.00	12.00	33.00	65.00	115.00	155.00	275.00
1895	5.00	7.00	25.00	35.00	70.00	120.00	195.00
1895O	11.00	17.00	40.00	70.00	125.00	190.00	345.00
1895S	18.00	27.00	70.00	110.00	165.00	240.00	360.00
1896	5.00	6.00	21.00	38.00	75.00	110.00	195.00
1896O	28.00	50.00	110.00	215.00	375.00	625.00	685.00
1896S	850.00	1400.00	2200.00	3000.00	4300.00	6000.00	9000.00
1897	5.00	6.00	18.00	30.00	60.00	95.00	175.00
1897O	18.00	36.00	115.00	225.00	345.00	· 515.00	725.00
1897S	60.00	95.00	180.00	250.00	375.00	575.00	850.00
1898	5.00	6.00	19.00	28.00	65.00	99.00	175.00
1898O	14.00	27.00	69.00	135.00	255.00	375.00	575.00
1898S	10.00	16.00	45.00	62.00	90.00	160.00	335.00
1899	5.00	6.00	20.00	32.00	65.00	95.00	175.00
1899O	12.00	20.00	34.00	66.00	125.00	250.00	350.00
1899S	15.00	25.00	65.00	85.00	125.00	250.00	375.00
1900	5.00	7.00	21.00	32.00	65.00	115.00	175.00
1900O	14.00	28.00	65.00	110.00	160.00	295.00	510.00
1900S	7.00	15.00	31.00	45.00	70.00	112.00	325.00
1901	10.00	11.00	22.00	38.00	66.00	110.00	180.00
1901O	36.00	55.00	125.00	225.00	380.00	560.00	750.00

	G	VG	F	VF	XF	AU	MS60
1901S	4800.00	11500.00	16500.00	25500.00	30000.00	35000.00	39000.00
1902	6.00	8.00	16.00	27.00	58.00	100.00	175.00
1902O	7.00	14.00	43.00	67.00	125.00	185.00	420.00
1902S	13.00	19.00	45.00	75.00	150.00	220.00	455.00
1903	6.00	7.00	17.00	30.00	54.00	99.00	175.00
1903O	7.00	12.00	34.00	55.00	105.00	215.00	420.00
1903S	14.00	22.00	38.00	66.00	120.00	250.00	425.00
1904	7.00	8.00	17.00	30.00	60.00	104.00	195.00
1904O	10.00	18.00	55.00	84.00	185.00	385.00	730.00
1905	12.00	14.00	22.00	35.00	60.00	100.00	200.00
1905O	15.00	28.00	70.00	150.00	225.00	300.00	400.00
1905S	12.00	14.00	37.00	55.00	99.00	200.00	300.00
1906	6.00	7.25	16.00	28.00	56.00	100.00	200.00
1906D	6.00	7.25	21.00	41.00	58.00	150.00	200.00
1906O	6.00	8.00	34.00	52.00	88.00	200.00	350.00
1907	5.00	6.50	15.00	27.00	53.00	93.00	170.00
1907D	5.00	6.50	22.00	42.00	66.00	145.00	205.00
1907O	5.00	7.50	16.00	33.00	56.00	110.00	175.00
1907S	8.50	16.00	40.00	63.00	112.00	225.00	420.00
1908	5.00	6.00	16.00	56.00	95.00	175.00	280.00
1908D	5.00	6.00	15.00	57.00	96.00	200.00	335.00
1908O	5.00	8.00	15.00	60.00	100.00	170.00	295.00
1908S	15.00	33.00	75.00	130.00	255.00	420.00	650.00
1909	5.00	6.00	15.00	25.00	47.00	95.00	195.00
1909D	6.00	7.00	18.00	33.00	72.00	130.00	195.00
1909O	15.00	32.00	75.00	165.00	275.00	440.00	675.00
1909S	7.00	12.00	33.00	46.00	79.00	165.00	255.00
1910	7.00	11.00	25.00	37.00	65.00	118.00	185.00
1910D	7.00	10.00	40.00	62.00	110.00	210.00	326.00
1911	6.00	8.00	18.00	27.00	60.00	100.00	175.00
1911D	8.00	17.00	85.00	190.00	290.00	410.00	555.00
1911S	6.00	12.00	45.00	80.00	130.00	245.00	335.00
1912	5.00	7.00	15.00	28.00	47.00	95.00	195.00
1912S	7.00	11.00	38.00	75.00	150.00	250.00	325.00
1913	13.00	22.00	60.00	165.00	335.00	450.00	825.00

	G	VG	F	VF	XF	AU	MS60
1913D	10.00	11.00	31.00	47.00	75.00	155.00	225.00
1913S	1600.00	2200.00	5000.00	7500.00	10000.00	12500.00	15000.00
1914	5.00	6.00	15.00	28.00	47.00	95.00	195.00
1914D	5.00	6.00	15.00	26.00	47.00	95.00	195.00
1914S	75.00	110.00	205.00	365.00	550.00	665.00	875.00
1915	5.00	6.00	15.00	25.00	55.00	95.00	195.00
1915D	5.00	6.00	15.00	25.00	55.00	95.00	195.00
1915S	8.00	11.00	31.00	46.00	88.00	180.00	255.00
1916	5.00	6.00	15.00	25.00	47.00	95.00	195.00
1916D	5.00	6.00	15.00	25.00	47.00	95.00	195.00

Standing Liberty Type Minted 1916-1930

TWENTY-FIVE CENT PIECES

STANDING LIBERTY QUARTER DOLLARS

	G	VG	F	VF	XF	AU	MS60
1916 BareBreast	2100.00	4800.00	7200.00	9500.00	11000.00	12250.00	15500.00
1917 BareBreast	19.00	40.00	58.00	80.00	110.00	160.00	220.00
1917D BareBreast	20.00	60.00	85.00	115.00	175.00	220.00	275.00
1917S BareBreast	23.00	60.00	89.00	130.00	195.00	250.00	300.00
1917 Cov.Breast	17.00	30.00	45.00	62.00	85.00	125.00	175.00
1917D Cov.Breast	33.00	38.00	75.00	100.00	140.00	180.00	240.00
1917S Cov.Breast	30.00	39.00	75.00	95.00	135.00	175.00	220.00
1918	13.00	16.00	25.00	26.00	37.00	70.00	110.00
1918D	19.00	34.00	65.00	70.00	125.00	175.00	250.00
1918S	14.00	17.00	28.00	29.00	45.00	75.00	150.00
1918/17S	1200.00	1600.00	3200.00	4000.00	6400.00	12000.00	16000.00
1919	27.00	38.00	55.00	62.00	75.00	110.00	160.00
1919D	62.00	88.00	170.00	330.00	550.00	675.00	850.00
1919S	55.00	86.00	160.00	240.00	430.00	480.00	600.00
1920	11.00	14.00	20.00	32.00	44.00	78.00	125.00
1920D	39.00	50.00	75.00	100.00	150.00	190.00	280.00

	G	VG	F	VF	XF	AU	MS60
1920S	14.00	19.00	24.00	30.00	52.00	90.00	200.00
1921	135.00	150.00	390.00	550.00	675.00	950.00	1400.00
1923	12.00	14.00	29.00	35.00	47.00	85.00	135.00
1923S	210.00	308.00	555.00	855.00	1250.00	1700.00	2400.00
1924	12.00	15.00	19.00	32.00	44.00	100.00	175.00
1924D	42.00	53.00	88.00	115.00	155.00	195.00	245.00
1924S	22.00	26.00	40.00	55.00	110.00	200.00	275.00
1925	4.00	4.50	5.00	15.00	35.00	70.00	120.00
1926	4.00	4.50	5.00	12.00	28.00	65.00	110.00
1926D	5.00	7.00	20.00	40.00	80.00	110.00	150.00
1926S	4.00	4.25	9.00	18.00	90.00	185.00	275.00
1927	4.00	4.25	5.00	9.00	26.00	52.00	90.00
1927D	11.00	16.00	26.00	66.00	135.00	195.00	225.00
1927S	35.00	40.00	100.00	275.00	850.00	2400.00	3900.00
1928	4.00	4.25	5.00	10.00	25.00	52.00	85.00
1928D	4.00	4.25	6.00	16.00	35.00	64.00	110.00
1928S	4.00	4.25	5.00	15.00	33.00	62.00	110.00
1929	4.00	4.25	5.00	10.00	25.00	55.00	85.00
1929D	4.00	4.25	5.00	12.00	29.00	65.00	110.00
1929S	4.00	4.25	5.00	12.00	26.00	60.00	110.00
1930	4.00	4.25	5.00	9.00	26.00	55.00	85.00
1930S	4.00	4.25	5.00	9.00	26.00	60.00	85.00

Since one of the high points of the Standing Liberty Quarter is the date, especially for pieces before 1925, items graded good generally have only a partial date and are thus not found desirable by most collectors.

WASHINGTON TYPE MINTED 1932 - DATE

WASHINGTON QUARTER DOLLARS

	G	VG	F	VF	XF	AU	MS60
1932	4.00	5.00	6.00	7.00	8.00	13.00	25.00
1932D	145.00	150.00	175.00	195.00	320.00	425.00	850.00
1932S	160.00	165.00	180.00	200.00	250.00	275.00	450.00
1934	4.00	4.00	4.00	4.00	4.00	7.00	22.00
1934D	4.00	5.00	5.00	8.00	18.00	66.00	210.00
1935	3.00	4.00	4.00	4.00	4.00	7.00	18.00
1935D	4.00	4.00	5.00	10.00	20.00	105.00	210.00
1935S	4.00	4.00	4.00	5.00	10.00	28.00	85.00
1936	3.00	3.00	3.00	3.00	3.00	7.00	22.00
1936D	4.00	4.00	5.00	15.00	40.00	200.00	500.00
1936S	4.00	4.00	4.00	5.00	10.00	35.00	95.00
1937	3.00	3.00	3.00	3.00	4.00	14.00	20.00
1937D	4.00	4.00	4.00	4.00	10.00	27.00	55.00
1937S	4.00	4.00	4.00	9.00	17.00	75.00	140.00
1938	3.00	3.00	3.00	5.00	11.00	30.00	80.00
1938S	4.00	4.00	5.00	6.00	11.00	33.00	95.00
1939	2.00	3.00	3.00	3.00	3.00	6.00	14.00
1939D	4.00	4.00	4.00	4.00	7.00	15.00	38.00
1939S	4.00	4.00	4.00	4.00	10.00	39.00	88.00
1940	3.00	3.00	3.00	3.00	3.00	5.00	16.00
1940D	4.00	4.00	5.00	7.00	15.00	49.00	110.00
1940S	3.00	3.00	3.00	4.00	5.00	13.00	26.00
1941	3.00	3.00	3.00	3.00	3.00	4.00	8.00
1941D	3.00	3.00	3.00	3.00	3.00	6.00	28.00
1941S	3.00	3.00	3.00	3.00	3.00	5.00	25.00
1942	3.00	3.00	3.00	3.00	3.00	3.00	5.00
1942D	3.00	3.00	3.00	3.00	3.00	3.00	16.00

	G	VG	F	VF	XF	AU	MS60
1942S	3.00	3.00	3.00	3.00	3.00	10.00	65.00
1943	3.00	3.00	3.00	3.00	3.00	3.00	4.00
1943D	3.00	3.00	3.00	3.00	3.00	9.00	25.00
1943S	3.00	3.00	3.00	3.00	3.00	9.00	23.00
1944	3.00	3.00	3.00	1.50	1.50	3.00	5.00
1944D	1.50	1.50	1.50	1.50	1.50	6.00	16.00
1944S	1.50	1.50	1.50	1.50	1.50	6.00	13.00
1945	1.50	1.50	1.50	1.50	1.50	3.00	5.00
1945D	1.50	1.50	1.50	1.50	1.50	7.00	16.00
1945S	1.50	1.50	1.50	1.50	1.50	4.00	8.00
1946	1.50	1.50	1.50	1.50	1.50	3.00	5.00
1946D	1.50	1.50	1.50	1.50	1.50	3.00	9.00
1946S	1.50	1.50	1.50	1.50	1.50	3.00	7.00
1947	1.50	1.50	1.50	1.50	1.50	3.00	10.00
1947D	1.50	1.50	1.50	1.50	1.50	3.00	10.00
1947S	1.50	1.50	1.50	1.50	1.50	3.00	8.00
1948	1.50	1.50	1.50	1.50	1.50	3.00	5.00
1948D	1.50	1.50	1.50	1.50	1.50	4.00	12.00
1948S	1.50	1.50	1.50	1.50	1.50	3.00	6.00
1949	1.50	1.50	1.50	1.50	1.50	11.00	32.00
1949D	1.50	1.50	1.50	1.50	1.50	4.00	15.00
1950	1.50	1.50	1.50	1.50	1.50	3.00	8.00
1950D	1.50	1.50	1.50	1.50	1.50	3.00	8.00
1950S	1.50	1.50	1.50	1.50	1.50	3.00	8.00
1951	1.50	1.50	1.50	1.50	1.50	3.00	8.00
1951D	1.50	1.50	1.50	1.50	1.50	3.00	8.00
1951S	1.50	1.50	1.50	1.50	1.50	3.00	8.00
1952	1.50	1.50	1.50	1.50	1.50	3.00	8.00
1952D	1.50	1.50	1.50	1.50	1.50	3.00	8.00
1952S	1.50	1.50	1.50	1.50	1.50	3.00	8.00
1953	1.50	1.50	1.50	1.50	1.50	2.00	8.00
1953D	1.50	1.50	1.50	1.50	1.50	2.00	8.00
1953S	1.50	1.50	1.50	1.50	1.50	2.00	8.00
1954	1.50	1.50	1.50	1.50	1.50	2.00	8.00
1954D	1.50	1.50	1.50	1.50	1.50	2.00	8.00

	G	VG	F	VF	XF	AU	MS60
1954S	1.50	1.50	1.50	1.50	1.50	2.00	8.00
1955	1.50	1.50	1.50	1.50	1.50	2.00	8.00
1955D	1.50	1.50	1.50	1.50	1.50	2.00	8.00
1956	1.50	1.50	1.50	1.50	1.50	2.00	8.00
1956D	1.50	1.50	1.50	1.50	1.50	2.00	8.00
1957	1.50	1.50	1.50	1.50	1.50	2.00	8.00
1957D	1.50	1.50	1.50	1.50	1.50	2.00	8.00
1958	1.50	1.50	1.50	1.50	1.50	2.00	8.00
1958D	1.50	1.50	1.50	1.50	1.50	1.50	8.00
1959	1.50	1.50	1.50	1.50	1.50	1.50	8.00
1959D	1.50	1.50	1.50	1.50	1.50	1.50	8.00
1960	1.50	1.50	1.50	1.50	1.50	1.50	8.00
1960D	1.50	1.50	1.50	1.50	1.50	1.50	8.00
1961	1.50	1.50	1.50	1.50	1.50	1.50	8.00
1961D	1.50	1.50	1.50	1.50	1.50	1.50	8.00
1962	1.50	1.50	1.50	1.50	1.50	1.50	8.00
1962D	1.50	1.50	1.50	1.50	1.50	1.50	8.00
1963	1.50	1.50	1.50	1.50	1.50	1.50	8.00
1963D	1.50	1.50	1.50	1.50	1.50	1.50	8.00
1964	1.50	1.50	1.50	1.50	1.50	1.50	8.00
1964D	1.50	1.50	1.50	1.50	1.50	1.50	8.00

BV = bullion value

Pieces minted after 1964 are sold in the 30-50 cents range if uncirculated. The only exceptions to this are the 1982P, 1983P&D, 1984D, 1985P&D, 1986P&D. In MS60 these are generally priced in the $2-$3 range. Also proof issues (1968-2002) are priced below.

WASHINGTON 25 CENT — PROOF COINS

Proof Coins	Proof 64	Proof Coins	Proof 64	Proof Coins	Proof 64
1968S	4.00	1980S	4.00	1992S Silver	6.00
1969S	4.00	1981S	4.00	1993S Clad	4.00
1970S	4.00	1982S	4.00	1993S Silver	6.00
1971S	4.00	1983S	3.00	1994S Clad	4.00
1972S	4.00	1984S	3.00	1994S Silver	6.00
1973S	4.00	1985S	3.00	1995S Clad	4.00
1974S	4.00	1986S	3.00	1995S Silver	6.00
1975S	4.00	1987S	3.00	1996S Clad	4.00
1976S	4.00	1988S	3.00	1996S Silver	6.00
1976S Silver	5.00	1989S	3.00	1997S Clad	4.00
1977S	4.00	1990S	3.00	1997S Silver	6.00
1978S	4.00	1991S	3.00	1998S Clad	4.00
1979S	4.00	1992S Clad	4.00	1998S Silver	6.00

50 STATE QUARTERS
The United States Mint 50 State Quarters Program

1999	2000	2001	2002	2003
Delaware	Massachusetts	New York	Tennessee	Illinois
Pennsylvania	Maryland	North Carolina	Ohio	Alabama
New Jersey	South Carolina	Rhode Island	Louisiana	Maine
Georgia	New	Vermont	Indiana	Missouri
Connecticut	Hampshire	Kentucky	Mississippi	Arkansas
	Virginia			

2004	2005	2006	2007	2008
Michigan	California	Nevada	Montana	Oklahoma
Florida	Minnesota	Nebraska	Washington	New Mexico
Texas	Oregon	Colorado	Idaho	Arizona
Iowa	Kansas	North Dakota	Wyoming	Alaska
Wisconsin	West Virginia	South Dakota	Utah	Hawaii

50 State Quarters
Redesigned Quarter Obverse

Beginning in 1999 the Washington quarter was redesigned with a more detailed portrait of Washington on the obverse and a design on the reverse featuring the unique heritage of each of the fifty states. The Mint issues five state quarters per year (about ten weeks apart) for ten years starting in 1999. These are to be sent to the Federal Reserve banks as needed or requested, and will not necessarily be seen first in the particular state commemorated. Both the Philadelphia and Denver mints will mint general circulation coins for each state. Also the program includes the inclusion of San Francisco proof coins in the yearly proof sets. Consequently, a total of 200 different coins will have been minted by the end of the program (50 P-mint, 50 D-mint, 50 S-mint, and 50 Silver S-mint). For more information visit www.USMINT.gov or call 1-800-USA-Mint. Special albums to hold all the 50-State quarters are already available.

Just when we thought the Statehood Quarter program had come to its end, Congress authorized the much debated and highly anticipated US Territory addition/extension program. During 2009, another year of Commemorative Quarters will appear, representing The District of Columbia and the US Territories of Puerto Rico, Guam, American Samoa, US Virgin Islands, and the Northern Mariana Islands. Signed into law by President George W. Bush, these 6 new coins will be minted in 2009 with the current George Washington obverse (same as the state quarters) but with artistic vignettes representing each of the 6 diverse territories. The first coin in the extended series will be the District of Columbia.

1999 Reverses

Delaware—Caesar Rodney cast the tiebreaker vote in favor of the Declaration
of Independence.

Pennsylvania—the state motto, "Virtue, Liberty, Independence," and the
statue atop the Pennsylvania Capitol dome, superimposed over
an outline of the state.

New Jersey—George Washington's crossing of the Delaware River to defeat
the British at Trenton.

Georgia—A peach, the state motto, "Wisdom, Justice, Moderation", and oak
sprigs superimposed upon an outline of the state.

Connecticut—The Charter Oak, hiding place of the colonial government's charter
after it was challenged by the government of King George in 1687.

	MS60	Proof	Silver Proof
Delaware (P&D mint state, S proof)	1.50	12.00	60.00
Pennsylvania (P&D mint state, S proof)	1.50	12.00	60.00
New Jersey (P&D mint state, S proof)	1.00	12.00	60.00
Georgia (P&D mint state, S proof)	1.00	12.00	60.00
Connecticut (P & D mint state, S proof)	1.00	12.00	60.00

2000 Reverses

Massachusetts—the state map and a minuteman.

Maryland—The Maryland statehouse.

South Carolina—the state map, bird, and flower.

New Hampshire—the Old Man of the Mountain and the state motto.

Virginia—the 400th anniversary of the ships arriving at Jamestown.

	MS60	Proof	Silver Proof
Massachusetts (P & D mint state, S proof)	.50	3.00	6.00
Maryland (P & D mint state, S proof)	.50	3.00	6.00
South Carolina (P & D mint state, S proof)	.50	3.00	6.00
New Hampshire (P & D mint state, S proof)	.50	3.00	6.00
Virginia (P & D mint state, S proof)	.50	3.00	6.00

2001 Reverses

New York—the Statue of Liberty superimposed over an outline of the state.

North Carolina—Kitty Hawk flight with drawing of the Wright Brothers craft, the Flyer.

Rhode Island—a vintage sailboat gliding through Rhode Island's famous Narragansett Bay.

Vermont—Maple sugar production against the background of Vermont's Green Mountains.

Kentucky—the stately mansion, Federal Hill, with thoroughbred racehorse in the foreground.

	MS60	Proof	Silver Proof
New York (P & D mint state, S proof)	.50	5.00	12.00
North Carolina (P & D mint state, S proof)	.50	5.00	12.00
Rhode Island (P & D mint state, S proof)	.50	5.00	12.00
Vermont (P & D mint state, S proof)	.50	5.00	12.00
Kentucky (P & D mint state, S proof)	.50	5.00	12.00

2002 REVERSES

Tennessee—various musical instruments.

Ohio—State map and an astronaut.

Louisiana—The Louisiana Purchase and a pelican superimposed on a map of the U.S.

Indiana—State map and Indianapolis 500 race car.

Mississippi—Magnolias.

2002 REVERSES

	MS60	Proof	Silver Proof
Tennessee (P & D mint state, S proof)	.50	3.00	6.00
Ohio (P & D mint state, S proof)	.50	3.00	6.00
Louisiana (P & D mint state, S proof)	.50	3.00	6.00
Indiana (P & D mint state, S proof)	.50	3.00	6.00
Mississippi (P & D mint state, S proof)	.50	3.00	6.00

2003 REVERSES

Illinois—Abe Lincoln, Map, Chicago and Farm.

Maine—Lighthouse and Sailing Ship.

Missouri—the Arch and Lewis and Clark

Alabama—Helen Keller.

Arkansas—Diamond and Wildlife Habitat.

	MS60	Proof	Silver Proof
Illinois (P & D mint state, S proof)	.50	3.00	5.00
Maine (P & D mint state, S proof)	.50	3.00	5.00
Missouri (P & D mint state, S proof)	.50	3.00	5.00
Alabama (P & D mint state, S proof)	.50	3.00	5.00
Arkansas (P & D mint state, S proof)	.50	3.00	5.00

2004 Reverses

Michigan—Map of Michigan surrounded by the Great Lakes

Florida—Space Shuttle, Palm Trees, and a Spanish Discovery Ship

Texas—Lone Star superimposed on the Map of Texas

Iowa—One-Room School House

Wisconsin—Dairy Cow, Cheese Wheel and Ear of Corn

	MS60	Proof	Silver Proof
Michigan (P & D mint state, S proof)	.50	3.00	5.00
Florida (P & D mint state, S proof)	.50	3.00	5.00
Texas (P & D mint state, S proof)	.50	3.00	5.00
Iowa (P & D mint state, S proof)	.50	3.00	5.00
Wisconsin (P & D mint state, S proof)	.50	3.00	5.00

2005 Reverses

California—John Muir admiring Yosemite Valley's "Half Dome" and a soaring California condor

Minnesota—A tree-lined lake, two people fishing, loon on the water, State outline

Oregon—Crater Lake incorporating Wizards Island

Kansas—Buffalo and sunflower motif

West Virginia—New River and the New River Gorge Bridge

	MS60	Proof	Silver Proof
California (P & D mint state, S proof)	.50	3.00	5.00
Oregon (P & D mint state, S proof)	.50	3.00	5.00
Minnesota (P & D mint state, S proof)	.50	3.00	5.00
Kansas (P & D mint state, S proof)	.50	3.00	5.00
West Virginia (P & D mint state, S proof)	.50	3.00	5.00

2006 State Quarter Reverses

		MS60	Proof	Silver Proof
Nevada	The Silver State	.50	2.00	4.00
Nebraska	Chimney Rock	.50	2.00	4.00
Colorado	Colorful Colorado	.50	2.00	4.00
North Dakota	Badlands with Bison	.50	2.00	4.00
South Dakota	Mount Rushmore And Pheasant	.50	2.00	4.00

2007 State Quarter Reverses

		MS60	Proof	Silver Proof
Montana	Big Sky Country	.50	2.00	4.00
Washington	The Evergreen State	.50	2.00	4.00
Idaho	Peregrine Falcon	.50	2.00	4.00
Wyoming	The Equality State	.50	2.00	4.00
Utah	Crossroads of the West	.50	2.00	4.00

2008 State Quarter Reverses

		MS60	Proof	Silver Proof
Oklahoma	Scissortail Flycatcher	.50	2.00	4.00
New Mexico	Land of Enchantment	.50	2.00	4.00
Arizona	Grant Canyon State	.50	2.00	4.00
Alaska	The Great Land	.50	2.00	4.00
Hawaii	King Kamehameha I	.50	2.00	4.00

HALF DOLLARS MINTED 1794 - DATE

EARLY TYPES MINTED 1794-1839

FLOWING HAIR 1794-1795

	G	VG	F	VF	XF	AU	MS60
1794	3500.00	5000.00	9000.00	15000.00	30000.00	60000.00	125000.00
1795	1000.00	1250.00	1750.00	4500.00	10500.00	18000.00	35000.00
1795 Recut Date	1200.00	1300.00	1850.00	5100.00	11000.00	19000.00	35000.00
1795 3 Leaves	2200.00	2900.00	4400.00	7500.00	14500.00	28000.00	50000.00

DRAPED BUST TYPE
EAGLE & SHIELD REVERSE

DRAPED BUST 1796-1807

	G	VG	F	VF	XF	AU	MS60
1796 15 stars	30000.00	37000.00	51000.00	60000.00	95000.00	140000.00	245000.00
1796 16 Stars	35000.00	40000.00	53000.00	75000.00	100000.00	145000.00	185000.00
1797 15 Stars	30000.00	37000.00	51000.00	65000.00	95000.00	142000.00	150000.00
1801	550.00	950.00	2000.00	3300.00	7000.00	12000.00	30000.00

HALF DOLLARS — HERALDIC EAGLE

	G	VG	F	VF	XF	AU	MS60
1802	550.00	950.00	2000.00	3300.00	7000.00	11000.00	29500.00
1803 Small 3	165.00	195.00	300.00	700.00	2000.00	4800.00	11000.00
1803 Large 3	155.00	180.00	240.00	550.00	1500.00	1600.00	9000.00
1805 5 over 4	165.00	240.00	300.00	800.00	2000.00	5500.00	26000.00
1805	155.00	180.00	240.00	550.00	1500.00	4500.00	8500.00
1806 6 over 5	155.00	196.00	250.00	540.00	1500.00	4450.00	9500.00
1806 6 over inverted 6	165.00	265.00	450.00	1000.00	2500.00	5500.00	11500.00
1806 Knob 6, Lg. Stars	155.00	190.00	200.00	500.00	1500.00	4300.00	8000.00
1806 Knob 6, Sm. Stars	155.00	190.00	200.00	500.00	1500.00	4300.00	8000.00
1806 Knob 6 (stemless claw)	16000.00	20000.00	30000.00	45000.00	75000.00	0.00	0.00
1806 Pointed 6	160.00	180.00	210.00	500.00	1500.00	4300.00	7900.00
1807	160.00	180.00	210.00	500.00	1500.00	4300.00	7800.00

CAPPED BUST 1807-1839

	G	VG	F	VF	XF	AU	MS60
	85.00	130.00	250.00	500.00	1200.00	3100.00	5100.00
1807 Small stars	65.00	102.00	195.00	400.00	1050.00	2600.00	4600.00
1807 Large stars	60.00	95.00	155.00	350.00	950.00	2500.00	4500.00
1807 50 over 20	55.00	75.00	100.00	180.00	350.00	960.00	2000.00
1808 8 over 7	55.00	60.00	80.00	120.00	275.00	450.00	1600.00
1808	55.00	60.00	70.00	110.00	225.00	420.00	1260.00
1809	65.00	70.00	80.00	100.00	240.00	390.00	1080.00
1810	65.00	78.00	85.00	95.00	265.00	330.00	1300.00
1811	55.00	59.00	90.00	165.00	250.00	570.00	2040.00
1812 2over1,Sm 8	1425.00	1800.00	3480.00	5100.00	7200.00	19000.00	0.00
1812 2 over 1, Lg 8	55.00	62.00	72.00	96.00	175.00	400.00	1200.00
1812	55.00	60.00	63.00	100.00	162.00	384.00	900.00
1813	70.00	75.00	100.00	145.00	260.00	660.00	1440.00
1813 50c over UNI	80.00	90.00	125.00	195.00	270.00	875.00	1920.00
1814 4 over 3	65.00	75.00	90.00	125.00	210.00	600.00	1020.00
1814 E over A in STATES	55.00	63.00	76.00	96.00	150.00	420.00	810.00
1814	950.00	1150.00	1800.00	3000.00	3300.00	5200.00	8800.00
1815 5 over 2	95.00	126.00	180.00	372.00	690.00	1450.00	3120.00
1817 7 over 3	35000.00	48000.00	95000.00	120000.00	155000.00	260000.00	0.00
1817 7 over 4	55.00	64.00	72.00	90.00	186.00	378.00	840.00
1817	75.00	82.00	92.00	120.00	198.00	708.00	1260.00
1818 8 over 7	52.00	58.00	64.00	84.00	162.00	342.00	840.00
1818	60.00	65.00	75.00	96.00	222.00	432.00	1200.00
1819 9 over 8	55.00	58.00	64.00	90.00	156.00	294.00	792.00
1819	80.00	90.00	100.00	160.00	324.00	792.00	1530.00
1820 20 over 19	55.00	64.00	72.00	102.00	282.00	510.00	990.00
1820	55.00	62.00	70.00	88.00	168.00	510.00	900.00
1821	69.00	80.00	105.00	150.00	270.00	600.00	960.00
1822 2 over 1	55.00	59.00	64.00	84.00	156.00	330.00	558.00

	G	VG	F	VF	XF	AU	MS60
1822	62.00	60.00	95.00	144.00	300.00	630.00	1170.00
1823 Broken 3	55.00	65.00	90.00	120.00	204.00	420.00	960.00
1823 Patched 3	55.00	59.00	65.00	75.00	138.00	306.00	850.00
1823	60.00	65.00	72.00	95.00	174.00	390.00	840.00
1824 4 over 1	50.00	55.00	64.00	72.00	138.00	282.00	850.00
1824	50.00	55.00	64.00	72.00	138.00	282.00	850.00
1825	50.00	55.00	64.00	72.00	138.00	282.00	850.00
1826	70.00	75.00	90.00	110.00	190.00	360.00	930.00
1827 7 over 6	50.00	55.00	64.00	72.00	138.00	282.00	850.00
1827	55.00	59.00	66.00	80.00	140.00	282.00	850.00
1828 Curl Base 2	50.00	55.00	64.00	72.00	138.00	282.00	432.00
1828 Square Base 2	61.00	69.00	75.00	95.00	170.00	342.00	900.00
1829 9 over 7	50.00	55.00	64.00	72.00	138.00	282.00	850.00
1829	50.00	55.00	64.00	72.00	138.00	282.00	850.00
1830	51.00	55.00	64.00	72.00	138.00	282.00	850.00
1831	51.00	55.00	64.00	72.00	138.00	282.00	850.00
1832	51.00	55.00	64.00	72.00	138.00	282.00	850.00
1833	51.00	55.00	64.00	72.00	138.00	282.00	850.00
1834	51.00	55.00	64.00	72.00	138.00	282.00	850.00
1835	51.00	55.00	64.00	72.00	138.00	282.00	850.00
1836	51.00	55.00	64.00	72.00	138.00	282.00	850.00
1836 50 over 00	65.00	60.00	88.00	114.00	258.00	720.00	1320.00

REEDED EDGE

	G	VG	F	VF	XF	AU	MS60
1836	750.00	950.00	1375.00	1700.00	2275.00	3250.00	6420.00
1837	55.00	65.00	75.00	11.00	162.00	312.00	850.00

"HALF DOLLAR" ON REVERSE

	G	VG	F	VF	XF	AU	MS60
1838	50.00	60.00	75.00	108.00	162.00	312.00	850.00
1838 O	125000.00	145000.00	165000.00	175000.00	185000.00	200000.00	225000.00
1839	54.00	64.00	80.00	114.00	180.00	360.00	900.00
1839 O	175.00	230.00	320.00	420.00	705.00	1020.00	2250.00

LIBERTY SEATED TYPE MINTED 1839 – 1891

LIBERTY SEATED FIFTY-CENT PIECE
NO DRAPERY

	G	VG	F	VF	XF	AU	MS60
1839	40.00	78.00	143.00	322.00	745.00	1730.00	4650.00

NO MOTTO WITH DRAPERY

	G	VG	F	VF	XF	AU	MS60
1839	25.00	36.00	55.00	85.00	136.00	242.00	534.00
1840 SMLetters Rev.1839	27.00	38.00	52.00	76.00	133.00	272.00	500.00
1840MDLettersRev.1838	106.00	156.00	227.00	310.00	565.00	1100.00	3030.00
1840 O	27.00	33.00	51.00	88.00	121.00	248.00	550.00
1841	43.00	54.00	83.00	136.00	223.00	326.00	1230.00
1841 O	26.00	33.00	51.00	82.00	127.00	248.00	690.00
1842OSMDateSmLetters	484.00	786.00	1175.00	1810.00	3625.00	7250.00	15750.00
1842 SM Date	27.00	46.00	71.00	94.00	127.00	308.00	1110.00
1842 MD Date	26.00	33.00	50.00	72.00	121.00	290.00	780.00
1842 O MD Date LG Letter	26.00	33.00	51.00	70.00	121.00	284.00	1050.00
1843	26.00	33.00	49.00	64.00	115.00	236.00	546.00
1843 O	26.00	33.00	53.00	64.00	115.00	236.00	546.00
1844	26.00	33.00	49.00	64.00	115.00	236.00	546.00
1844 O	26.00	33.00	49.00	64.00	115.00	236.00	630.00
1844 O Double Date	424.00	606.00	815.00	1060.00	2185.00	5330.00	7950.00
1845	28.00	42.00	58.00	112.00	181.00	320.00	870.00
1845 O	26.00	33.00	49.00	64.00	115.00	236.00	630.00
1845 O No Drapery	28.00	52.00	70.00	104.00	181.00	320.00	1290.00
1846	26.00	33.00	49.00	58.00	115.00	120.00	600.00
1846Over Horizon.6	124.00	168.00	215.00	340.00	505.00	1070.00	3150.00
1846 O MD Date	28.00	33.00	49.00	58.00	121.00	270.00	1050.00
1846 O Tall Date	130.00	246.00	323.00	538.00	925.00	1850.00	6150.00
1847 over 46	1324.00	2046.00	2885.00	3610.00	5425.00	8750.00	16950.00
1847	26.00	33.00	49.00	64.00	115.00	240.00	530.00
1847 O	25.00	33.00	49.00	58.00	115.00	250.00	710.00
1848	37.00	59.00	81.00	142.00	229.00	470.00	990.00

	G	VG	F	VF	XF	AU	MS60
1848 O	25.00	33.00	49.00	64.00	115.00	250.00	740.00
1849	31.00	41.00	55.00	78.00	145.00	370.00	960.00
1849 O	25.00	30.00	49.00	64.00	115.00	260.00	810.00
1850	172.00	258.00	383.00	490.00	625.00	830.00	1560.00
1850 O	26.00	33.00	49.00	64.00	115.00	240.00	570.00
1851	256.00	366.00	413.00	520.00	625.00	770.00	1700.00
1851 O	29.00	42.00	55.00	78.00	145.00	250.00	540.00
1852	304.00	450.00	545.00	730.00	955.00	1250.00	1650.00
1852 O	50.00	102.00	143.00	208.00	445.00	800.00	1770.00
1853 O 3 known	135004.00	145006.00	150005.00	192010.00	350025.00	50.00	150.00
ARROWS & RAYS							
1853	28.00	39.00	51.00	88.00	253.00	560.00	1530.00
1853 O	28.00	40.00	53.00	118.00	283.00	710.00	2310.00
ARROWS AT DATE							
1854	28.00	39.00	51.00	70.00	133.00	320.00	690.00
1854 O	28.00	39.00	51.00	70.00	133.00	320.00	690.00
1855 over 1854	62.00	84.00	149.00	238.00	355.00	590.00	2130.00
1855	28.00	39.00	51.00	70.00	133.00	320.00	750.00
1855 O	28.00	39.00	51.00	70.00	133.00	320.00	690.00
1855 S	262.00	426.00	635.00	1030.00	2365.00	5930.00	12750.00
NO MOTTO							
1856	24.00	33.00	49.00	64.00	115.00	250.00	570.00
1856 O	24.00	33.00	49.00	64.00	115.00	240.00	530.00
1856 S	43.00	60.00	101.00	202.00	397.00	920.00	3570.00
1857	24.00	33.00	49.00	64.00	115.00	240.00	530.00
1857 O	24.00	33.00	49.00	64.00	115.00	240.00	1020.00
1857 S	49.00	72.00	113.00	196.00	415.00	1010.00	3690.00
1858	24.00	33.00	49.00	64.00	115.00	240.00	530.00
1858 O	24.00	33.00	49.00	58.00	115.00	240.00	530.00
1858 S	33.00	42.00	51.00	100.00	193.00	350.00	840.00
1859	28.00	42.00	53.00	88.00	133.00	250.00	530.00
1859 O	24.00	33.00	49.00	64.00	115.00	240.00	530.00
1859 S	32.00	34.00	50.00	88.00	169.00	320.00	690.00
1860	25.00	33.00	49.00	62.00	115.00	290.00	680.00
1860 O	24.00	34.00	49.00	64.00	115.00	180.00	530.00
1860 S	26.00	33.00	49.00	64.00	115.00	240.00	780.00

	G	VG	F	VF	XF	AU	MS60
1861	24.00	33.00	49.00	64.00	115.00	240.00	590.00
1861 O	26.00	35.00	49.00	64.00	115.00	240.00	570.00
1861 S	28.00	36.00	49.00	64.00	115.00	240.00	600.00
1862	29.00	46.00	61.00	112.00	169.00	310.00	600.00
1862 S	24.00	33.00	49.00	64.00	115.00	250.00	600.00
1863	29.00	38.00	51.00	76.00	121.00	250.00	600.00
1863 S	26.00	33.00	49.00	64.00	115.00	250.00	600.00
1864	29.00	38.00	55.00	91.00	157.00	310.00	600.00
1864 S	27.00	33.00	49.00	64.00	115.00	260.00	750.00
1865	28.00	36.00	53.00	76.00	145.00	310.00	600.00
1865 S	26.00	33.00	49.00	64.00	115.00	260.00	630.00
1866 S	400.00	495.00	750.00	1100.00	2100.00	2750.00	4250.00

WITH MOTTO

	G	VG	F	VF	XF	AU	MS60
1866	27.00	33.00	50.00	64.00	115.00	220.00	510.00
1866 S	24.00	33.00	49.00	58.00	107.00	230.00	630.00
1867	28.00	40.00	53.00	112.00	163.00	280.00	510.00
1867 S	24.00	33.00	49.00	64.00	109.00	230.00	570.00
1868	40.00	51.00	80.00	124.00	199.00	280.00	630.00
1868 S	24.00	33.00	49.00	64.00	115.00	230.00	600.00
1869	24.00	34.00	50.00	64.00	119.00	220.00	510.00
1869 S	24.00	33.00	49.00	64.00	133.00	240.00	840.00
1870	25.00	33.00	50.00	68.00	130.00	220.00	600.00
1870 CC	454.00	950.00	2500.00	5500.00	27500.00	75000.00	135000.00
1870 S	26.00	33.00	50.00	67.00	127.00	250.00	930.00
1871	26.00	33.00	49.00	64.00	109.00	220.00	490.00
1871 CC	112.00	198.00	401.00	658.00	1345.00	2330.00	11750.00
1871 S	24.00	33.00	49.00	64.00	109.00	220.00	500.00
1872	26.00	33.00	49.00	64.00	107.00	220.00	550.00
1872 CC	64.00	90.00	167.00	346.00	625.00	1490.00	3650.00
1872 S	28.00	42.00	59.00	106.00	187.00	340.00	1050.00
1873 closed 3	26.00	44.00	62.00	100.00	145.00	280.00	630.00
1873 open 3	3100.00	3700.00	4600.00	5800.00	6750.00	8300.00	12750.00
1873 CC	118.00	180.00	305.00	538.00	1105.00	2930.00	8070.00

	G	VG	F	VF	XF	AU	MS60
ARROWS AT DATE							
1873	30.00	42.00	53.00	88.00	229.00	430.00	980.00
1873 CC	118.00	222.00	335.00	760.00	1765.00	2450.00	6600.00
1873 S	46.00	72.00	107.00	208.00	397.00	710.00	2310.00
1874	30.00	42.00	53.00	88.00	229.00	430.00	980.00
1874 CC	268.00	438.00	755.00	1270.00	2500.00	4405.00	9750.00
1874 S	33.00	48.00	71.00	166.00	337.00	650.00	1710.00
WITH MOTTO							
1875	24.00	35.00	49.00	64.00	107.00	220.00	540.00
1875 CC	34.00	42.00	57.00	82.00	163.00	280.00	690.00
1875 S	24.00	36.00	49.00	64.00	115.00	220.00	480.00
1876	24.00	33.00	49.00	64.00	109.00	220.00	480.00
1876 CC	34.00	42.00	57.00	76.00	157.00	260.00	700.00
1876 S	24.00	33.00	49.00	64.00	109.00	220.00	480.00
1877	24.00	33.00	49.00	64.00	109.00	220.00	480.00
1877 CC	34.00	42.00	57.00	69.00	145.00	260.00	750.00
1877 S	24.00	33.00	49.00	64.00	109.00	220.00	480.00
1878	26.00	40.00	51.00	82.00	127.00	220.00	540.00
1878 CC	294.00	406.00	565.00	850.00	1765.00	2930.00	4950.00
1878 S	16800.00	29000.00	35000.00	38000.00	42000.00	58000.00	70000.00
1879	214.00	258.00	293.00	334.00	415.00	530.00	750.00
1880	174.00	206.00	235.00	280.00	325.00	460.00	750.00
1881	184.00	206.00	255.00	290.00	325.00	460.00	750.00
1882	264.00	286.00	315.00	340.00	385.00	530.00	750.00
1883	244.00	276.00	295.00	330.00	375.00	470.00	720.00
1884	294.00	306.00	345.00	380.00	415.00	500.00	750.00
1885	294.00	326.00	345.00	360.00	405.00	490.00	750.00
1886	304.00	426.00	455.00	490.00	555.00	650.00	840.00
1887	434.00	486.00	555.00	590.00	685.00	770.00	960.00
1888	184.00	216.00	245.00	280.00	315.00	470.00	720.00
1889	184.00	246.00	275.00	300.00	325.00	470.00	750.00
1890	184.00	216.00	245.00	300.00	345.00	500.00	770.00
1891	42.00	52.00	85.00	105.00	145.00	240.00	540.00

LIBERTY HEAD TYPE MINTED 1892 -1915

BARBER HALF DOLLARS 1892 - 1915

	G	VG	F	VF	XF	AU	MS60
1892	24.00	34.00	57.00	102.00	168.00	235.00	400.00
1892O	275.00	345.00	4540.00	500.00	595.00	635.00	780.00
1892S	205.00	288.00	350.00	435.00	485.00	575.00	810.00
1893	17.00	25.00	60.00	110.00	186.00	288.00	468.00
1893O	30.00	48.00	110.00	175.00	270.00	365.00	510.00
1893S	130.00	170.00	245.00	390.00	445.00	480.00	1050.00
1894	27.00	41.00	95.00	155.00	235.00	324.00	438.00
1894O	18.00	25.00	72.00	140.00	216.00	288.00	450.00
1894S	15.00	22.00	56.00	103.00	186.00	312.00	426.00
1895	15.00	20.00	60.00	120.00	174.00	265.00	516.00
1895O	19.00	30.00	88.00	145.00	222.00	330.00	516.00
1895S	25.00	43.00	110.00	190.00	246.00	330.00	498.00
1896	17.00	22.00	75.00	120.00	216.00	300.00	492.00
1896O	34.00	44.00	142.00	235.00	360.00	600.00	1200.00
1896S	75.00	105.00	170.00	288.00	372.00	600.00	1200.00
1897	11.00	14.00	39.00	82.00	138.00	288.00	402.00
1897O	135.00	190.00	410.00	688.00	888.00	1080.00	1500.00
1897S	125.00	174.00	335.00	450.00	702.00	900.00	1320.00
1898	11.00	13.00	33.00	77.00	144.00	288.00	384.00
1898O	30.00	62.00	185.00	295.00	408.00	505.00	990.00
1898S	23.00	42.00	70.00	135.00	198.00	350.00	840.00
1899	12.00	15.00	32.00	84.00	138.00	282.00	384.00
1899O	21.00	30.00	65.00	135.00	235.00	330.00	570.00
1899S	18.00	27.00	60.00	110.00	180.00	312.00	576.00
1900	12.00	14.00	32.00	77.00	138.00	270.00	378.00
1900O	15.00	19.00	50.00	140.00	240.00	330.00	750.00
1900S	13.00	15.00	42.00	90.00	180.00	276.00	570.00
1901	12.00	13.00	30.00	78.00	144.00	258.00	425.00

	G	VG	F	VF	XF	AU	MS60
1901O	14.00	22.00	65.00	170.00	282.00	420.00	1170.00
1901S	28.00	44.00	132.00	295.00	498.00	870.00	1620.00
1902	11.00	13.00	27.00	76.00	144.00	252.00	395.00
1902O	12.00	14.00	47.00	87.00	180.00	318.00	636.00
1902S	14.00	16.00	53.00	125.00	210.00	350.00	660.00
1903	12.00	13.00	41.00	84.00	180.00	300.00	420.00
1903O	11.00	14.00	46.00	98.00	186.00	300.00	600.00
1903S	12.50	15.00	45.00	100.00	204.00	336.00	522.00
1904	10.00	11.00	29.00	70.00	138.00	270.00	384.00
1904O	17.00	26.00	70.00	180.00	318.00	462.00	960.00
1904S	32.00	55.00	225.00	450.00	875.00	1550.00	5500.00
1905	19.00	23.00	75.00	150.00	210.00	300.00	498.00
1905O	24.00	40.00	105.00	195.00	276.00	384.00	660.00
1905S	13.00	14.00	42.00	105.00	198.00	318.00	564.00
1906	10.00	11.00	27.00	70.00	144.00	258.00	395.00
1906D	10.00	11.00	30.00	75.00	138.00	264.00	384.00
1906O	10.00	11.00	39.00	82.00	150.00	288.00	540.00
1906S	11.00	13.00	48.00	90.00	192.00	276.00	540.00
1907	10.00	11.00	27.00	76.00	138.00	258.00	395.00
1907D	10.00	11.00	27.00	66.00	138.00	264.00	395.00
1907O	10.00	11.00	28.00	75.00	138.00	288.00	480.00
1907S	14.00	19.00	72.00	135.00	282.00	570.00	1110.00
1908	10.00	11.00	26.00	70.00	138.00	252.00	372.00
1908D	10.00	11.00	26.00	70.00	138.00	252.00	384.00
1908O	10.00	11.00	27.00	76.00	138.00	288.00	468.00
1908S	16.00	21.00	60.00	140.00	235.00	330.00	690.00
1909	11.00	15.00	35.00	70.00	144.00	252.00	395.00
1909O	14.00	19.00	45.00	120.00	270.00	462.00	660.00
1909S	10.00	11.00	32.00	82.00	168.00	306.00	516.00
1910	17.00	24.00	70.00	132.00	264.00	360.00	540.00
1910S	12.00	14.00	30.00	85.00	162.00	300.00	570.00
1911	10.00	11.00	27.00	75.00	138.00	258.00	420.00
1911D	11.00	12.00	35.00	80.00	168.00	252.00	498.00
1911S	12.00	13.00	34.00	83.00	150.00	294.00	504.00
1912	10.00	11.00	27.00	72.00	138.00	258.00	395.00

1912D	11.00	13.00	26.00	68.00	138.00	270.00	395.00
1912S	13.00	17.00	33.00	85.00	160.00	294.00	480.00
1913	60.00	75.00	170.00	335.00	420.00	690.00	960.00
1913D	13.00	18.00	38.00	82.00	174.00	276.00	420.00
1913S	16.00	22.00	42.00	90.00	180.00	324.00	540.00
1914	125.00	135.00	270.00	408.00	570.00	810.00	1140.00
1914S	13.00	16.00	33.00	85.00	162.00	270.00	504.00
1915	80.00	115.00	210.00	330.00	465.00	720.00	1020.00
1915D	10.00	11.00	26.00	68.00	138.00	252.00	395.00
1915S	13.00	16.00	34.00	80.00	138.00	252.00	395.00

Liberty Walking Type Minted 1916 -1947

LIBERTY WALKING FIFTY-CENT PIECE

WALKING LIBERTY HALF DOLLARS

	G	VG	F	VF	XF	AU	MS60
1916	45.00	52.00	85.00	155.00	225.00	245.00	300.00
1916D MM On Obverse	48.00	52.00	70.00	120.00	190.00	225.00	325.00
1916S MM On Obverse	98.00	125.00	245.00	380.00	550.00	650.00	975.00
1917	8.00	9.00	11.00	20.00	42.00	65.00	110.00
1917D MM On Obverse	22.00	30.00	70.00	145.00	225.00	300.00	550.00
1917S MM On Obverse	24.00	38.00	125.00	310.00	655.00	1100.00	1900.00
1917D	10.00	15.00	33.00	102.00	222.00	500.00	800.00
1917S	8.00	9.00	15.00	30.00	48.00	140.00	290.00
1918	8.00	9.00	14.00	60.00	140.00	225.00	475.00
1918D	8.50	11.00	32.00	80.00	210.00	420.00	1225.00
1918S	8.00	9.00	14.00	29.00	65.00	175.00	450.00
1919	23.00	27.00	66.00	235.00	475.00	760.00	1245.00
1919D	22.50	33.00	90.00	275.00	660.00	1550.00	5200.00
1919S	15.00	25.00	65.00	275.00	750.00	1500.00	3200.00
1920	8.00	9.00	15.00	40.00	75.00	140.00	280.00
1920D	9.00	16.00	60.00	245.00	410.00	810.00	1300.00
1920S	8.00	9.00	18.00	75.00	250.00	420.00	795.00

	G	VG	F	VF	XF	AU	MS60
1921	150.00	180.00	310.00	650.00	1380.00	2400.00	3650.00
1921D	250.00	310.00	455.00	800.00	1920.00	2760.00	4450.00
1921S	40.00	65.00	205.00	630.00	3200.00	7560.00	12400.00
1923S	8.00	12.00	23.00	95.00	265.00	582.00	1200.00
1927S	8.00	9.00	12.00	40.00	120.00	350.00	850.00
1928S	8.00	9.00	14.00	61.00	170.00	400.00	850.00
1929D	8.00	9.00	13.00	28.00	90.00	180.00	350.00
1929S	8.00	9.00	12.00	26.00	110.00	190.00	350.00
1933S	8.00	10.00	12.00	16.00	52.00	240.00	525.00
1934	8.00	8.50	8.75	9.00	10.00	25.00	80.00
1934D	8.00	8.50	8.75	9.00	29.00	75.00	135.00
1934S	8.00	8.50	8.75	9.00	27.00	102.00	340.00
1935	8.00	8.50	8.75	9.00	10.00	22.00	40.00
1935D	8.00	8.50	8.75	9.00	31.00	62.00	125.00
1935S	8.00	8.50	8.75	9.00	28.00	96.00	255.00
1936	8.00	8.50	8.75	9.00	10.00	24.00	33.00
1936D	8.00	8.50	8.75	9.00	18.00	52.00	75.00
1936S	8.00	8.50	8.75	9.00	21.00	64.00	125.00
1937	8.00	8.50	8.75	9.00	10.00	24.00	38.00
1937D	8.00	8.50	8.75	9.00	28.00	90.00	210.00
1937S	8.00	8.50	8.75	9.00	21.00	78.00	165.00
1938	8.00	8.50	8.75	9.00	10.00	46.00	68.00
1938D	105.00	125.00	145.00	175.00	200.00	222.00	465.00
1939	8.00	8.50	8.75	9.00	10.00	24.00	38.00
1939D	8.00	8.50	8.75	9.00	10.00	28.00	43.00
1939S	8.00	8.50	8.75	9.00	10.00	70.00	140.00
1940	8.00	8.50	8.75	9.00	10.00	10.00	30.00
1940S	8.00	8.50	8.75	9.00	10.00	20.00	44.00
1941	8.00	8.50	8.75	9.00	10.00	10.00	32.00
1941D	8.00	8.50	8.75	9.00	10.00	15.00	33.00
1941S	8.00	8.50	8.75	9.00	10.00	24.00	75.00
1942	8.00	8.50	8.75	9.00	10.00	10.00	28.00
1942D	8.00	8.50	8.75	9.00	10.00	17.00	34.00
1942S	8.00	8.50	8.75	9.00	10.00	15.00	33.00
1943	8.00	8.50	8.75	9.00	10.00	10.00	30.00

1943D	8.00	8.50	8.75	9.00	10.00	21.00	38.00
1943S	8.00	8.50	8.75	9.00	10.00	17.00	40.00
1944	8.00	8.50	8.75	9.00	10.00	10.00	31.00
1944D	8.00	8.50	8.75	9.00	10.00	18.00	34.00
1944S	8.00	8.50	8.75	9.00	10.00	15.00	33.00
1945	8.00	8.50	8.75	9.00	10.00	10.00	29.00
1945D	8.00	8.50	8.75	9.00	10.00	18.00	32.00
1945S	8.00	8.50	8.75	9.00	10.00	15.00	31.00
1946	8.00	8.50	8.75	9.00	10.00	11.00	35.00
1946D	8.00	8.50	8.75	9.00	13.00	34.00	44.00
1946S	8.00	8.50	9.00	9.50	10.00	18.00	42.00
1947	8.00	8.50	9.00	9.50	10.00	20.00	45.00
1947D	8.00	8.50	9.00	9.50	10.00	28.00	47.00

FRANKLIN TYPE MINTED 1948 - 1963

FRANKLIN FIFTY-CENT PIECE

FRANKLIN HALF DOLLARS

	G	VG	F	VF	XF	AU	MS60
1948	7.00	8.00	9.00	10.00	11.00	12.00	15.00
1948D	7.00	8.00	9.00	10.00	11.00	12.00	13.00
1949	7.00	8.00	9.00	10.00	11.00	12.00	33.00
1949D	7.00	8.00	9.00	11.00	15.00	25.00	35.00
1949S	7.00	8.00	9.00	11.00	13.00	32.00	55.00
1950	7.00	8.00	9.00	10.00	11.00	12.00	20.00
1950D	7.00	8.00	9.00	10.00	11.00	12.00	17.00
1951	7.00	8.00	9.00	10.00	11.00	12.00	14.00
1951D	7.00	8.00	9.00	10.00	14.00	18.00	21.00
1951S	7.00	8.00	9.00	10.00	12.00	13.00	19.00
1952	7.00	8.00	9.00	10.00	11.00	12.00	13.00
1952D	7.00	8.00	9.00	10.00	11.00	12.00	13.00
1952S	7.00	8.00	9.00	10.00	16.00	25.00	43.00
1953	7.00	8.00	9.00	10.00	11.00	15.00	20.00

	G	VG	F	VF	XF	AU	MS60
1953D	7.00	8.00	9.00	10.00	11.00	12.00	13.00
1953S	7.00	8.00	9.00	10.00	11.00	15.00	22.00
1954	7.00	8.00	9.00	10.00	11.00	12.00	13.00
1954D	7.00	8.00	9.00	10.00	11.00	12.00	13.00
1954S	7.00	8.00	9.00	10.00	11.00	12.00	16.00
1955	7.00	8.00	9.00	10.00	11.00	12.00	27.00
1956	7.00	8.00	9.00	10.00	11.00	12.00	11.00
1957	7.00	8.00	9.00	10.00	11.00	12.00	13.00
1957D	7.00	8.00	9.00	10.00	11.00	12.00	13.00
1958	7.00	8.00	9.00	10.00	11.00	12.00	13.00
1958D	7.00	8.00	9.00	10.00	11.00	12.00	13.00
1959	7.00	8.00	9.00	10.00	11.00	12.00	13.00
1959D	7.00	8.00	9.00	10.00	11.00	12.00	13.00
1960	7.00	8.00	9.00	10.00	11.00	12.00	13.00
1960D	7.00	8.00	9.00	10.00	11.00	12.00	13.00
1961	7.00	8.00	9.00	10.00	11.00	12.00	13.00
1961D	7.00	8.00	9.00	10.00	11.00	12.00	13.00
1962	7.00	8.00	9.00	10.00	11.00	12.00	13.00
1962D	7.00	8.00	9.00	10.00	11.00	12.00	13.00
1963	7.00	8.00	9.00	10.00	11.00	12.00	13.00
1963D	7.00	8.00	9.00	10.00	11.00	12.00	13.00

BV = bullion value

Virtually all Franklin Halves survive in better than "good" condition.

KENNEDY TYPE MINTED 1964 – DATE

KENNEDY FIFTY-CENT PIECE   **1976 BICENTENNIAL DESIGN**
KENNEDY HALF DOLLARS

		BU	Proof			BU	Proof
1964	90% Silver	5.00	7.25	1976D		2.00	
1964D	90% Silver	5.00		1976S	Proof		3.00
1965	40% Silver	3.00		1976S	40% Silver	4.50	6.25
1965	SMS	7.00		1977		2.25	
1966	40% Silver	7.00		1977D		2.25	
1966	SMS	7.00		1977S	Proof Only		2.00
1967	40% Silver	7.00		1978		3.45	
1967	SMS	14.75		1978D		3.85	
1968D	40% Silver	3.00		1978S	Proof Only		2.00
1968S	Proof Only		6.00	1979		2.35	
1969D	40% Silver	3.00		1979D		2.35	
1969S	Proof Only		6.00	1979S	Proof Only		2.00
1970D		17.50		1980P		2	
1970S	Proof Only		12.00	1980D		2	
1971		2.00		1980S	Proof Only		3.00
1971D		2.00		1981P		2.00	
1971S	Proof Only		3.00	1981D		2.00	
1972		2.00		1981S	Proof Only		3.00
1972D		2.00		1982P		4.85	
1972S	Proof Only		3.00	1982D		4.85	
1973		2.00		1982S	Proof Only		3.00
1973D		2.00		1983P		5.95	
1973S	Proof Only		3.00	1983D		5.95	
1974		2.00		1983S	Proof Only		4.00
1974D		2.00		1984P		4.85	
1974S	Proof Only		3.00	1984D		4.40	
1976		2.00		1984S	Proof Only		4.50

		BU	Proof			BU	Proof
1985P		4.25		1995D		2.00	
1985D		4.25		1995S	Proof Only		40.00
1985S	Proof Only		4.00	1995S	Silver Proof		100.00
1986P		7.85		1996P		2	
1986D		7.85		1996D		2.00	
1986S	Proof Only		8.75	1996S	Proof Only		14.00
1987P		4.35		1996S	Silver Proof		40.00
1987D		4.35		1997P		2.00	
1987S	Proof Only		3.50	1997D		2.00	
1988P		4.75		1997S	Proof Only		30.00
1988D		3.85		1997S	Silver Proof		85.00
1988S	Proof Only		4.00	1998P		2.40	
1989P		3.50		1998D		2.40	
1989D		3.50		1998S	Proof Only		20.00
1989S	Proof Only		6.00	1998S	Silver Proof		35.00
1990P		3.65		1999P		2.70	
1990D		4.40		1999D		2.70	
1990S	Proof Only		6.00	1999S	Proof Only		25.00
1991P		3.95		1999S	Silver Proof		62.00
1991D		6.50		2000P		2.85	
1991S	Proof Only		11.00	2000D		2.85	
1992P		2.40		2000S	Proof Only		8.00
1992D		3.85		2000S	Silver Proof		25.00
1992S	Proof Only		5.00	2001P		2.80	
1992S	Silver Proof		14.00	2001D		2.80	
1993P		2.65		2001S	Proof Only		12.00
1993D		2.65		2001S	Silver Proof		24.00
1993S	Proof Only		15.00	2002P		3.25	
1993S	Silver Proof		40.00	2002D		3.25	
1994P		2.45		2002S	Proof Only		8.00
1994D		2.45		2002S	Silver Proof		25.00
1994S	Proof Only		12.00	2003P		2.85	
1994S	Silver Proof		45.00	2003D		2.85	
1995P		2		2003S	Proof Only		8.00

	BU	Proof			BU	Proof
2003S	Silver Proof	11.00	207p			
2004P	2.85		2007d			
2004D	2.85		2007s	Proof Only		6.00
2004S	Proof Only	16.00	2007s	Silver Proof		9.00
2004S	Silver Proof	10.00	2008p			
2005P	2.85		2008d			
2005D	2.85		2008s	Proof Only		4.00
2005S	Proof Only	6.00	2008s	Silver Proof		8.00
2005S	Silver Proof	9.00	2009p			
2006P	2.85		2009d			
2006D	2.85		2009s	Proof Only		10.00
2006S	Proof Only	6.00	2009s	Silver Proof		20.00
2006S	Silver Proof	9.00				

Dollars Minted 1794 - 1981

EARLY TYPES MINTED 1794-1804

FLOWING HAIR TYPE

	G	VG	F	VF	XF	AU	MS60
1794	48000.00	78000.00	98000.00	150000.00	215000.00	325000.00	500000.00
1795	1400.00	1800.00	3500.00	6500.00	13500.00	19500.00	70000.00

DRAPED BUST TYPE

SMALL EAGLE

	G	VG	F	VF	XF	AU	MS60
1795	1100.00	1700.00	3000.00	5000.00	10000.00	13000.00	40000.00
1796	1120.00	1650.00	2950.00	5000.00	10500.00	13500.00	51000.00

**DRAPED BUST TYPE
EAGLE & SHIELD REVERSE**

LARGE EAGLE

	G	VG	F	VF	XF	AU	MS60
1798	800.00	900.00	1350.00	2160.00	4200.00	7200.00	22000.00
1799	800.00	900.00	1375.00	2160.00	4200.00	7200.00	21500.00
1800	800.00	910.00	1360.00	2160.00	4440.00	7320.00	21500.00
1801	850.00	1100.00	1700.00	2650.00	4440.00	7320.00	22000.00
1802	900.00	950.00	1600.00	2500.00	4500.00	8500.00	22000.00
1803	975.00	1125.00	2000.00	3000.00	4740.00	8400.00	23000.00
1804						Proof 63	1-6 Million

LIBERTY SEATED TYPE MINTED 1840-1873

LIBERTY SEATED DOLLAR

LIBERTY SEATED TYPE

	G	VG	F	VF	XF	AU	MS60
1840	200.00	225.00	250.00	300.00	450.00	750.00	2000.00
1841	180.00	210.00	230.00	270.00	360.00	600.00	1700.00
1842	180.00	210.00	230.00	270.00	360.00	600.00	1500.00
1843	180.00	210.00	230.00	260.00	330.00	600.00	1550.00
1844	190.00	210.00	240.00	330.00	450.00	720.00	2450.00
1845	245.00	275.00	320.00	375.00	600.00	1000.00	6500.00
1846	180.00	200.00	240.00	290.00	410.00	560.00	1650.00
1846O	180.00	210.00	260.00	300.00	480.00	870.00	4400.00
1847	180.00	210.00	220.00	290.00	330.00	600.00	1500.00
1848	250.00	300.00	390.00	500.00	660.00	1080.00	2760.00
1849	180.00	200.00	230.00	270.00	360.00	600.00	1900.00
1850	320.00	410.00	560.00	720.00	960.00	1760.00	4760.00
1850O	245.00	290.00	375.00	575.00	1050.00	3000.00	10500.00
1851	2600.00	3200.00	3850.00	5500.00	10000.00	16800.00	33000.00

Year		G	VG	F	VF	XF	AU	MS60
1852		2250.00	2650.00	3550.00	5050.00	9000.00	16800.00	30000.00
1853		250.00	300.00	400.00	475.00	600.00	930.00	2040.00
1854		870.00	1200.00	1740.00	2400.00	3480.00	4800.00	6240.00
1855		660.00	1020.00	1260.00	1860.00	2760.00	3360.00	5880.00
1856		290.00	360.00	420.00	540.00	960.00	1740.00	3240.00
1857		330.00	410.00	470.00	600.00	1040.00	1200.00	2040.00
1858		2880.00	3120.00	3600.00	4200.00	4800.00	6840.00	0.00
1859		210.00	240.00	320.00	410.00	480.00	620.00	1320.00
1859O		180.00	190.00	220.00	270.00	350.00	580.00	1450.00
1859S		230.00	290.00	360.00	540.00	1200.00	2760.00	12000.00
1860		190.00	225.00	270.00	410.00	480.00	570.00	1400.00
1860O		180.00	190.00	220.00	260.00	330.00	570.00	1250.00
1861		450.00	600.00	720.00	840.00	1080.00	1500.00	2400.00
1862		330.00	480.00	720.00	840.00	960.00	1350.00	2400.00
1863		265.00	350.00	390.00	460.00	560.00	840.00	2160.00
1864		245.00	260.00	300.00	420.00	540.00	960.00	2100.00
1865		220.00	240.00	300.00	420.00	520.00	960.00	2200.00
1866					2 Known			

MOTTO ADDED

Year		G	VG	F	VF	XF	AU	MS60
1866		225.00	240.00	320.00	450.00	480.00	780.00	1400.00
1867		200.00	230.00	300.00	390.00	420.00	780.00	1350.00
1868		205.00	240.00	300.00	420.00	450.00	810.00	1500.00
1869		200.00	220.00	280.00	390.00	430.00	600.00	1400.00
1870		195.00	220.00	210.00	270.00	360.00	600.00	1350.00
1870	CC	350.00	390.00	605.00	810.00	1380.00	2640.00	10500.00
1870S		55000.00	95000.00	185000.00	450000.00	800000.00	1200000.00	1500000.00
1871		170.00	180.00	210.00	260.00	320.00	540.00	1200.00
1871	CC	1140.00	2160.00	3000.00	4560.00	9000.00	16200.00	48000.00
1872		170.00	180.00	210.00	270.00	380.00	540.00	1200.00
1872	CC	780.00	1170.00	1920.00	2640.00	4340.00	7920.00	18000.00
1872S		230.00	290.00	390.00	540.00	960.00	2160.00	7200.00
1873		180.00	235.00	265.00	290.00	390.00	570.00	1500.00
1873	CC	3120.00	4080.00	5640.00	8400.00	13200.00	24000.00	66000.00

Trade Dollar Type Minted 1873-1885

TRADE DOLLAR

SILVER DOLLARS — TRADE DOLLARS

		G	VG	F	VF	XF	AU	MS60
1873		85.00	100.00	120.00	150.00	180.00	260.00	675.00
1873	CC	190.00	225.00	275.00	350.00	550.00	1150.00	9000.00
1873S		85.00	95.00	120.00	160.00	210.00	280.00	950.00
1874		85.00	95.00	120.00	150.00	200.00	240.00	650.00
1874	CC	190.00	225.00	260.00	300.00	450.00	550.00	3000.00
1874S		75.00	100.00	110.00	125.00	150.00	240.00	650.00
1875		95.00	120.00	270.00	330.00	420.00	690.00	1620.00
1875	CC	175.00	210.00	235.00	270.00	400.00	650.00	2000.00
1875S		70.00	100.00	110.00	140.00	160.00	260.00	650.00
1875S/ CC		180.00	210.00	300.00	450.00	800.00	1200.00	3750.00
1876		75.00	100.00	110.00	140.00	150.00	240.00	650.00
1876	CC	180.00	220.00	240.00	290.00	425.00	825.00	5000.00
1876S		75.00	100.00	115.00	140.00	170.00	310.00	600.00
1877		80.00	95.00	110.00	140.00	160.00	225.00	650.00
1877	CC	190.00	230.00	270.00	350.00	560.00	625.00	2100.00
1877S		75.00	95.00	110.00	140.00	150.00	240.00	600.00
1878 Impaired Proof			0.00	0.00	900.00	1050.00		
1878	CC	325.00	365.00	575.00	825.00	1750.00	3400.00	9750.00
1878S		75.00	95.00	110.00	140.00	160.00	240.00	600.00
roof Only 1879 Impaired Proof			725.00	825.00	925.00	1000.00	Proof60	1100.00
roof Only 1880 Impaired Proof			725.00	825.00	925.00	1000.00	Proof60	1080.00
oof Only 1881 Impaired Proof			725.00	825.00	925.00	1000.00	Proof60	1200.00
oof Only 1882 Impaired Proof			725.00	825.00	925.00	1000.00	Proof60	1080.00
roof Only 1883 Impaired Proof			725.00	825.00	925.00	1000.00	Proof60	1200.00
roof Only 1884							Proof60	96000.00
roof Only 1885							Proof60	420000.00

LIBERTY HEAD TYPE MINTED 1878 -1921

SILVER DOLLARS—MORGAN DOLLARS

		G	VG	F	VF	XF	AU55	MS60
1878	BF	15.00	27.00	28.00	32.00	39.00	72.00	110.00
1878	7F	15.00	20.00	21.00	22.00	23.00	36.00	62.00
1878	7/8F	15.00	20.00	22.00	23.00	33.00	65.00	135.00
1878	CC	65.00	85.00	88.00	94.00	110.00	120.00	210.00
1878 S		15.00	20.00	21.00	22.00	24.00	30.00	45.00
1879		15.00	18.00	19.00	20.00	21.00	25.00	32.00
1879	CC	90.00	150.00	160.00	240.00	625.00	1700.00	3800.00
1879 O		15.00	16.00	17.00	18.00	20.00	70.00	180.00
1879 S		15.00	18.00	19.00	20.00	21.00	35.00	45.00
1880		15.00	18.00	19.00	20.00	21.00	24.00	30.00
1880	CC	90.00	145.00	175.00	195.00	240.00	295.00	455.00
1880 O		15.00	18.00	19.00	20.00	21.00	23.00	52.00
1880 S		15.00	18.00	19.00	20.00	21.00	23.00	32.00
1881		15.00	18.00	19.00	20.00	21.00	23.00	32.00
1881	CC	240.00	340.00	350.00	360.00	370.00	380.00	475.00
1881 O		15.00	18.00	19.00	20.00	21.00	23.00	35.00
1881S		15.00	18.00	19.00	20.00	21.00	23.00	32.00
1882		15.00	18.00	19.00	20.00	21.00	23.00	32.00
1882	CC	60.00	85.00	95.00	110.00	120.00	125.00	200.00
1882 O		15.00	18.00	19.00	20.00	21.00	23.00	32.00
1882 S		15.00	18.00	19.00	20.00	21.00	23.00	31.00
1883		15.00	18.00	19.00	20.00	21.00	23.00	31.00
1883	CC	40.00	85.00	88.00	93.00	96.00	100.00	185.00
1883 O		15.00	18.00	19.00	20.00	21.00	23.00	30.00
1883 S		15.00	18.00	19.00	20.00	21.00	23.00	550.00
1884		15.00	18.00	19.00	20.00	21.00	23.00	31.00
1884	CC	65.00	115.00	120.00	145.00	160.00	175.00	200.00
1884 O		15.00	18.00	19.00	20.00	21.00	23.00	30.00

		G	VG	F	VF	XF	AU	MS60
1884 S		15.00	18.00	19.00	20.00	21.00	23.00	4995.00
1885		15.00	18.00	19.00	20.00	21.00	23.00	30.00
1885	CC	400.00	495.00	525.00	550.00	560.00	575.00	625.00
1885 O		15.00	18.00	19.00	20.00	21.00	23.00	30.00
1885 S		15.00	18.00	19.00	20.00	21.00	23.00	200.00
1886		15.00	18.00	19.00	20.00	21.00	23.00	30.00
1886 O		15.00	18.00	19.00	20.00	21.00	23.00	30.00
1886 S		11.00	40.00	52.00	70.00	75.00	155.00	275.00
1887		15.00	18.00	19.00	20.00	21.00	23.00	30.00
1887 O		15.00	18.00	19.00	20.00	21.00	23.00	44.00
1887 S		15.00	18.00	19.00	20.00	21.00	23.00	99.00
1888		15.00	18.00	19.00	20.00	21.00	23.00	30.00
1888 O		15.00	18.00	19.00	20.00	21.00	23.00	31.00
1888 S		55.00	115.00	160.00	180.00	190.00	200.00	255.00
1889		15.00	18.00	19.00	20.00	21.00	23.00	30.00
1889	CC	375.00	575.00	860.00	1410.00	2600.00	5800.00	21000.00
1889 O		15.00	18.00	19.00	20.00	21.00	23.00	135.00
1889 S		18.00	32.00	48.00	55.00	70.00	100.00	175.00
1890		15.00	18.00	19.00	20.00	21.00	23.00	30.00
1890	CC	40.00	85.00	90.00	95.00	135.00	175.00	400.00
1890 O		15.00	18.00	19.00	20.00	21.00	23.00	50.00
1890 S		15.00	18.00	19.00	20.00	21.00	23.00	46.00
1891		15.00	18.00	19.00	20.00	21.00	23.00	50.00
1891	CC	40.00	85.00	90.00	100.00	135.00	175.00	320.00
1891 O		15.00	18.00	19.00	20.00	21.00	23.00	125.00
1891 S		15.00	18.00	19.00	20.00	21.00	23.00	50.00
1892		15.00	18.00	19.00	20.00	21.00	23.00	135.00
1892	CC	90.00	170.00	185.00	275.00	450.00	670.00	1375.00
1892 O		15.00	18.00	19.00	20.00	21.00	23.00	135.00
1892 S		15.00	18.00	19.00	20.00	21.00	23.00	29000.00
1893		50.00	210.00	220.00	230.00	240.00	340.00	650.00
1893	CC	60.00	225.00	275.00	610.00	1440.00	1900.00	3250.00
1893 O		40.00	175.00	225.00	320.00	550.00	900.00	1655.00
1893 S		2000.00	3500.00	4400.00	6100.00	9600.00	21000.00	82000.00
1894		1000.00	1350.00	1550.00	1625.00	2100.00	2900.00	4500.00

	G	VG	F	VF	XF	AU	MS60
1894-O	15.00	18.00	19.00	20.00	21.00	23.00	505.00
1894-S	15.00	18.00	19.00	20.00	21.00	23.00	625.00
1895 Proof	17000.00	17250.00	25000.00	28000.00	31000.00	37000.00	45000.00
1895-O	50.00	300.00	370.00	525.00	750.00	1250.00	15800.00
1895S	80.00	400.00	450.00	750.00	1050.00	1900.00	3500.00
1896	15.00	18.00	19.00	20.00	21.00	23.00	30.00
1896-O	15.00	18.00	19.00	20.00	21.00	23.00	900.00
1896-S	15.00	18.00	19.00	20.00	21.00	23.00	1430.00
1897	15.00	18.00	19.00	20.00	21.00	23.00	30.00
1897-O	15.00	18.00	19.00	20.00	21.00	23.00	600.00
1897-S	15.00	18.00	19.00	20.00	21.00	23.00	50.00
1898	15.00	18.00	19.00	20.00	21.00	23.00	30.00
1898-O	15.00	18.00	19.00	20.00	21.00	23.00	31.00
1898-S	15.00	18.00	19.00	20.00	21.00	23.00	245.00
1899	75.00	155.00	165.00	180.00	200.00	245.00	300.00
1899-O	15.00	18.00	19.00	20.00	21.00	23.00	30.00
1899-S	15.00	18.00	19.00	20.00	21.00	23.00	275.00
1900	15.00	18.00	19.00	20.00	21.00	23.00	30.00
1900-O	15.00	18.00	19.00	20.00	21.00	23.00	30.00
1900-S	15.00	18.00	19.00	20.00	21.00	23.00	250.00
1901	11.00	24.00	30.00	50.00	94.00	300.00	1850.00
1901-O	15.00	18.00	19.00	20.00	21.00	23.00	31.00
1901-S	15.00	18.00	19.00	20.00	21.00	23.00	340.00
1902	15.00	18.00	19.00	20.00	21.00	23.00	40.00
1902-O	15.00	18.00	19.00	20.00	21.00	23.00	30.00
1902-S	15.00	58.00	78.00	140.00	185.00	260.00	375.00
1903	15.00	44.00	47.00	50.00	55.00	60.00	65.00
1903-O	110.00	295.00	310.00	340.00	360.00	375.00	425.00
1903-S	15.00	50.00	65.00	145.00	290.00	1720.00	3750.00
1904	15.00	21.00	22.00	23.00	25.00	35.00	75.00
1904-O	15.00	21.00	22.00	23.00	25.00	27.00	33.00
1904-S	15.00	30.00	40.00	75.00	200.00	475.00	975.00
1921	15.00	18.00	19.00	20.00	21.00	23.00	21.00
1921-D	15.00	18.00	19.00	20.00	21.00	23.00	41.00
1921-S	15.00	18.00	19.00	20.00	21.00	23.00	31.00

PEACE TYPE MINTED 1921 -1935

SILVER DOLLARS—PEACE DOLLARS

	G	VG	F	VF	XF	AU	MS60
1921	90.00	115.00	120.00	125.00	130.00	140.00	220.00
1922	13.00	13.50	14.00	14.50	15.00	16.00	20.00
1922-D	13.00	13.50	14.00	14.50	15.00	16.00	23.00
1922-S	13.00	13.50	14.00	14.50	15.00	16.00	23.00
1923	13.00	13.50	14.00	14.50	15.00	16.00	19.00
1923-D	13.00	13.50	14.00	14.50	15.00	16.00	46.00
1923-S	13.00	13.50	14.00	14.50	15.00	16.00	25.00
1924	13.00	13.50	14.00	14.50	15.00	16.00	19.00
1924-S	13.00	16.00	15.00	33.00	35.00	50.00	175.00
1925	13.00	13.50	14.00	14.50	15.00	16.00	20.00
1925-S	13.00	13.50	14.00	14.50	15.00	16.00	65.00
1926	13.00	13.50	14.00	14.50	15.00	16.00	35.00
1926-D	13.00	13.50	14.00	14.50	15.00	16.00	55.00
1926-S	13.00	13.50	14.00	14.50	15.00	16.00	35.00
1927	13.00	20.00	21.00	26.00	27.00	45.00	60.00
1927-D	13.00	25.00	27.00	28.00	30.00	16.00	125.00
1927-S	13.00	20.00	22.00	24.00	25.00	66.00	114.00
1928	190.00	390.00	410.00	424.00	450.00	475.00	550.00
1928-S	13.00	28.00	29.00	31.00	36.00	55.00	130.00
1934	13.00	16.00	17.00	18.00	20.00	40.00	100.00
1934-D	13.00	16.00	17.00	18.00	19.00	40.00	120.00
1934-S	13.00	26.00	18.00	60.00	150.00	430.00	1500.00
1935	13.00	16.00	17.00	18.00	19.00	26.00	55.00
1935-S	13.00	16.00	17.00	15.00	20.00	90.00	225.00

EISENHOWER TYPE MINTED 1971 - 1978

EISENHOWER DOLLARS   **1976 BICENTENNIAL DESIGN**

	MS60	Proof		MS60	Proof
1971	3.00		1974S Clad		5.00
1971D	2.00		1974S 40% Silver	5.00	15.00
1971S 40% Silver	6.00	7.00	1976	5.00	
1972	2.00		1976D	2.50	
1972D	2.00		1976S Clad		8.00
1972S 40% Silver	6.00	7.00	1976S 40% Silver	12.00	14.00
1973	10.00		1977	3.50	
1973D	10.00		1977D	3.00	
1973S Clad		8.00	1977S Clad		6.00
1973S 40% Silver	7.00	22.00	1978	2.00	
1974	2.50		1978D	2.50	
1974D	2.50		1978S Clad		7.00

ANTHONY TYPE MINTED 1979 - 1981, 1999

REDUCED SIZE DOLLAR COINS—SUSAN B. ANTHONY 1979 - 1999

	BU	Proof		BU	Proof
1979P	1.50		1981P	4.00	
1979D	1.50		1981D	4.00	
1979S	1.50	6.00	1981S	4.00	6.00
1980P	1.50		1999P	2.00	
1980D	1.50		1999D	2.00	
1980S	1.50	5.00	1999P Proof		32.00

Sacagawea Type Minted Beginning 2000 - Present

REEDUCED SIZE SECAGAWEA DOLLAR

	BU	Proof		BU	Proof
2000P	1.50		2005P	2.75	
2000D	1.50		2005D	3.00	
2000S		6.00	20005S		8.00
2001P	1.50		2006p	3.00	
2001D	1.75		2006d	7.00	
2001S		60.00	2006s		8.50
2002P	1.85		2007p	1.75	
2002D	1.85		2007d	1.75	
2002S		21.00	2007s		6.00
2003P	7.00		2008p	1.75	
2003D	7.00		2008d	1.75	
2003S		5.00	2008s		6.00
2004P	6.50		2009p		
2004D	6.50		2009d		
2004S		6.00	2009s		

Presidential Dollars

Beginning in 2007 and continuing through 2016, Former Presidents of the United States will be honored on circulating coins. Each year, four presidents, in the order in which they held office, will each have a separate coin minted in their honor. Thus, in 2007, Washington, Adams, Jefferson and Madison dollars were minted. The coins are dollars, similar in size, color, and denomination to the Sacagawea coins which will be minted along side the Presidential Dollars. Each dollar coin will have the portrait of a President on the obverse with a rendition of the Statue of Liberty on the reverse. In addition, some of the devices, including the date and mint mark have been moved to the edge of the coin. Each President will have a business strke coin minted at the Philadelphia and Denver Mints, as well as a Proof strike from the San Francisco Mint.

2007 Presidents	**2008 Presidents**	**2009 Presidents**
George Washington	James Monroe	William Henry Harrison
John Adams	John Quincy Adams	John Tyler
Thomas Jefferson	Andrew Jackson	James Polk
James Madison	Martin Van Buren	Zachary Taylor

SMALL SIZE DOLLAR COINS — PRESIDENTIAL TYPE 2007 - 2016

		BU	Proof			BU	Proof
2007p	G Washington	1.25		2009p	W Harrison	1.25	
2007d		1.25		2009d		1.25	
2007s			5.00	2009s			5.00
2007p	J Adams	1.25		2009p	J Tyler	1.25	
2007d		1.25		2009d		1.25	
2007s			5.00	2009s			5.00
2007p	T. Jefferson	1.25		2009p	J Polk	1.25	
2007d		1.25		2009d		1.25	
2007s			5.00	2009s			5.00
2007p	Madison	1.25		2009p	Z Taylor	1.25	
2007d		1.25		2009d		1.25	
2007s			5.00	2009s			5.00
2008p	Monroe	1.25		2010p	M Fillmore	1.25	
2008d		1.25		2010d		1.25	
2008s			5.00	2010s			5.00
2008p	JQ Adams	1.25		2010p	J Buchanan	1.25	
2008d		1.25		2010d		1.25	
2008s			5.00	2010s			5.00
2008p	A Jackson	1.25		2010p	F Pierce	1.25	
2008d		1.25		2010d		1.25	
2008s			5.00	2010s			5.00
2008p	M Van Buren	1.25		2010p	A Lincoln	1.25	
2008d		1.25		2010d		1.25	
2008s			5.00	2010s			5.00

CHAPTER 5

GOLD COINS
What About Gold Coins

The U.S. government has minted coins in gold since 1792 (some pattern pieces) when the first authorizing act was passed permitting the mintage of gold coins with the values of $2.50, $5 and $10. Until 1933, when gold coins were discontinued for general circulation, over four and one-half billion dollars' worth of gold coins had been made. Pursuant to the gold law, many of these were melted down and were for a time in bars at Fort Knox.

Naturally, people were quick to ask whether they could still collect gold coins and keep those they already owned. The law made provision for keeping coins of recognized value to collectors which involved dates and mint marks, as well as recognized conditions, like those coins of metals other than gold. Many coins of marginal collector value found their way overseas. With the rise in price of the metal and the loosening of restrictions for Americans who wanted to hold gold, many of these coins have, since 1974, found their way back into the United States.

However, no provision was made for the expanded interest in coin collecting that was due to come. The best way to understand the ramifications of the gold act is to read the following copy of the law relating to "Hoarding of Gold."
Values of the various dates are covered later in this chapter.

The following is a copy of the law relating to gold coins:

HOARDING OF GOLD—EXECUTIVE ORDER NO. 6260

Section 4, Acquisition of gold coin and gold bullion.

"No person other than a Federal Reserve bank shall after the date of this order acquire in the United States any gold coin, gold bullion, or gold certificates except under license therefore issued pursuant to this Executive Order, provided that member banks of the Federal Reserve System may accept delivery of such coin, bullion, and certificates, for surrender promptly to a Federal Reserve bank and provided further that persons requiring gold for use in industry, profession or art in which they are regularly engaged may replenish their stocks of gold up to an aggregate amount of $100, by acquisitions of gold bullion held under licenses issued under Section 5 (b), without necessity of obtaining a license for such acquisitions; and provided further that collectors of rare and unusual coin may acquire from one another and hold without necessity of obtaining a license therefore gold coin having a recognized special value to collectors of rare and unusual coin may acquire from one another and hold without necessity of obtaining a license thereof gold coin having a recognized special value to collectors of rare and unusual gold (but not including quarter eagles, otherwise known as $2.50 pieces, unless held, together with rare and unusual coin, as part of a collection for historical, scientific or numismatic purposes, containing not more than four quarter eagles of the same date and design and struck by the same mint)."

On December 31, 1974, the gold law was rescinded after being in effect for a full 40 years. Since that period, the price of gold has soared to many times what it was in 1933, reaching a high of $900/ oz. in early 1980. In a sense, this means that all gold coins could be regarded as collector's items, regardless of rarity or condition. Of course, the fluctuations of the gold market figure in such calculations. Gold would have to sell at about $205 an ounce for U.S. coins to be worth ten times their face value. At the time the above law was written, gold had only approached that figure. A week after the law was rescinded, the U.S. Treasury was accepting all bids of $153 to $185 an ounce, which meant specifically that a $5 gold piece would be worth about $37.50 to $44.75; a $10 gold piece from about $75 to $89.50; and a $20 gold piece from $150 to $179. That, however, applied only to the value of the metal; anyone acquiring gold U.S. coins at those prices could sell them at whatever profit the demand by collectors would bring.

Today a $20 gold piece can be purchased for just a nominal amount above its gold content value. Also, more recently, the U.S. government has decided to get back into the gold coin business. It currently has sold a variety of commemorative and bullion gold pieces.

VALUES OF GOLD COINS
GOLD DOLLARS MINTED 1849-1889

LIBERTY HEAD TYPE GOLD DOLLAR
LIBERTY HEAD TYPE MINTED 1849-1854

	F	VF	XF	AU	MS60
1849 Open wreath	105.00	147.00	210.00	241.50	399.00
1849 Closed wreath	105.00	147.00	199.50	220.50	367.50
1849 C Closed wreath	682.50	871.50	1197.00	1701.00	8379.00
1849 C Open	126000.00	220500.00	308700.00	453600.00	525000.00
1849 D Open wreath	882.00	1050.00	1627.50	2625.00	4567.50

	F	VF	XF	AU	MS60
1849 O Open wreath	126.00	157.50	241.50	325.50	693.00
1850	105.00	147.00	199.50	220.50	357.00
1850 C	708.75	871.50	1197.00	2079.00	7938.00
1850 D	892.50	1092.00	1491.00	3465.00	10473.75
1850 O	189.00	252.00	367.50	756.00	2772.00
1851	105.00	147.00	199.50	220.50	252.00
1851 C	708.75	882.00	1197.00	1449.00	2677.50
1851D	892.50	1044.75	1506.75	1890.00	4662.00
1851 O	147.00	168.00	220.50	241.50	756.00
1852	105.00	147.00	199.50	220.50	252.00
1852 C	708.75	871.50	1197.00	1449.00	3906.00
1852 D	892.50	1092.00	1491.00	1858.50	8064.00
1852 O	126.00	147.00	241.50	336.00	1102.50
1853	105.00	147.00	199.50	220.50	252.00
1853 C	708.75	871.50	1197.00	1638.00	5166.00
1853 D	892.50	1092.00	1491.00	2142.00	8316.00
1853 O	136.50	157.50	220.50	241.50	609.00
1854	105.00	147.00	199.50	220.50	262.50
1854 D	892.50	1092.00	1491.00	5040.00	11340.00
1854 S	252.00	304.50	430.50	682.50	2079.00

Indian Head Small Gold Dollar

SMALL INDIAN HEAD 1854-1856

	F	VF	XF	AU	MS60
1854	210.00	294.00	430.50	567.00	3433.50
1855	210.00	294.00	430.50	567.00	3433.50
1855 C	735.00	1155.00	3360.00	19950.00	27825.00
1855 D	3150.00	4410.00	7875.00	20160.00	47250.00
1855 O	346.50	409.50	556.50	3832.50	6825.00
1856 S	462.00	756.00	1260.00	4509.75	7875.00

Indian Head Large Gold Dollar

LARGE INDIAN HEAD 1856-1889

	F	VF	XF	AU	MS60
1856 Upright 5	126.00	157.50	210.00	241.50	472.50
1856 Slanted 5	136.50	147.00	199.50	220.50	273.00
1856 D	2268.00	3528.00	5544.00	7245.00	27720.00
1857	115.50	147.00	199.50	220.50	273.00
1857 C	708.75	871.50	1197.00	2709.00	11025.00
1857 D	892.50	1092.00	1491.00	3528.00	9450.00
1857 S	252.00	514.50	609.00	1102.50	5796.00
1858	115.50	147.00	199.50	220.50	273.00
1858 D	840.00	1044.75	1417.50	2142.00	9450.00
1858 S	283.50	378.00	504.00	1134.00	5292.00
1859	115.50	147.00	199.50	220.50	273.00
1859 C	708.75	871.50	1197.00	3024.00	9450.00
1859 D	892.50	1092.00	1491.00	2488.50	9450.00
1859 S	189.00	241.50	504.00	1060.50	5040.00
1860	115.50	147.00	199.50	220.50	357.00
1860 D	2079.00	2394.00	3780.00	6300.00	15120.00
1860 S	294.00	336.00	483.00	714.00	2331.00
1861	115.50	147.00	199.50	220.50	273.00
1861 D	4725.00	6615.00	9450.00	17010.00	28980.00
1862	115.50	147.00	199.50	220.50	273.00
1863	346.50	441.00	850.50	1638.00	3780.00
1864	283.50	367.50	462.00	787.50	945.00
1865	283.50	367.50	567.00	724.50	1512.00
1866	283.50	367.50	441.00	661.50	945.00
1867	315.00	409.50	504.00	630.00	1123.50
1868	252.00	283.50	409.50	483.00	945.00
1869	315.00	346.50	504.00	630.00	1071.00
1870	252.00	283.50	399.00	483.00	808.50
1870 S	294.00	462.00	756.00	1134.00	2205.00

1871	252.00	283.50	378.00	472.50	724.50
1872	252.00	283.50	367.50	451.50	882.00
1873 Closed 3	315.00	409.50	787.50	913.50	1575.00
1873 Open 3	115.50	147.00	199.50	220.50	273.00
1874	115.50	147.00	199.50	220.50	273.00
1875	1606.50	1890.00	3780.00	4851.00	6048.00
1876	231.00	283.50	346.50	462.00	630.00
1877	147.00	178.50	336.00	462.00	619.50
1878	178.50	210.00	357.00	462.00	630.00
1879	157.50	189.00	273.00	315.00	504.00
1880	147.00	157.50	210.00	231.00	409.50
1881	147.00	157.50	210.00	231.00	409.50
1882	157.50	178.50	210.00	231.00	409.50
1883	147.00	157.50	210.00	231.00	409.50
1884	136.50	157.50	210.00	231.00	409.50
1885	147.00	157.50	210.00	231.00	409.50
1886	147.00	157.50	210.00	231.00	409.50
1887	147.00	157.50	210.00	231.00	409.50
1888	147.00	157.50	210.00	231.00	409.50
1889	147.00	157.50	210.00	231.00	336.00

$2.50 Gold Pieces Minted 1796 - 1839
EARLY TYPES MINTED 1796-1839

CAPPED BUST TYPE (FACING RIGHT)

CAPPED BUST TO RIGHT MINTED 1796-1807

	F	VF	XF	AU	MS60
1796 No Stars	45000.00	60000.00	85000.00	100000.00	200000.00
1796 Stars	30000.00	40000.00	60000.00	90000.00	160000.00
1797	14490.00	17010.00	22050.00	50400.00	100800.00
1798	4410.00	6300.00	7812.00	20790.00	48510.00
1802 2 over 1	4410.00	6300.00	7560.00	9513.00	18900.00
1804 13 Stars	23940.00	31500.00	69300.00	126000.00	0.00
1804 14 Stars	4410.00	6300.00	7560.00	10080.00	20286.00

1805	4410.00	6300.00	7560.00	9639.00	19845.00
1806 6 over 4	4536.00	6426.00	7686.00	9765.00	21420.00
1806 6 over 5	5670.00	7875.00	11970.00	26460.00	69300.00
1807	4410.00	6300.00	7560.00	9450.00	18900.00

$2.50 GOLD PIECES — CAPPED BUST TYPE (FACING LEFT)
CAPPED BUST TO LEFT MINTED 1808-1834

	F	VF	XF	AU	MS60
1808 Large Size	23310.00	30240.00	44100.00	65520.00	83160.00
1821	5040.00	6300.00	7686.00	9828.00	21420.00
1824 4over 1	5040.00	6300.00	7560.00	9702.00	18900.00
1825	5040.00	6300.00	7560.00	9450.00	19687.50
1826 6 over 5	5292.00	6552.00	8190.00	10080.00	31489.50
1827 Small Size	5418.00	6930.00	8820.00	10458.00	20580.00
1829	4725.00	5670.00	6615.00	8820.00	11970.00
1830	4725.00	5670.00	6615.00	8820.00	11970.00
1831	4725.00	5670.00	6615.00	8820.00	13125.00
1832	4725.00	5670.00	6615.00	9009.00	11970.00
1833	4725.00	5670.00	6678.00	9009.00	12285.00
1834 Motto	6930.00	9828.00	15750.00	21420.00	39375.00

$2.50 GOLD PIECES — CLASSIC HEAD TYPE

CLASSIC HEAD MINTED 1834-1839

	F	VF	XF	AU	MS60
1834 No Motto	262.50	346.50	504.00	756.00	2268.00
1835	262.50	346.50	504.00	756.00	2268.00
1836	262.50	346.50	504.00	756.00	2268.00
1837	315.00	294.00	661.50	1197.00	3276.00
1838	262.50	346.50	504.00	756.00	2268.00
1838 C	882.00	1260.00	2142.00	6174.00	23940.00
1839/8	273.00	367.50	661.50	1449.00	4284.00
1839 C	882.00	1134.00	2142.00	3528.00	22680.00
1839/8 D	882.00	1165.50	2772.00	5985.00	21420.00
1839 O	378.00	504.00	913.50	1386.00	5670.00

$2.50 GOLD PIECES — LIBERTY 1840-1907

LIBERTY MINTED 1840-1907

	VF	XF	AU	MS60
1840	200.00	882.00	2520.00	6195.00
1840 C	1312.50	1785.00	4200.00	11655.00
1840 D	2772.00	8190.00	1260.00	36540.00
1840 O	252.00	840.00	1890.00	10395.00
1841 Proof Only	50400.00	94500.00	100800.00	0.00
1841 C	1312.50	1837.50	3465.00	17640.00
1841 D	1842.75	4200.00	10290.00	26460.00
1842	945.00	2520.00	6300.00	20790.00
1842 C	1680.00	3045.00	7245.00	26460.00
1842 D	1680.00	3570.00	11025.00	37800.00
1842 O	420.00	1155.00	2205.00	11340.00

	VF	XF	AU	MS60
1843	178.50	231.00	378.00	1197.00
1843 C Small Date	2205.00	5250.00	8505.00	22680.00
1843 C Large Date	1391.25	1785.00	3150.00	8400.00
1843 D Small Date	1522.50	1890.00	2835.00	9765.00
1843 O Small Date	189.00	241.50	367.50	1680.00
1843 O Large Date	241.50	441.00	1680.00	6300.00
1844	378.00	882.00	1995.00	7560.00
1844 C	1417.50	2016.00	6930.00	17640.00
1844 D	1496.25	1890.00	2730.00	6825.00
1845	252.00	304.50	420.00	1260.00
1845 D	1496.25	1890.00	3024.00	13860.00
1845 O	976.50	2205.00	6090.00	15120.00
1846	273.00	504.00	945.00	5460.00
1846 C	1422.75	2520.00	8820.00	17640.00
1846 D	1522.50	1890.00	2730.00	10605.00
1846 O	294.00	409.50	1155.00	6195.00
1847	231.00	367.50	840.00	3570.00
1847 C	1391.25	1638.00	2415.00	6300.00
1847 D	1617.00	1890.00	2730.00	10080.00
1847 O	231.00	378.00	1050.00	3360.00
1848	504.00	850.50	1785.00	5985.00
1848 "CAL"	14175.00	24675.00	32550.00	46725.00
1848 C	1296.75	1968.75	3150.00	13860.00
1848 D	1506.75	1890.00	3045.00	10605.00
1849	283.50	483.00	840.00	2520.00
1849 C	1296.75	1785.00	5040.00	23310.00
1849 D	1506.75	1890.00	3570.00	16380.00
1850	178.50	220.50	367.50	1050.00
1850 C	1296.75	1680.00	3570.00	17640.00
1850 D	1506.75	1890.00	3150.00	15120.00
1850 O	220.50	462.00	1260.00	4725.00
1851	178.50	210.00	241.50	325.50
1851 C	1296.75	1680.00	4725.00	12180.00
1851 D	1506.75	2100.00	3990.00	11970.00
1851 O	189.00	220.50	945.00	4725.00
1852	178.50	210.00	241.50	336.00

	VF	XF	AU	MS60
1852 C	1296.75	1785.00	4410.00	17640.00
1852 D	1506.75	2520.00	7560.00	17010.00
1852 O	189.00	315.00	945.00	5040.00
1853	178.50	210.00	241.50	367.50
1853 D	1785.00	3360.00	5040.00	17010.00
1854	178.50	210.00	241.50	367.50
1854 C	1417.50	2100.00	5040.00	15120.00
1854 D	2835.00	5355.00	11340.00	35448.00
1854 O	178.50	220.50	430.50	1575.00
1854 S	67200.00	116550.00	189000.00	0.00
1855	178.50	210.00	241.50	378.00
1855 C	1386.00	4410.00	19425.00	36750.00
1855 D	3276.00	7560.00	23625.00	47250.00
1856	178.50	210.00	241.50	399.00
1856 C	1155.00	2310.00	4095.00	15120.00
1856 D	6510.00	10080.00	25200.00	75600.00
1856 O	220.50	735.00	1260.00	7875.00
1856 S	210.00	378.00	913.50	4410.00
1857	178.50	210.00	241.50	399.00
1857 D	1417.50	2520.00	3780.00	12600.00
1857 O	210.00	367.50	1050.00	4410.00
1857 S	210.00	346.50	882.00	5544.00
1858	178.50	252.00	346.50	1260.00
1858 C	1837.50	2940.00	4194.75	17325.00
1859	178.50	252.00	399.00	1260.00
1859 D	1785.00	3045.00	4830.00	18900.00
1859 S	315.00	945.00	2520.00	6510.00
1860	178.50	252.00	462.00	1134.00
1860 C	1417.50	1890.00	3675.00	21420.00
1860 S	199.50	661.50	1155.00	3990.00
1861	178.50	210.00	241.50	336.00
1861 S	346.50	945.00	3045.00	7560.00
1862 2 over 1	882.00	1785.00	3465.00	8085.00
1862	210.00	315.00	525.00	1260.00
1862 S	882.00	2205.00	4305.00	17640.00
1863 Proof Only	0.00	0.00	0.00	44100.00

$2.50 GOLD PIECES — QUARTER EAGLES CONTINUED 1850-1907

	VF	XF	AU	MS60
1863 S	493.50	1480.50	3150.00	13860.00
1864	5670.00	11340.00	22680.00	37800.00
1865	4788.00	7560.00	18900.00	37800.00
1865 S	220.50	619.50	1386.00	4410.00
1866	1260.00	3570.00	5040.00	11970.00
1866 S	283.50	661.50	1449.00	6174.00
1867	378.00	819.00	1165.50	4914.00
1867 S	241.50	619.50	1638.00	4200.00
1868	231.00	409.50	661.50	1575.00
1868 S	189.00	304.50	1071.00	4095.00
1869	241.50	462.00	724.50	3087.00
1869 S	220.50	472.50	819.00	4410.00
1870	231.00	420.00	756.00	3780.00
1870 S	189.00	430.50	756.00	4725.00
1871	241.50	336.00	598.50	2310.00
1871 S	189.00	283.50	535.50	2310.00
1872	378.00	840.00	1155.00	4725.00
1872 S	189.00	420.00	945.00	4536.00
1873 Closed 3	180.00	220.50	273.00	525.00
1873 Open 3	180.00	210.00	252.00	294.00
1873 S	220.50	378.00	871.50	2835.00
1874	252.00	378.00	724.50	2079.00
1875	3465.00	5040.00	8442.00	13860.00
1875 S	178.50	304.50	756.00	4410.00
1876	283.50	651.00	913.50	3402.00
1876 S	241.50	535.50	966.00	3360.00
1877	378.00	787.50	1060.50	3087.00
1877 S	180.00	210.00	241.50	630.00
1878	180.00	210.00	241.50	283.50
1878 S	180.00	210.00	241.50	346.50
1879	180.00	210.00	241.50	283.50
1879 S	210.00	283.50	504.00	2205.00
1880	189.00	346.50	630.00	1365.00

	VF	XF	AU	MS60
1881	1890.00	2940.00	4436.25	8820.00
1882	199.50	315.00	420.00	682.50
1883	199.50	399.00	997.50	2310.00
1884	189.00	399.00	598.50	1575.00
1885	630.00	1764.00	2457.00	4305.00
1886	180.00	273.00	441.00	1102.50
1887	180.00	252.00	336.00	693.00
1888	180.00	231.00	283.50	315.00
1889	180.00	220.50	262.50	336.00
1890	180.00	231.00	294.00	504.00
1891	180.00	210.00	241.50	420.00
1892	180.00	241.50	336.00	756.00
1893	180.00	210.00	241.50	294.00
1894	180.00	231.00	325.50	787.50
1895	180.00	220.50	283.50	399.00
1896	180.00	210.00	241.50	294.00
1897	180.00	210.00	241.50	294.00
1898	180.00	210.00	241.50	294.00
1899	180.00	210.00	241.50	294.00
1900	180.00	252.00	378.00	430.50
1901	180.00	210.00	231.00	283.50
1902	180.00	210.00	231.00	283.50
1903	180.00	210.00	231.00	283.50
1904	180.00	210.00	231.00	283.50
1905	180.00	210.00	231.00	283.50
1906	180.00	210.00	231.00	283.50
1907	180.00	210.00	231.00	283.50

INDIAN HEAD $2.50 GOLD PIECE
INDIAN HEAD TYPE MINTED 1908-1929

	XF	AU	MS60
1908	210.00	230.00	275.00
1909	210.00	230.00	275.00
1910	210.00	230.00	275.00
1911	210.00	230.00	275.00
1911D	2400.00	4750.00	7200.00
1912	210.00	230.00	275.00
1913	210.00	230.00	275.00
1914	210.00	230.00	400.00
1914D	210.00	230.00	275.00
1915	210.00	230.00	275.00
1925D	210.00	230.00	275.00
1926	210.00	230.00	275.00
1927	210.00	230.00	275.00
1928	210.00	230.00	275.00
1929	210.00	230.00	350.00

$3.00 Gold Pieces Minted 1854 -1889

INDIAN HEAD $3.00 GOLD PIECE
INDIAN HEAD TYPE MINTED 1854-1889

	VF	XF	AU	MS60
1854	715.00	1250.00	1750.00	3000.00
1854 D	8580.00	17250.00	33000.00	78000.00
1854 O	990.00	2250.00	3750.00	22500.00
1855	726.00	1250.00	1750.00	3000.00
1855 S	1056.00	2625.00	6500.00	28500.00
1856	726.00	1250.00	1750.00	3000.00
1856 S	781.00	1500.00	2750.00	10875.00
1857	726.00	1250.00	1750.00	3500.00

	VF	XF	AU	MS60
1857 S	847.00	2000.00	5750.00	18750.00
1858	891.00	1875.00	3500.00	8625.00
1859	748.00	1500.00	1875.00	3250.00
1860	792.00	1375.00	2125.00	4250.00
1860 S	924.00	2125.00	7875.00	18000.00
1861	825.00	1375.00	2125.00	4125.00
1862	825.00	1375.00	2125.00	4125.00
1863	825.00	1375.00	2125.00	4125.00
1864	825.00	1375.00	2125.00	4125.00
1865	1188.00	2875.00	5750.00	9000.00
1866	825.00	1375.00	2125.00	4125.00
1867	825.00	1375.00	2125.00	4125.00
1868	825.00	1375.00	2125.00	4125.00
1869	825.00	1375.00	2125.00	4125.00
1870	792.00	1250.00	2125.00	4750.00
1870 S	528000.00	1200000.00	0.00	0.00
1871	902.00	1375.00	2125.00	4500.00
1872	825.00	1375.00	2125.00	4125.00
1873 Closed 3	3036.00	5500.00	10250.00	30000.00
1873 Open 3 Proof only	0.00	0.00	9500.00	0.00
1874	715.00	1250.00	1750.00	3000.00
1875 Proof only	0.00	0.00	56250.00	0.00
1876 Proof only	0.00	0.00	16500.00	0.00
1877	1276.00	3375.00	6375.00	13875.00
1878	715.00	1250.00	1750.00	3000.00
1879	715.00	1250.00	1875.00	3000.00
1880	792.00	2000.00	2625.00	3625.00
1881	1320.00	2875.00	5125.00	8437.50
1882	891.00	1375.00	2125.00	3625.00
1883	858.00	1625.00	2625.00	3750.00
1884	1188.00	1875.00	2750.00	3750.00
1885	1188.00	2000.00	3000.00	4125.00
1886	1188.00	2125.00	2750.00	5125.00
1887	759.00	1375.00	2125.00	3750.00
1888	759.00	1375.00	2125.00	3250.00
1889	748.00	1375.00	1875.00	3250.00

$4.00 Gold Pieces Minted 1879-1880

$4.00 GOLD STELLAS

1879	Flowing Hair	Proof Only	Proof60	80000.00
1879	Coiled Hair	Proof Only	Proof60	125000.00
1880	Flowing Hair	Proof Only	Proof60	95000.00
1880	Coiled Hair	Proof Only	Proof60	210000.00

$5.00 Gold Pieces Minted 1795-1929

CAPPED BUST TYPE (EAGLE & SHIELD REVERSE)
CAPPED BUST TO RIGHT MINTED 1795-1807
SMALL EAGLE

	F	VF	XF	AU	MS60
1795	16000.00	21000.00	26000.00	36500.00	60000.00
1796 6 over 5	16500.00	22000.00	33000.00	63000.00	97000.00
1797 15 Stars	18000.00	24000.00	40000.00	85000.00	160000.00
1797 16 Stars	17000.00	22000.00	35000.00	72000.00	150000.00
1798	84000.00	125000.00	264000.00	348000.00	0.00

HERALDIC EAGLE

	F	VF	XF	AU	MS60
1795	8200.00	14000.00	19000.00	37800.00	78000.00
1797 7 over 5	8000.00	13800.00	20000.00	51000.00	144000.00
1797 16 Star Obverse					
1798 Small 8	4200.00	5000.00	9000.00	17000.00	32000.00
1798 Large 8, 13 Stars	3500.00	4000.00	7200.00	10800.00	28000.00
1798 Large 8, 14 Stars	3600.00	4400.00	9000.00	22000.00	100000.00
1799	3500.00	4000.00	6500.00	10500.00	22000.00
1800	3400.00	3900.00	6200.00	9000.00	13000.00
1802 2 over 1	3400.00	3900.00	6200.00	9000.00	13000.00
1803 3 over 2	3400.00	3900.00	6200.00	9000.00	13000.00

	F	VF	XF	AU	MS60
1804 Small 8	3400.00	3900.00	6200.00	9000.00	13000.00
1804 Small 8 over Lg.8	3400.00	3900.00	6200.00	9000.00	1300.00
1805	3400.00	3900.00	6200.00	9000.00	1300.00
1806 Pointed Top 6	3400.00	3900.00	6200.00	9000.00	1300.00
1806 Round Top 6	3400.00	3900.00	6200.00	9000.00	1300.00
1807	3400.00	3900.00	6200.00	9000.00	1300.00

CAPPED HEAD TYPE
CAPPED BUST TO LEFT MINTED 1807-1812

	F	VF	XF	AU	MS60
1807	2700.00	3300.00	4700.00	7500.00	11000.00
1808 8 over 7	2800.00	3800.00	5200.00	7800.00	16000.00
1808	2700.00	3300.00	4700.00	7500.00	11000.00
1809 9 over 8	2700.00	3300.00	4700.00	7500.00	11000.00
1810 Sm. Date Sm. 5	9000.00	19800.00	30600.00	43200.00	90000.00
1810 Sm. Date Tall 5	2700.00	3300.00	4700.00	7500.00	11000.00
1810 Lg. Date Small 5	12000.00	22200.00	32400.00	54000.00	108000.00
1810 Lg. Date Lg. 6	2700.00	3300.00	4700.00	7500.00	11000.00
1811	2700.00	3300.00	4700.00	7500.00	11000.00
1812	2700.00	3300.00	4700.00	7500.00	11000.00

$5.00 GOLD PIECES — LARGE SIZE BUST

	F	VF	XF	AU	MS60
1813	2500.00	2600.00	4800.00	7500.00	9500.00
1814 4 over 3	4400.00	5800.00	7500.00	11000.00	17000.00
1815	33000.00	46200.00	69000.00	96000.00	114000.00
1818	4400.00	5800.00	7500.00	11000.00	17000.00
1818 5D over 50	4400.00	5800.00	7500.00	11000.00	17000.00
1819	8400.00	14400.00	24000.00	33600.00	54000.00
1819 5D over 50	4500.00	9000.00	17500.00	32400.00	60000.00
1820	4400.00	5800.00	7500.00	11000.00	17000.00
1821	11000.00	18000.00	24000.00	35000.00	75000.00
1822	480000.00	800000.00	1000000.00	0.00	0.00
1823	4400.00	5800.00	7500.00	11000.00	17000.00

	F	VF	XF	AU	MS60
1824	4400.00	9000.00	13800.00	19200.00	28500.00
1825 5 over 1	4500.00	7200.00	10200.00	16800.00	28500.00
1825 5 over 4	0.00	0.00	0.00	0.00	500000.00
1826	4400.00	5800.00	7500.00	11000.00	17000.00
1827	5000.00	8400.00	10800.00	16800.00	30000.00
1828 8 over 7	12000.00	21000.00	30000.00	60000.00	90000.00
1828	4800.00	10800.00	16800.00	26400.00	57000.00
1829 LG Date	12000.00	22000.00	32000.00	50000.00	85000.00

$5.00 GOLD PIECES — SMALL SIZE BUST

	F	VF	XF	AU	MS60
1829 SM Date	32100.00	45000.00	72000.00	0.00	0.00
1830	12600.00	15600.00	18000.00	22000.00	34000.00
1831	12600.00	15600.00	18000.00	23000.00	35000.00
1832 12 Stars	36000.00	54000.00	78000.00	102000.00	0.00
1832 13 stars	12900.00	15600.00	18000.00	22000.00	34000.00
1833 LG Date	12600.00	15600.00	18000.00	28000.00	35000.00
1833 SM Date	12900.00	15600.00	18000.00	20400.00	0.00
1834 Plain 4	12600.00	15600.00	18000.00	20400.00	34000.00
1834 Crosslet 4	12600.00	15600.00	18000.00	20400.00	34000.00

CLASSIC HEAD TYPE
$5.00 GOLD PIECES — CLASSIC HEAD 1834-1838

	F	VF	XF	AU	MS60
1834 Plain 4	290.00	400.00	550.00	900.00	3500.00
1834 Crosslet 4	840.00	1440.00	2400.00	4800.00	22000.00
1835	290.00	400.00	550.00	900.00	3600.00
1836	290.00	400.00	550.00	900.00	3600.00
1837	300.00	400.00	650.00	2000.00	4000.00
1838	300.00	425.00	700.00	1900.00	4200.00
1838 C	1100.00	1800.00	3400.00	9400.00	33600.00
1838 D	1000.00	1700.00	3200.00	7000.00	22000.00

$5.00 GOLD PIECES — LIBERTY HEAD 1839-1908
NO MOTTTO

	VF	XF	AU	MS60
1839	325.00	410.00	1100.00	3500.00
1839 C	1600.00	2400.00	5100.00	17400.00
1839 D	1550.00	2000.00	4500.00	16200.00
1840	325.00	375.00	1200.00	3300.00
1840 C	1500.00	2200.00	6000.00	21600.00
1840 D	1450.00	2550.00	5900.00	12600.00
1840 O	325.00	750.00	1600.00	9600.00
1841	340.00	810.00	1600.00	4400.00
1841 C	1400.00	1700.00	2700.00	14400.00
1841 D	1500.00	1700.00	2700.00	12600.00
1842 SM Letters	325.00	1000.00	2700.00	12000.00
1842 LG Letters	600.00	1800.00	2600.00	9600.00
1842 C SM Date	7800.00	19800.00	38400.00	126000.00
1842 C LG Date	1400.00	1700.00	3000.00	15000.00
1842 D SM Date	1500.00	1700.00	2400.00	13200.00
1842 D LG Date	2000.00	5100.00	11400.00	42000.00
1842 O	900.00	2700.00	8400.00	19200.00
1843	285.00	300.00	325.00	1700.00
1843 C	1400.00	1750.00	3400.00	10200.00
1843 D	1500.00	1850.00	2500.00	10200.00
1843 O SM Letters	450.00	1200.00	1900.00	19200.00
1843 O LG Letters	285.00	300.00	325.00	1700.00
1844	285.00	300.00	325.00	1700.00
1844 C	1400.00	2250.00	5700.00	22000.00
1844 D	1500.00	1900.00	2800.00	9600.00
1844 O	230.00	330.00	530.00	3500.00
1845	285.00	300.00	325.00	1700.00
1845 D	1500.00	1900.00	2800.00	10400.00
1845 O	360.00	630.00	2400.00	8700.00

	VF	XF	AU	MS60
1846	285.00	300.00	325.00	1700.00
1846 C	1450.00	2520.00	5600.00	19800.00
1846 D	1500.00	1800.00	3200.00	11100.00
1846 O	330.00	840.00	2800.00	10200.00
1847	285.00	300.00	325.00	1700.00
1847 C	1450.00	1800.00	3000.00	11400.00
1847 D	1500.00	1900.00	2800.00	10500.00
1847 O	1600.00	6600.00	8400.00	22800.00
1848	285.00	300.00	325.00	1700.00
1848 C	1450.00	2520.00	2760.00	16800.00
1848 D	1500.00	1800.00	2800.00	12600.00
1849	285.00	300.00	325.00	1700.00
1849 C	1450.00	2520.00	2800.00	11700.00
1849 D	1500.00	1800.00	2900.00	12000.00
1850	285.00	300.00	325.00	1700.00
1850 C	1450.00	2520.00	2700.00	10100.00
1850 D	1500.00	1800.00	3500.00	25200.00
1851	285.00	300.00	325.00	1700.00
1851 C	1450.00	2520.00	2700.00	14400.00
1851 D	1500.00	1800.00	2700.00	12600.00
1851 O	500.00	1320.00	3500.00	10500.00
1852	285.00	300.00	325.00	1700.00
1852 C	1450.00	2520.00	2700.00	5900.00
1852 D	1500.00	1800.00	2800.00	11100.00
1853	285.00	300.00	325.00	1700.00
1853 C	1450.00	2520.00	2700.00	7400.00
1853 D	1500.00	1800.00	2800.00	9000.00
1854	285.00	300.00	325.00	1700.00
1854 C	1450.00	2520.00	3400.00	12400.00
1854 D	1500.00	1800.00	2800.00	9300.00
1854 O	285.00	300.00	325.00	1700.00
1854 S			240000.00	
1855	285.00	300.00	325.00	1700.00
1855 C	1450.00	2520.00	2900.00	13200.00
1855 D	1500.00	1800.00	2900.00	14400.00
1855 O	540.00	1860.00	4100.00	18000.00

	VF	XF	AU	MS60
1855 S	350.00	840.00	1900.00	13800.00
1856	285.00	300.00	325.00	1700.00
1856 C	1450.00	2520.00	2900.00	18000.00
1856 D	1500.00	1800.00	3300.00	9200.00
1856 O	570.00	1080.00	4100.00	10800.00
1856 S	335.00	540.00	1100.00	6000.00
1857	285.00	300.00	325.00	1700.00
1857 C	1450.00	2520.00	2900.00	7800.00
1857 D	1500.00	1800.00	3000.00	11400.00
1857 O	560.00	1230.00	4100.00	14400.00
1857 S	325.00	470.00	1000.00	11700.00
1858	325.00	480.00	630.00	3400.00
1858 C	1450.00	2520.00	2800.00	9000.00
1858 D	1500.00	1800.00	2700.00	10800.00
1858 S	620.00	2040.00	4800.00	27000.00
1859	325.00	540.00	720.00	6400.00
1859 C	1450.00	2520.00	3300.00	13200.00
1859 D	1500.00	1800.00	2700.00	12600.00
1859 S	1080.00	3120.00	4700.00	25200.00
1860	325.00	510.00	1000.00	3600.00
1860 C	1450.00	2520.00	2900.00	11100.00
1860 D	1500.00	1800.00	3200.00	15000.00
1860 S	960.00	1860.00	5100.00	22200.00
1861	325.00	470.00	1000.00	11700.00
1861 C	1750.00	3360.00	6200.00	20400.00
1861 D	3840.00	6120.00	14400.00	46800.00
1861 S	900.00	3960.00	5700.00	31800.00
1862	600.00	1470.00	2800.00	18000.00
1862 S	2700.00	5520.00	9300.00	54000.00
1863	1050.00	3300.00	5400.00	24000.00
1863 S	1260.00	3600.00	8900.00	31200.00
1864	560.00	1620.00	3600.00	12900.00
1864 S	4260.00	13800.00	26400.00	48000.00
1865	1160.00	3600.00	7700.00	17400.00
1865 S	1140.00	2400.00	4500.00	15000.00
1866 S	1440.00	3480.00	11000.00	35400.00

$5.00 GOLD PIECES — WITH MOTTO

	VF	XF	AU	MS60
1866	690.00	1320.00	3000.00	13200.00
1866 S	840.00	2400.00	7000.00	22200.00
1867	440.00	1380.00	3300.00	9300.00
1867 S	1110.00	2280.00	7000.00	30000.00
1868	600.00	900.00	3000.00	9600.00
1868 S	360.00	1320.00	3500.00	17400.00
1869	810.00	2100.00	3300.00	14400.00
1869 S	440.00	1530.00	3500.00	24000.00
1870	690.00	1800.00	2500.00	15600.00
1870 CC	4440.00	11280.00	22800.00	96000.00
1870 S	720.00	2280.00	6800.00	25200.00
1871	840.00	1620.00	2900.00	10800.00
1871 CC	980.00	2880.00	9600.00	54000.00
1871 S	450.00	870.00	2800.00	11400.00
1872	750.00	1680.00	2700.00	1200.00
1872 CC	980.00	4200.00	18000.00	54000.00
1872 S	390.00	690.00	3200.00	11400.00
1873 Closed 3	265.00	270.00	360.00	1100.00
1873 Open 3	265.00	270.00	330.00	800.00
1873 CC	2200.00	10800.00	24000.00	54000.00
1873 S	470.00	1260.00	3000.00	19200.00
1874	580.00	1470.00	2300.00	11400.00
1874 CC	720.00	1500.00	7800.00	33000.00
1874 S	560.00	1860.00	4000.00	19800.00
1875	30000.00	36000.00	51600.00	168000.00
1875 CC	1200.00	3840.00	10100.00	45000.00
1875 S	590.00	2040.00	4200.00	14400.00
1876	960.00	2190.00	3600.00	9600.00
1876 CC	1040.00	4320.00	12600.00	40800.00
1876 S	1440.00	3120.00	8100.00	27000.00
1877	780.00	2400.00	3500.00	12000.00
1877 CC	890.00	2520.00	9600.00	45600.00
1877 S	350.00	570.00	1300.00	8100.00
1878	265.00	275.00	290.00	380.00

	VF	XF	AU	MS60
1878 CC	2640.00	6300.00	17400.00	54000.00
1878 S	265.00	275.00	285.00	600.00
1879	265.00	275.00	285.00	350.00
1879 CC	470.00	1320.00	2800.00	19200.00
1879 S	265.00	275.00	290.00	380.00
1880	265.00	275.00	290.00	380.00
1880 CC	380.00	680.00	1200.00	8640.00
1880 S	265.00	275.00	290.00	380.00
1881 1 over 0	300.00	480.00	630.00	1320.00
1881	265.00	275.00	290.00	380.00
1881 CC	450.00	1260.00	6000.00	19800.00
1881 S	265.00	275.00	290.00	380.00
1882	265.00	275.00	290.00	380.00
1882 CC	350.00	480.00	710.00	6600.00
1882 S	265.00	275.00	290.00	380.00
1883	265.00	275.00	290.00	380.00
1883 CC	410.00	920.00	2800.00	15000.00
1883 S	265.00	275.00	290.00	380.00
1884	265.00	275.00	290.00	380.00
1884 CC	490.00	860.00	2700.00	15000.00
1884 S	265.00	275.00	290.00	380.00
1885	265.00	275.00	290.00	380.00
1885 S	265.00	275.00	290.00	380.00
1886	265.00	275.00	290.00	380.00
1886 S	265.00	275.00	290.00	380.00
1887 Proof Only			12600.00	
1887 S	265.00	275.00	290.00	380.00
1888	265.00	275.00	290.00	380.00
1888 S	265.00	275.00	290.00	380.00
1889	260.00	390.00	450.00	1000.00
1890	360.00	440.00	480.00	2000.00
1890 CC	290.00	360.00	500.00	1200.00
1891	265.00	275.00	290.00	380.00
1891 CC	280.00	370.00	470.00	650.00
1892	265.00	275.00	290.00	380.00

	VF	XF	AU	MS60
1892 CC	280.00	370.00	510.00	1350.00
1892 O	450.00	870.00	1200.00	2900.00
1892 S	265.00	275.00	290.00	380.00
1893	265.00	275.00	290.00	380.00
1893 CC	280.00	400.00	680.00	1200.00
1893 O	265.00	275.00	290.00	380.00
1893 S	265.00	275.00	290.00	380.00
1894	265.00	275.00	290.00	380.00
1894 O	265.00	275.00	290.00	380.00
1894 S	265.00	330.00	510.00	2600.00
1895	265.00	275.00	290.00	380.00
1895 S	265.00	275.00	290.00	380.00
1896	265.00	275.00	290.00	380.00
1896 S	265.00	275.00	300.00	1170.00
1897	265.00	275.00	290.00	380.00
1897 S	265.00	275.00	290.00	380.00
1898	265.00	275.00	290.00	380.00
1898 S	265.00	275.00	290.00	380.00
1899	265.00	275.00	290.00	380.00
1899 S	265.00	275.00	290.00	380.00
1900	265.00	275.00	290.00	380.00
1900 S	265.00	275.00	290.00	380.00
1901	265.00	275.00	290.00	380.00
1901 S, 1 over 0	265.00	275.00	290.00	380.00
1901 S	265.00	275.00	290.00	380.00
1902	265.00	275.00	290.00	380.00
1902 S	265.00	275.00	290.00	380.00
1903	265.00	275.00	290.00	380.00
1903 S	265.00	275.00	290.00	380.00
1904	265.00	275.00	290.00	380.00
1904 S	265.00	275.00	290.00	380.00
1905	265.00	275.00	290.00	380.00
1905S	265.00	275.00	290.00	380.00
1906	265.00	275.00	290.00	380.00
1906 D	265.00	275.00	290.00	380.00

	VF	XF	AU	MS60
1906 S	265.00	275.00	290.00	380.00
1907	265.00	275.00	290.00	380.00
1907 D	265.00	275.00	290.00	380.00
1908	265.00	275.00	290.00	380.00

INDIAN HEAD $5.00 GOLD PIECE
$5.00 GOLD PIECES —INDIAN HEAD TYPE MINTED 1908-1929

	VF	XF	AU	MS60
1908	275.00	290.00	320.00	375.00
1908D	275.00	290.00	320.00	375.00
1908S	300.00	335.00	500.00	1200.00
1909	275.00	290.00	320.00	375.00
1909D	275.00	290.00	320.00	375.00
1909O	1600.00	2700.00	9500.00	22000.00
1909S	275.00	290.00	350.00	1200.00
1910	275.00	290.00	320.00	375.00
1910D	275.00	290.00	320.00	375.00
1910S	275.00	300.00	450.00	870.00
1911	275.00	290.00	320.00	375.00
1911D	375.00	430.00	1600.00	3800.00
1911S	275.00	325.00	410.00	1800.00
1912	275.00	290.00	320.00	375.00
1912S	275.00	290.00	575.00	1500.00
1913	275.00	290.00	320.00	375.00
1913S	275.00	280.00	650.00	1230.00
1914	275.00	290.00	320.00	375.00
1914D	275.00	290.00	320.00	375.00
1914S	275.00	290.00	520.00	1200.00
1915	275.00	290.00	320.00	375.00
1915S	275.00	360.00	685.00	1790.00
1916S	275.00	325.00	345.00	530.00
1929	5000.00	10000.00	12000.00	14000.00

$10.00 Gold Pieces Minted 1795-1933

CAPPED BUST TYPE
CAPPED BUST TO RIGHT MINTED 1795-1804

	F	VF	XF	AU	MS60
1795 9 Leaves	28000.00	40700.00	61600.00	115500.00	247500.00
1795 13 Leaves	25000.00	29000.00	42000.00	52000.00	95000.00
1796	26000.00	30000.00	45000.00	63000.00	100000.00
1797 SM Eagle	29000.00	34100.00	48000.00	88000.00	178200.00
1797	8195.00	9900.00	11880.00	20350.00	37400.00

HERALDIC EAGLE REVERSE

	F	VF	XF	AU	MS60
1798 over 7, 9 stars left	11300.00	16700.00	26400.00	35640.00	96800.00
1798 over 7, 7 stars left	27000.00	35000.00	59400.00	132000.00	217800.00
1799	8030.00	9350.00	11770.00	15950.00	27500.00
1800	8195.00	9350.00	12100.00	16500.00	26400.00
1801	8195.00	9350.00	12100.00	16500.00	26400.00
1803	8195.00	9350.00	12100.00	16500.00	26950.00
1804 Crosslet 4	14500.00	20200.00	26000.00	40000.00	90000.00
1804 Plain 4 Proof Only	0.00	0.00	0.00	0.00	0.00

LIBERTY $10.00 GOLD PIECE
$10 GOLD PIECES — LIBERTY HEAD 1838 - 1907

No Motto	VF	XF	AU	MS60
1838	2400.00	6000.00	13000.00	36500.00
1839 LG Letters Type of 1838	1000.00	1800.00	4500.00	27000.00
1839 SM Letters Type of 1840	1400.00	3200.00	6000.00	30000.00
1840	575.00	625.00	1300.00	9300.00
1841	575.00	625.00	1000.00	6800.00
1841 O	2000.00	4400.00	10700.00	30000.00

	VF	XF	AU	MS60
1842	575.00	625.00	1100.00	14400.00
1842 O	350.00	420.00	2100.00	15600.00
1843	600.00	440.00	1400.00	16500.00
1843 O	600.00	420.00	1000.00	9900.00
1844	1100.00	2700.00	4900.00	14400.00
1844 O	600.00	450.00	1440.00	13200.00
1845	600.00	700.00	1900.00	16200.00
1845 O	600.00	660.00	2100.00	12600.00
1846	630.00	920.00	4400.00	21000.00
1846 O	600.00	720.00	3000.00	14400.00
1847	600.00	650.00	800.00	2800.00
1847 O	600.00	650.00	800.00	5100.00
1848	600.00	650.00	800.00	4600.00
1848 O	600.00	1020.00	3000.00	12600.00
1849	600.00	650.00	800.00	3200.00
1849 O	600.00	1920.00	4800.00	21000.00
1850 LG Date	600.00	650.00	800.00	3600.00
1850 SM Date	600.00	750.00	1560.00	9000.00
1850 O	600.00	710.00	2700.00	15000.00
1851	600.00	650.00	800.00	5000.00
1851 O	600.00	650.00	840.00	5600.00
1852	600.00	650.00	800.00	4200.00
1852 O	600.00	960.00	3500.00	22800.00
1853 3 over 2	600.00	690.00	1620.00	13800.00
1853	600.00	650.00	800.00	3500.00
1853 O	600.00	650.00	900.00	12000.00
1854	600.00	650.00	800.00	5800.00
1854 O	600.00	640.00	1500.00	8400.00
1854 S	600.00	650.00	750.00	9600.00
1855	600.00	650.00	840.00	3500.00
1855 O	600.00	1200.00	4800.00	20400.00
1855 S	1200.00	1920.00	6600.00	30000.00
1856	550.00	650.00	795.00	3500.00
1856 O	600.00	1200.00	3600.00	14400.00
1856 S	600.00	650.00	1000.00	9000.00

	VF	XF	AU	MS60
1857	550.00	810.00	1740.00	12300.00
1857 O	840.00	1700.00	2900.00	18000.00
1857 S	550.00	780.00	1920.00	10500.00
1858	4500.00	6300.00	9900.00	28000.00
1858 0	550.00	720.00	1560.00	8400.00
1858 S	1320.00	2820.00	4700.00	30000.00
1859	550.00	600.00	1140.00	9000.00
1859 O	3900.00	6600.00	13200.00	46800.00
1859 S	1800.00	4500.00	11400.00	42000.00
1860	550.00	660.00	1140.00	7800.00
1860 O	600.00	1080.00	2160.00	13200.00
1860 S	2220.00	4560.00	13800.00	42000.00
1861	550.00	630.00	800.00	2900.00
1861 S	1320.00	2800.00	5600.00	33000.00
1862	625.00	930.00	2200.00	12600.00
1862 S	1560.00	2900.00	5000.00	36000.00
1863	3720.00	7700.00	14400.00	48000.00
1863 S	1260.00	3100.00	8100.00	23400.00
1864	1600.00	3600.00	6600.00	13800.00
1864 S	4400.00	10700.00	25200.00	54000.00
1865	1700.00	3500.00	6200.00	33000.00
1865 S	3120.00	8100.00	14400.00	46800.00
1865 S Over Inverted 186	3000.00	5900.00	9000.00	47400.00
1866 S	2220.00	3000.00	10800.00	45600.00

WITH MOTTO

1866	800.00	1600.00	4100.00	20400.00
1866 S	1320.00	3300.00	6200.00	23600.00
1867	1400.00	2400.00	4400.00	27000.00
1867 S	2200.00	5600.00	7700.00	42000.00
1868	625.00	720.00	1410.00	12900.00
1868 S	1200.00	2100.00	3400.00	24000.00
1869	1380.00	2400.00	4400.00	33000.00
1869 S	1200.00	2300.00	4800.00	22800.00
1870	780.00	1100.00	1900.00	16200.00
1870 CC	7700.00	21600.00	43200.00	96000.00

	VF	XF	AU	MS60
1870 S	900.00	2200.00	5600.00	33000.00
1871	1320.00	2600.00	3800.00	18000.00
1871 CC	1800.00	4700.00	13800.00	57600.00
1871 S	990.00	1400.00	5300.00	26400.00
1872	2220.00	3100.00	9000.00	15600.00
1872 CC	1980.00	7400.00	19200.00	57600.00
1872 S	625.00	800.00	1700.00	21600.00
1873	3840.00	9000.00	14400.00	45000.00
1873 CC	3120.00	8300.00	21600.00	60000.00
1873 S	900.00	1600.00	4000.00	24000.00
1874	625.00	650.00	850.00	1700.00
1874 CC	770.00	2100.00	7400.00	42000.00
1874S	960.00	2800.00	5700.00	42000.00
1875	36000.00	45000.00	58800.00	0.00
1875 CC	3000.00	8100.00	20400.00	66000.00
1876	2640.00	5800.00	11400.00	54000.00
1876 CC	2760.00	6600.00	16800.00	54000.00
1876 S	1170.00	1500.00	4900.00	38400.00
1877	2160.00	4700.00	6600.00	28800.00
1877 CC	1920.00	4700.00	12000.00	48000.00
1877 S	625.00	700.00	1800.00	23400.00
1878	530.00	550.00	600.00	740.00
1 878 CC	3000.00	8100.00	18600.00	48000.00
1878 S	625.00	700.00	1500.00	15000.00
1879	550.00	620.00	800.00	900.00
1879 CC	5100.00	9900.00	19200.00	66000.00
1879 O	1700.00	3700.00	7700.00	30600.00
1879 S	550.00	575.00	600.00	1000.00
1880	550.00	620.00	800.00	900.00
1880 CC	800.00	720.00	1400.00	12600.00
1880 O	625.00	630.00	1300.00	7200.00
1880 S	550.00	570.00	580.00	600.00
1881	550.00	570.00	580.00	600.00
1881 CC	530.00	600.00	900.00	5300.00
1881 O	550.00	750.00	1100.00	6300.00

	VF	XF	AU	MS60
1881 S	550.00	570.00	580.00	600.00
1882	550.00	570.00	580.00	600.00
1882 CC	600.00	1100.00	2700.00	13200.00
1882 O	550.00	600.00	1100.00	5300.00
1882 S	550.00	570.00	580.00	600.00
1883	550.00	570.00	580.00	600.00
1883 CC	470.00	720.00	1920.00	12000.00
1883 O	2160.00	6900.00	9300.00	31800.00
1883 S	350.00	375.00	400.00	870.00
1884	550.00	570.00	580.00	600.00
1884 CC	500.00	840.00	2100.00	10800.00
1884 S	550.00	570.00	580.00	600.00
1885	550.00	570.00	580.00	600.00
1885 S	550.00	570.00	580.00	600.00
1886	525.00	530.00	540.00	650.00
1886 S	525.00	530.00	540.00	650.00
1887	525.00	530.00	540.00	650.00
1887 S	525.00	530.00	540.00	650.00
1888	525.00	530.00	540.00	650.00
1888 O	525.00	530.00	540.00	650.00
1888 S	525.00	530.00	540.00	650.00
1889	525.00	530.00	540.00	2000.00
1889 S	525.00	530.00	540.00	650.00
1890	525.00	530.00	540.00	650.00
1890 CC	525.00	530.00	540.00	1700.00
1891	525.00	530.00	540.00	650.00
1891 CC	525.00	530.00	540.00	1500.00
1892	525.00	530.00	540.00	650.00
1892 CC	525.00	530.00	540.00	34000.00
1892 O	525.00	530.00	540.00	650.00
1892 S	525.00	530.00	540.00	650.00
1893	525.00	530.00	540.00	650.00
1893 CC	525.00	530.00	1500.00	6500.00
1893 O	525.00	530.00	540.00	650.00
1893 S	525.00	530.00	540.00	650.00
1894	525.00	530.00	540.00	650.00

	VF	XF	AU	MS60
1894 O	525.00	530.00	540.00	650.00
1894 S	525.00	530.00	540.00	3200.00
1895	525.00	530.00	540.00	650.00
1895 O	525.00	530.00	540.00	650.00
1895 S	525.00	530.00	540.00	2990.00
1896	525.00	530.00	540.00	650.00
1896 S	525.00	530.00	540.00	1900.00
1897	525.00	530.00	540.00	650.00
1897 O	525.00	530.00	540.00	650.00
1897 S	525.00	530.00	540.00	650.00
1898	525.00	530.00	540.00	650.00
1898 S	525.00	530.00	540.00	650.00
1899	525.00	530.00	540.00	650.00
1899 O	525.00	530.00	540.00	650.00
1899 S	525.00	530.00	540.00	650.00
1900	525.00	530.00	540.00	650.00
1900 S	525.00	530.00	540.00	650.00
1901	525.00	530.00	540.00	650.00
1901 O	525.00	530.00	540.00	650.00
1901 S	525.00	530.00	540.00	650.00
1902	525.00	530.00	540.00	650.00
1902 S	525.00	530.00	540.00	650.00
1903	525.00	530.00	540.00	650.00
1903 O	525.00	530.00	540.00	650.00
1903 S	525.00	530.00	540.00	650.00
1904	525.00	530.00	540.00	650.00
1904 O	525.00	530.00	540.00	650.00
1905	525.00	530.00	540.00	650.00
1905 S	525.00	530.00	540.00	650.00
1906	525.00	530.00	540.00	650.00
1906 D	525.00	530.00	540.00	650.00
1906 O	525.00	530.00	540.00	650.00
1906 S	525.00	530.00	540.00	650.00
1907	525.00	530.00	540.00	650.00
1907 D	525.00	530.00	540.00	650.00
1907 S	525.00	530.00	540.00	650.00

INDIAN HEAD $10.00 GOLD PIECE
INDIAN HEAD TYPE MINTED 1907-1933

				XF	AU	MS60
1907	Wire	Edge	With Periods	12000.00	13500.00	17500.00
1907			W/O Stars	Unique--1	exists	
1907	Rolled	Edge	With Periods	32000.00	41000.00	62000.00
1907			W/O Periods	585.00	600.00	690.00
1908			W/O Motto	585.00	600.00	690.00
1908D			W/O Motto	585.00	600.00	610.00
Motto Added					AU	MS60
1908				585.00	600.00	685.00
1908D				585.00	600.00	685.00
1908S				415.00	1600.00	2350.00
1909				585.00	600.00	685.00
1909D				585.00	600.00	685.00
1909S				585.00	600.00	685.00
1910				585.00	600.00	685.00
1910D				585.00	600.00	685.00
1910S				585.00	600.00	685.00
1911				585.00	600.00	685.00
1911D				690.00	720.00	3200.00
1911S				500.00	580.00	910.00
1912				585.00	600.00	685.00
1912S				585.00	600.00	685.00
1913				585.00	600.00	685.00
1913S				580.00	720.00	3000.00
1914				585.00	600.00	685.00
1914D				585.00	600.00	685.00
1914S				585.00	600.00	685.00
1915				585.00	600.00	685.00
1915S				640.00	720.00	2500.00
1916S				585.00	600.00	685.00

1920S	6600.00	7300.00	15000.00
1926	585.00	600.00	685.00
1930S	5500.00	7200.00	8200.00
1932	585.00	600.00	685.00
1933	110000.00	125000.00	160000.00

$20.00 Gold Pieces Minted 1849 -1907

LIBERTY $20.00 GOLD PIECE
LIBERTY TYPE MINTED 1849-1907

No Motto Ty 1	VF	XF	AU	MS60
1849 (1 Minted)	NA	NA	NA	NA
1850	1300.00	1350.00	2500.00	7500.00
1850 O	1300.00	3300.00	7500.00	40000.00
1851	1175.00	1200.00	1250.00	2500.00
1851 O	1175.00	1250.00	1700.00	14400.00
1852	1175.00	1250.00	780.00	2900.00
1852 O	1175.00	1295.00	1620.00	13200.00
1853 3 over 2	1175.00	1140.00	2900.00	34200.00
1853	1175.00	1250.00	1500.00	3900.00
1853 O	1175.00	1250.00	2500.00	23000.00
1854	1175.00	1250.00	1500.00	5200.00
1854 O	65000.00	110000.00	180000.00	375000.00
1854 S	1175.00	1200.00	1250.00	3400.00
1855	1175.00	1200.00	1020.00	7200.00
1855 O	2040.00	5040.00	18000.00	66000.00
1855 S	1175.00	1200.00	1250.00	6300.00
1856	1175.00	1200.00	1250.00	7800.00
1856 O	75000.00	120000.00	240000.00	360000.00
1856 S	1175.00	1200.00	1250.00	3400.00
1857	1175.00	1200.00	1250.00	3000.00
1857 O	1175.00	1600.00	3800.00	19200.00
1857 S	1175.00	1200.00	1250.00	3000.00

	VF	XF	AU	MS60
1858	1175.00	1200.00	1250.00	4400.00
1858 O	1200.00	1800.00	4675.00	34000.00
1858 S	1175.00	1200.00	1250.00	6900.00
1859	1175.00	1860.00	3600.00	27600.00
1859 O	3000.00	8500.00	23000.00	76000.00
1859 S	1175.00	1200.00	1250.00	4400.00
1860	1175.00	1200.00	1250.00	3500.00
1860 O	2900.00	5300.00	18000.00	82000.00
1860 S	1175.00	1200.00	1250.00	5400.00
1861	1175.00	1200.00	1250.00	2200.00
1861 O	2200.00	3600.00	16500.00	78000.00
1861 S	1175.00	1235.00	1410.00	7400.00
1861 Paquet Rev.	NA	NA	NA	NA
1861 S. Paquet Rev.	10000.00	19500.00	38000.00	130000.00
1862	1175.00	1320.00	3200.00	13800.00
1862 S	1175.00	1200.00	1500.00	9300.00
1863	1175.00	1200.00	2200.00	15000.00
1863 S	1175.00	1200.00	1200.00	6600.00
1864	1175.00	1200.00	1600.00	12000.00
1864 S	1175.00	1200.00	1500.00	5800.00
1865	1175.00	1200.00	1350.00	5300.00
1865 S	1175.00	1200.00	1350.00	3500.00
1866 S	1500.00	3100.00	23500.00	84000.00
No Motto Ty 2	VF	XF	AU	MS60
1866	1150.00	1200.00	1450.00	4400.00
1866 S	1150.00	1200.00	1450.00	13800.00
1867	1150.00	1200.00	1450.00	2000.00
1867 S	1150.00	1200.00	1450.00	11400.00
1868	1150.00	1200.00	1700.00	8700.00
1868 S	1150.00	1200.00	1450.00	7500.00
1869	1150.00	1200.00	1450.00	5300.00
1869 S	1150.00	1200.00	1450.00	4500.00
1870	1150.00	1200.00	1400.00	8000.00
1870 CC	88000.00	120000.00	230000.00	500000.00
1870 S	1150.00	1200.00	1400.00	4600.00

	VF	XF	AU	MS60
1871	1150.00	1200.00	1400.00	3500.00
1871 CC	4600.00	8500.00	22000.00	65000.00
1871 S	1150.00	1200.00	1400.00	3100.00
1872	1150.00	1200.00	1400.00	2400.00
1872 CC	1600.00	2100.00	4700.00	21600.00
1872 S	1150.00	1200.00	1400.00	2600.00
1873 Closed 3	1150.00	1200.00	1400.00	2200.00
1873 Open 3	1150.00	1200.00	1400.00	1600.00
1873 CC Closed 3	1750.00	2750.00	5500.00	24500.00
1873 S Closed 3	1150.00	1200.00	1400.00	1500.00
1874	1150.00	1200.00	1400.00	1600.00
1874 CC	950.00	1200.00	2100.00	6600.00
1874 S	1150.00	1200.00	1400.00	1200.00
1875	1150.00	1200.00	1400.00	1600.00
1875 CC	950.00	1100.00	1320.00	2100.00
1875 S	1150.00	1200.00	1400.00	1600.00
1876	1150.00	1200.00	1400.00	1600.00
1876 CC	1150.00	1200.00	1320.00	3400.00
1876 S	1150.00	1200.00	1320.00	1600.00

$20.00 GOLD PIECES — DOLLARS ON REV TYPE 3

	VF	XF	AU	MS60
1877	1075.00	1085.00	1095.00	1400.00
1877 CC	1075.00	1175.00	2200.00	13800.00
1877 S	1075.00	1175.00	1275.00	1600.00
1878	1075.00	1175.00	1275.00	1600.00
1878 CC	1600.00	2400.00	3600.00	19000.00
1878 S	1075.00	1175.00	1275.00	1600.00
1879	1975.00	1175.00	1275.00	1600.00
1879 CC	1700.00	2600.00	4800.00	25500.00
1879 O	5750.00	7750.00	24500.00	65000.00
1879 S	1075.00	1175.00	1275.00	1500.00
1880	1075.00	1175.00	1275.00	2700.00
1880 S	1075.00	1175.00	1275.00	1400.00
1881	4100.00	6000.00	12000.00	38400.00
1881 S	1075.00	1175.00	1275.00	1400.00

	VF	XF	AU	MS60
1882	6300.00	13200.00	24600.00	54000.00
1882 CC	1100.00	1200.00	1600.00	5600.00
1882 S	1075.00	1175.00	1275.00	1400.00
1883 Proof Only		0.00	0.00	0.00
1883 CC	1075.00	1000.00	1200.00	3300.00
1883 S	1075.00	1175.00	1275.00	1400.00
1884 Proof Only		0.00	0.00	0.00
1884 CC	1075.00	1050.00	1225.00	2400.00
1884 S	1075.00	1175.00	1275.00	1400.00
1885	6000.00	7500.00	9800.00	27000.00
1885 CC	1800.00	2600.00	4700.00	9900.00
1885 S	1075.00	1175.00	1275.00	1400.00
1886	7200.00	10080.00	20400.00	38400.00
1887 Proof Only		0.00	0.00	0.00
1887 S	1075.00	1175.00	1275.00	1400.00
1888	1075.00	1175.00	1275.00	1400.00
1888 S	1075.00	1175.00	1275.00	1400.00
1889	1075.00	1175.00	1275.00	1400.00
1889 CC	1100.00	1230.00	1800.00	2800.00
1889 S	1075.00	1175.00	1275.00	1400.00
1890	1075.00	1175.00	1275.00	1400.00
1890 CC	1075.00	1175.00	1200.00	2040.00
1890 S	1075.00	675.00	700.00	800.00
1891	2500.00	4500.00	7800.00	39500.00
1891 CC	2900.00	6300.00	7200.00	14250.00
1891 S	1075.00	1175.00	1275.00	1400.00
1892	1075.00	1440.00	2300.00	4800.00
1892 CC	1075.00	1200.00	1620.00	2760.00
1892 S	1075.00	1175.00	1275.00	1400.00
1893	1075.00	1175.00	1275.00	1400.00
1893 CC	1200.00	1500.00	1700.00	3400.00
1893 S	1075.00	1100.00	1150.00	1400.00
1894	1075.00	1100.00	1150.00	1400.00
1894 S	1075.00	1100.00	1150.00	1400.00
1895	1075.00	1100.00	1150.00	1400.00

	VF	XF	AU	MS60
1895 S	1075.00	1100.00	1150.00	1400.00
1896	1075.00	1100.00	1150.00	1400.00
1896 S	1075.00	1100.00	1150.00	1400.00
1897	1075.00	1100.00	1150.00	1400.00
1897 S	1075.00	1100.00	1150.00	1400.00
1898	1075.00	1100.00	1150.00	1400.00
1898 S	1075.00	1100.00	1150.00	1400.00
1899	1075.00	1100.00	1150.00	1400.00
1899 S	1075.00	1100.00	1150.00	1400.00
1900	1075.00	1100.00	1150.00	1400.00
1900 S	1075.00	1100.00	1150.00	1400.00
1901	1075.00	1100.00	1150.00	1400.00
1901 S	1075.00	1100.00	1150.00	1400.00
1902	1075.00	1100.00	1150.00	1400.00
1902 S	1075.00	1100.00	1150.00	1400.00
1903	1075.00	1100.00	1150.00	1400.00
1903 S	1075.00	1100.00	1150.00	1400.00
1904	1075.00	1100.00	1150.00	1400.00
1904 S	1075.00	1100.00	1150.00	1400.00
1905	1075.00	1100.00	1150.00	1400.00
1905 S	1075.00	1100.00	1150.00	1400.00
1906	1075.00	1100.00	1150.00	1400.00
1906 D	1075.00	1100.00	1150.00	1400.00
1906 S	1075.00	1100.00	1150.00	1400.00
1907	1075.00	1100.00	1150.00	1400.00
1907 D	1075.00	1100.00	1150.00	1400.00
1907 S	1075.00	1100.00	1150.00	1400.00

SAINT-GAUDENS $20.00 GOLD PIECE

SAINT-GAUDENS TYPE MINTED 1907-1933

		XF	AU	MS60
1907	Plain Edge Ex. High Relief	Unique--1 exists		
1907	Lettered Edge High Relief	$1,000,000+		
1907	Roman Numerals Plain Edge High Relief	150000.00		
1907	Roman Numerals Wire Rim High Relief	6600.00	7700.00	8800.00
1907	Roman Numerals Flat Rim LG Letters			
1907	On Edge Small Letters	6600.00	7700.00	8800.00
1907	No Motto	Unique--1 exists		
1907	No Motto	1090.00	1100.00	1135.00
1908	No Motto	1090.00	1100.00	1135.00
1908D		1090.00	1100.00	1135.00

Motto added	XF	AU	MS60
1908	1090.00	1100.00	1135.00
1908D	1090.00	1100.00	1135.00
1908S	1540.00	1650.00	4750.00
1909	1090.00	1100.00	1135.00
1909D	1090.00	1100.00	1500.00
1909S	1090.00	1100.00	1135.00
1910	1090.00	1100.00	1135.00
1910D	1090.00	1100.00	1135.00
1910S	1090.00	1100.00	1135.00
1911	1090.00	1100.00	1135.00
1911D	1090.00	1100.00	1135.00
1911S	1090.00	1100.00	1135.00
1912	1090.00	1100.00	1135.00
1913	1090.00	1100.00	1135.00
1913D	1090.00	1100.00	1135.00
1913S	1090.00	1100.00	1135.00
1914	1090.00	1100.00	1135.00
1914D	1090.00	1100.00	1135.00

	XF	AU	MS60
1914S	1090.00	1100.00	1135.00
1915	1090.00	1100.00	1135.00
1915S	1090.00	1100.00	1135.00
1916S	1090.00	1100.00	1135.00
1920	1090.00	1100.00	1135.00
1920S	12100.00	17500.00	32000.00
1921	19000.00	22500.00	42000.00
1922	1090.00	1100.00	1135.00
1922S	1090.00	1100.00	1850.00
1923	1090.00	1100.00	1135.00
1923D	1090.00	1100.00	1135.00
1924	1090.00	1100.00	1135.00
1924D	1300.00	1400.00	2400.00
1924S	1320.00	1430.00	2310.00
1925	1090.00	1100.00	1135.00
1925D	1870.00	1980.00	2860.00
1925S	1540.00	2200.00	7000.00
1926	1090.00	1100.00	1135.00
1926D	3950.00	5000.00	12500.00
1926S	1320.00	1430.00	1650.00
1927	1090.00	1100.00	1135.00
1927D	187000.00	215000.00	290000.00
1927S	5500.00	6050.00	11000.00
1928	1090.00	1100.00	1135.00
1929	7150.00	7700.00	10500.00
1930S	16500.00	18700.00	22000.00
1931	9900.00	11000.00	17500.00
1931D	9900.00	13200.00	24000.00
1932	12100.00	13200.00	17000.00
1933		MS65	$8 Million

CHAPTER 6

COMMEMORATIVE COINS

B y Act of Congress, the mint over the years has been authorized to issue commemorative coins, each celebrating a current or historic event or honoring an outstanding citizen. Such coins show a great variety of design and inscription. Most would not be recognizable to the public as legal tender, although some issues were placed in general circulation.

Usually, these coins are offered to the public at a premium over their face value. For example, the Columbian Exposition half dollar was sold for $1 at the World's Columbian Exposition in Chicago during 1893. The fact that the mintage of commemorative coins is usually quite small also is a factor that puts them at a premium with collectors.

Since commemoratives were generally not issued to circulate, most pieces are well preserved and grade toward the high end of the scale that we have used for previous coins. Consequently, in what follows, pricing for two grades has been used, XF-AU which can even apply to an uncirculated coin that has been knocking around in a desk drawer for a few decades, and MS60, the lowest of the uncirculated grades. As with other coins, high-end uncirculated specimens can easily command prices in excess of five to ten times that of MS60.

Quarter Dollars
Isabella Quarter

Minted in 1893, this was the first U.S. coin portraying a foreign monarch. The obverse shows Queen Isabella of Spain who helped Columbus finance his voyage of discovery. The reverse displays a kneeling female who represents women's industry.

XF-AU	MS60
575.00	675.00

Half Dollar
Columbian Exposition

Issued in 1892 and 1893 in celebration of the 400th anniversary of the discovery of America by Columbus, and the Chicago World's Fair of 1893. The obverse shows a portrait of Columbus; the reverse the ship, Santa Maria, spanning the two hemispheres.

	XF-AU	MS60
1892	16.00	23.00
1893	14.00	23.00

Panama-Pacific

Issued by the Panama-Pacific International Exposition in 1915 to commemorate the completion of the Panama Canal. The obverse shows Columbia. The reverse displays the eagle and shield.

XF-AU	MS60
425.00	500.00

Illinois Centennial

Issued in 1918 to commemorate the 100th anniversary of the admission of Illinois into the Union. The obverse shows a bust of Lincoln. The reverse depicts portions of the Illinois state seal.

XF-AU	MS60
175.00	225.00

Maine Centennial

Issued in 1920 to commemorate the 100th anniversary of the admission of Maine into the Union. The obverse reproduces the Great Seal of the state. The reverse places the inscription "Maine Centennial, 1820-1920" within a wreath.

XF-AU	MS60
125.00	150.00

Pilgrim Tercentenary

Issued in 1920 and 1921 to commemorate the 300th anniversary of the landing of the Pilgrims. The obverse is a portrait of Governor Bradford. The reverse shows the Mayflower.

	XF-AU	MS60
1920 (No Date on Obverse)	75.00	100.00
1921 (Date on Obverse)	160.00	205.00

Alabama

Issued in 1921 two years late for the 100th anniversary of the admission of Alabama into the Union. The obverse shows the busts of the first (W.W. Bibb) and the then current (T.E. Kilby) governors of the State. Two varieties of the coin exist. The first has the St. Andrews cross between the number "22" (Alabama was the 22nd state) in the field of the obverse behind the governors' heads. The reverse shows an eagle.

	XF-AU	MS60
1921 with 22	270.00	300.00
1921 without 22	175.00	200.00

MISSOURI CENTENNIAL

Issued in 1921 to commemorate the 100th anniversary of Missouri's admission into the Union the obverse displays the bust of a frontiers-man. The reverse shows a standing frontiersman and an Indian. One variety has a small "2 x 4" on the obverse below the chin of the frontiersman, as Missouri was the 24th state.

	XF-AU	MS60
1921 with 24	350.00	670.00
1921 without 24	280.00	600.00

GRANT MEMORIAL

Issued in 1922 to commemorate the 100th anniversary of Grant's birth, the obverse is a bust of Grant. The reverse is a portrait of Grant's log cabin boyhood home. One variety has a star on the obverse above Grant's last name.

	XF/AU	MS60
1922 with star	500.00	1200.00
1922 without star	100.00	120.00

MONROE DOCTRINE CENTENNIAL

Issued in 1923 to mark the 100th anniversary of the proclamation of the Monroe Doctrine. The obverse shows the busts of Monroe and John Quincy Adams. The reverse shows the Western Hemisphere, the portion of the world the European powers were warned against interfering in.

XF-AU	MS60
60.00	75.00

Huguenot-Walloon Tercentenary

Issued in 1924 to commemorate the 300th anniversary of the arrival of the Huguenots and Walloons, Protestant refugees from Belgium. The obverse shows the busts of Admiral Coligny and William the Silent. The reverse depicts the ship, New Netherlands.

XF-AU	MS60
125.00	145.00

California Jubilee

Issued in 1925 to commemorate the 75th anniversary of the admission of California into the Union. The obverse shows a kneeling gold miner. The reverse displays the emblem of the state, a California grizzly bear.

XF-AU	MS60
180.00	200.00

Lexington-Concord Sesquicentennial

Issued in 1925 to mark the 150th anniversary of these two famous Revolutionary War battles. The obverse bears a portrait of a standing Minute Man. The reverse depicts the Old Belfry in Lexington.

XF-AU	MS60
90.00	105.00

STONE MOUNTAIN MEMORIAL

Issued in 1925 to raise funds for sculpturing figures of Confederate heroes on Stone Mountain in Georgia. The obverse shows Lee and Jackson on horseback. The reverse has an eagle perched on the mountain.

XF-AU	MS60
60.00	75.00

VANCOUVER CENTENNIAL

Issued in 1925 to mark the 100th anniversary of the building of Fort Vancouver. The obverse shows a bust of the builder, Dr. John McLaughlin. The reverse has a frontiersman standing with a rifle. In the background is the old fort and mountains.

XF-AU	MS60
300.00	360.00

SESQUICENTENNIAL OF AMERICAN INDEPENDENCE

Issued in 1926 to commemorate the 150th anniversary of the signing of the Declaration of Independence. The obverse has busts of Washington and Coolidge facing right. The reverse shows the Liberty Bell.

XF-AU	MS60
80.00	105.00

OREGON TRAIL MEMORIAL

Issued first in 1926, and subsequently in 1928, 1933, 1934, 1936-1939, to commemorate the memory of the pioneers who died along the Oregon Trail. The obverse depicts a covered wagon moving west. The reverse shows an American Indian superimposed on a map of the U.S.

	XF-AU	MS60
1926	105.00	145.00
1926 S	105.00	145.00
1928	170.00	205.00
1933 D	305.00	332.00
1934 D	140.00	180.00
1936	118.00	155.00
1936 S	130.00	155.00
1937 D	130.00	170.00
1938 P, D, S(Set)	365.00	450.00
1939 P, D, S(Set)	1,065.00	1,500.00

VERMONT SESQUICENTENNIAL

Issued in 1927 to mark the 150th anniversary of the independence of Vermont. The obverse shows the bust of Ira Allen, founder of Vermont. The reverse captures a stalking mountain lion.

XF-AU	MS60
225.00	250.00

HAWAIIAN SESQUICENTENNIAL

Issued in 1928 to mark the 150th anniversary of the landing of Captain Cook in the Hawaiian Islands. The obverse carries a bust of Captain Cook. The reverse displays a full-length statue of a native chief.

XF-AU	MS60
1500.00	2300.00

Boone Bicentennial

Issued first in 1934 and subsequently through 1938, these coins mark the 100th anniversary of Daniel Boone's birth. The obverse has Boone facing left. The reverse has standing figures of Boone and Chief Black Fish.

	XF-AU	MS60
1934	100.00	108.00
1934 P,D,S (Set)	800.00	825.00
(Actually issued In 1935 Small "1934" on reverse.)		
1935 P,D,S	310.00	325.00
1936 P,D,S	310.00	325.00
1937 P,D,S	375.00	775.00
1938 P,D,S	740.00	1000.00

Maryland Tercentenary

Issued in 1934 to commemorate the 300th anniversary of the granting of the original charter of Maryland to Lord Baltimore. The reverse displays Maryland's coat of arms.

XF-AU	MS60
135.00	160.00

Texas Centennial

Issued from 1934 through 1938 to commemorate the revolt of Texas from Mexico in 1836. The obverse has an eagle superimposed on the "Lone Star." The reverse contains small portraits of Sam Houston and Stephen Austin flanking a figure of winged Victory.

	XF-AU	MS60
1934	102.00	122.00
1935 P,D,S (Set)	310.00	375.00
1936 P,D,S (Set)	310.00	375.00
1937 P,D,S (Set)	310.00	375.00
1938 P,D,S (Set)	375.00	665.00

Arkansas Centennial

First issued in 1935, a year before the actual centennial, and then through 1939, these coins commemorate the 100th anniversary of the admission of Arkansas into the Union. The obverse shows a soaring eagle; reverse, the heads of an Indian chief and a then contemporary American girl.

	XF-AU	MS60
Type coin (any year)	70.00	88.00
1935 P,D,S (Set)	210.00	265.00
1936 P,D,S (Set)	210.00	265.00
1937 P,D,S (Set)	210.00	265.00
1938 P,D,S (Set)	275.00	465.00
1939 P,D,S (Set)	485.00	960.00

Connecticut Tercentenary

Issued in 1935 to commemorate the 300th anniversary of the founding of the colony of Connecticut. The obverse bears a standing eagle reminiscent of the Peace Dollar. The reverse bears a representation of the oak tree in Hartford where, according to tradition, the state's charter was hidden from the British governor in 1687.

XF-AU	MS60
225.00	250.00

Hudson Sesquicentennial

Issued in 1935 to mark the 150th anniversary of the founding of Hudson, New York. The obverse shows Henry Hudson's ship, the Half Moon. The seal of the city of Hudson, depicting a mythical sea scene, is found on the reverse.

XF-AU	MS60
650.00	800.00

SAN DIEGO EXPOSITION

Issued with the dates 1935 and 1936 for the opening of the exposition, the obverse shows a seated female warrior with a bear in the back-ground. The reverse displays the State of California building at the exposition.

	XF-AU	MS60
1935 S	78.00	108.00
1936 D	78.00	125.00

SPANISH TRAIL

Issued in 1935 to commemorate the 400th anniversary of the blazing of the "Old Spanish Trail" by de Vaca in 1535. The obverse portrays a longhorn cow from the explorer's name. The reverse maps the trail from Florida to Texas on which is superimposed a yucca tree.

XF-AU	MS60
1050.00	1200.00

ALBANY CHARTER

Issued in 1936 to mark the 250th anniversary of the charter of the City of Albany, New York. The obverse depicts a beaver at work. The reverse shows Peter Schuyler and Robert Livingston with Governor Dongan of New York after receiving the city's charter.

XF-AU	MS60
245.00	275.00

BRIDGEPORT CENTENNIAL

Issued in 1936 to commemorate the 100th anniversary of the incorporation of the city of Bridgeport, Connecticut. The obverse shows the portrait of P.T. Barnum, once mayor and Bridgeport's most famous citizen. The reverse shows an eagle about to soar.

XF-AU	MS60
120.00	150.00

CINCINNATI MUSIC CENTER

Issued in 1936 to commemorate the 50th anniversary of Cincinnati as a music center. The obverse carries a portrait of Stephen Foster. The reverse shows an allegorical figure representing music.

	XF-AU	MS60
1936 Type single	275.00	290.00
1936 P,D,S (Set)	815.00	850.00

CLEVELAND EXPOSITION

Issued in 1936 to mark the 100th anniversary of the founding of Cleveland as part of the Great Lakes Exposition held in Cleveland during that year. The obverse portrays General Moses Cleveland (old spelling), and ancestor of President Grover Cleveland. The reverse shows a map of nine large cities on the Great Lakes.

XF-AU	MS60
120.00	125.00

COLUMBIA SESQUICENTENNIAL

Issued in 1936 on the 150th anniversary of the founding of the city of Columbia, South Carolina. The obverse shows justice with sword and scales. The reverse shows a palmetto tree, emblem of the state of South Carolina.

	XF-AU	MS60
1936 type single	215.00	225.00
1936 P,D,S (Set)	650.00	675.00

DELAWARE TERCENTENARY

Issued in 1936 on the 300th anniversary of the landing of Swedish immigrants in Delaware. The obverse shows the Old Swedes Church in Wilmington. The reverse displays the vessel, Kalmor Nyckel, used for the journey.

XF-AU	MS60
245.00	290.00

ELGIN CENTENNIAL

Issued in 1936 to mark the 100th anniversary of the founding of Elgin, Illinois. The obverse shows a pioneer's portrait. The reverse depicts a Pioneer Memorial Statue to be fashioned from the monies received by the commemorative coin.

XF-AU	MS60
185.00	215.00

GETTYSBURG

Issued in 1936 to commemorate the Battle of Gettysburg. The obverse shows a Union and Confederate soldier. The reverse displays the shields of the Union and Confederacy.

XF-AU	MS60
320.00	380.00

LONG ISLAND TERCENTENARY

Issued in 1936 to commemorate the 300th anniversary of the Dutch Settlement of Jamaica Bay, Long Island, New York. The obverse shows a Dutch settler and a Native American. A Dutch sailing vessel is depicted on the reverse.

XF-AU	MS60
70.00	82.00

LYNCHBURG SESQUICENTENNIAL

Issued in 1936 to mark the 150th anniversary of the charter for Lynchburg, Virginia. The obverse portrays Carter Glass, long-time U.S. Senator from Virginia and Secretary of the Treasury under Woodrow Wilson. The reverse shows Liberty standing before the city courthouse.

XF-AU	MS60
195.00	225.00

NORFOLK BICENTENNIAL

Issued in 1936 to commemorate the 200th anniversary of the borough of Norfolk. The obverse is a representation of the city's Great Seal. On the reverse is found the Royal Mace of Norfolk.

	XF-AU	MS60
	410.00	460.00

RHODE ISLAND TERCENTENARY

Issued in 1936 to commemorate the 300th anniversary of the founding of Providence. The obverse shows the founder, Roger Williams, welcomed by a Native American. Rhode Island's state motto, "Hope," and an anchor are found on the reverse.

	XF-AU	MS60
1936 Type single	78.00	85.00
1936 P,D,S (Set)	235.00	255.00

ROBINSON ARKANSAS CENTENNIAL

Issued in 1936 to commemorate the 100th anniversary of Arkansas statehood. (See the previous commemoration.) The obverse again shows a soaring eagle. The reverse (even though it contains a portrait, usually considered the mark of the obverse of a coin) depicts then Senator Joseph T. Robinson.

	XF-AU	MS60
	130.00	145.00

San Francisco Bay Bridge

Issued in 1936 to celebrate the opening of the bridge connecting San Francisco to Oakland. The obverse has a California grizzly bear facing front. The reverse shows the bridge—then the worlds largest.

XF-AU	MS60
150.00	170.00

Wisconsin Centennial

Issued in 1936 to commemorate the 100th anniversary of the Wisconsin Territorial government. The obverse has a badger superimposed over the state emblem. The Territorial Seal, depicting the mining industry, is found on the reverse.

XF-AU	MS60
170.00	210.00

York County Tercentenary

Issued in 1936 to commemorate the 300th anniversary of the founding of York County, the first county in Maine. The obverse is of the old fort on the Saco River. The reverse depicts the York County Seal.

XF-AU	MS60
200.00	210.00

ANTIETAM

Issued in 1937 for the 75th anniversary of the Battle of Antietam. The obverse shows the opposing commanders of the Civil War battle, Lee and McClellan. The reverse shows a critical objective of the battle, the Burnside Bridge.

XF-AU	MS60
625.00	650.00

ROANOKE ISLAND

Issued in 1937 to mark the 350th anniversary of the attempt to colonize Roanoke Island, North Carolina. The obverse shows Sir Walter Raleigh who was active in the early attempts to colonize Virginia. The reverse commemorates the birth of Virginia Dare, supposedly the first white person born in the American colonies.

XF-AU	MS60
225.00	250.00

NEW ROCHELLE

Issued in 1938 to mark the 250th anniversary of the founding of New Rochelle, New York. The obverse shows a calf which was to be given away every year as part of the terms of gaining title to the land. The re-verse depicts the fleur-de-lys, the national symbol of France, since it was the French Huguenots who purchased the land.

XF-AU	MS60
360.00	385.00

Iowa Centennial

Issued in 1946 to commemorate the 100th anniversary of Iowa's en-trance into the Union. The obverse shows the first capitol building in Iowa City. The reverse depicts the state seal.

XF-AU	MS60
95.00	110.00

Booker T. Washington Memorial

Issued from 1946 to 1951 to further the views and ideals of this great black American educator. The obverse is the bust of Washington. The reverse has at its center the legend, "From Slave Cabin to Hall of Fame."

	XF-AU	MS60
Single Type Coin	14.00	18.00
1946 P,D,S (Set)	38.00	85.00
1947 P,D,S (Set)	90.00	110.00
1948 P,D,S (Set)	125.00	175.00
1949 P,D,S (Set)	185.00	225.00
1950 P,D,S (Set)	100.00	150.00
1951 P,D,S (Set)	100.00	150.00

Washington Carver

Issued from 1951 to 1954 to honor the memories of two distinguished black Americans, Booker T.Washington and George Washington Carver. The obverse shows the busts of the two men. The reverse is a map of the United States.

	XF-AU	MS60
Single Type Coin	13.00	17.00
1951 P,D,S (Set)	90.00	125.00
1952 P,D,S (Set)	90.00	125.00
1953 P,D,S (Set)	90.00	125.00
1954 P,D,S (Set)	90.00	125.00

Silver Dollar Commemorative
Lafayette Dollar

Issued in 1900 in memory of Lafayette's contributions to the United States during the revolution. The obverse has Washington's profile superimposed over Lafayette's. The reverse is a reproduction of a monument in Paris showing Lafayette astride his horse.

	XF-AU	MS60
	575.00	850.00

Louisiana Purchase Centennial

Dated 1903 and issued for the Louisiana Purchase Exposition held in St. Louis in 1904. Two obverses exist: One with the bust of Jefferson, the other with that of McKinley. The reverse is the same on both, showing the denomination and dates.

	XF-AU	MS60
$1.00 Gold (Both varieties)	575.00	625.00

Lewis & Clark Centennial

Issued in 1904 and 1905 to mark the 100th anniversary of the exploration by these two famous men. Their portraits appear on the obverse and reverse.

	XF-AU	MS60
$1.00 Gold 1904	870.00	1200.00
$1.00 Gold 1905	1100.00	1400.00

PANAMA PACIFIC EXPOSITION

$1.00 Gold $2.50 Gold

$50.00 Gold(Round) $50.00 Gold(Octagonal)

Issued in three denominations to commemorate the opening of the Panama Canal in 1915. The obverse of the $1 coin shows the bust of a canal laborer. The reverse has two dolphins surrounding the denomination. The obverse of the $2.50 coin shows Columbia astride a hippocampus. On the reverse is an eagle facing left. The $50 coin was issued in both a round and octagonal variety. The obverse of both shows a bust of Minerva. The reverse displays an owl.

PANAMA PACIFIC EXPOSITION

	XF-AU	MS60
$1.00 Gold 1915 S	505.00	615.00
$2.50 Gold 1915 S	1500.00	1800.00
$50.00 Gold 1915 S (Round)	50,000.00	55,000.00
$50.00 Gold 1915 S (Octagonal)	48,000.00	52,000.00

McKINLEY MEMORIAL

Dated 1916 and 1917 and issued to mark the death of President McKinley and to raise funds for a memorial building at his birthplace, the obverse is a bust of the slain president. The reverse is a replica of the structure to be built in his honor.

	XF-AU	MS60
$1.00 Gold 1916	500.00	565.00
$1.00 Gold 1917	675.00	700.00

GRANT MEMORIAL

Issued in 1922 to commemorate the 100th anniversary of Grant's birth. The obverse and reverse designs are the same as the half dollar.

	XF-AU	MS60
$1.00 Gold 1922 w/star	1500.00	1600.00
$1.00 Gold 1922 w/o star	1650.00	1699.00

SESQUICENTENNIAL OF AMERICAN INDEPENDENCE

Issued in 1926 to commemorate the 150th anniversary of the signing of the Declaration of Independence. The obverse has Liberty holding a scroll of the Declaration of Independence. The reverse shows Independence Hall.

	XF-AU	MS60
$2.50 Gold 1926	450.00	475.00

MODERN COMMEMORATIVES
GEORGE WASHINGTON MEMORIAL

Dated 1982 to commemorate the 150th anniversary of the birth of George Washington, the obverse shows Washington in full uniform mounted on a horse. While the reverse depicts his home at Mt. Vernon, Virginia.

	MS60	Proof
1982 D	8.00	
1982 S		8.00

Los Angeles Olympic

1984 PDS $10.00 Gold Olympic Coins
Issued to commemorate the 23rd Olympiad.

	MS60	Proof
1983 P Silver Dollar (Discus Thrower/Eagle)	18.00	
1983 D Silver Dollar (Discus Thrower/Eagle)	18.00	
1983 S Silver Dollar (Discus Thrower/Eagle)	18.00	18.00.
1984 P Silver Dollar (Coliseum/Eagle)	18.00	
1984 D Silver Dollar (Coliseum/Eagle)	18.00	
1984 S Silver Dollar (Coliseum/Eagle)	18.00	18.00
1984 P $10.00 Gold (Runners/Eagle)		450.00
1984 D $10.00 Gold (Runners/Eagle)		450.00
1984 S $10.00 Gold (Runners/Eagle)		450.00
1984 W $10.00 Gold (Runners/Eagle)	450.00	450.00

Statue of Liberty

1986 Dollar, Half Dollar and $5.00 Statue of Liberty Coins

Issued in 1986 on the 100th anniversary of the giving of the statue by France to the United States. The half dollar is clad with the obverse showing the statue welcoming a boatload of immigrants. The reverse shows an immigrant family on Ellis Island facing New York City. The dollar is stuck in .900 fine silver and shows the statue on the obverse. The reverse displays Liberty's torch. The gold $5 coin has Liberty's face on the obverse. The reverse shows a landing eagle.

	MS60	Proof
1986 D Clad Half	6.00	
1986 S " "		6.00
1986 P Silver Dollar	18.00	
1986 S " "		18.00
1986 W $5.00 Gold	235.00	235.00

CONSTITUTIONAL

Issued in 1987 to commemorate the 200th anniversary of the signing of the Constitution. The obverse of the $1 coin features the inscrip-tion, "We the People," superimposed on a sheaf of parchment and a quill pen. The reverse shows a cross-section of Americans from the past and present representing our country's political heritage. The obverse of the $5 gold coin shows an American eagle holding a quill pen. The reverse also displays the pen with a "We the People" inscription.

	MS60	Proof
1987 P Silver Dollar	18.00	
1987 S Silver Dollar	18.00	
1987 W $5.00 Gold	235.00	235.00

1988 OLYMPIC

Two U.S. coins were minted to commemorate the 1988 Olympics in Seoul, South Korea. The silver $1 coin depicts the passing of the Olympic flame to the Statue of Liberty torch. The reverse shows the Olympic rings. The obverse of the $5 gold coin portrays the Greek goddess of victory and the reverse displays the five Olympic rings above the Olympic flame.

	MS60	Proof
1988D Silver Dollar	18.00	
1988S Silver Dollar	18.00	
1988W $5.00 Gold	235.00	235.00

CONGRESSIONAL

Three coins were issued to celebrate the bicentennial of Congress. The obverse of the half dollar displays the bust of the statue atop the Capitol Building; the reverse shows the entire building. The dollar coin shows the entire statue, while on the reverse is found the mace of Congress. On the obverse of the $5 coin is the dome of the Capitol Building with a perched eagle on the reverse.

	MS60	Proof
1989D Half Dollar	8.00	
1989S Half Dollar		8.00
1989D Silver Dollar	18.00	
1989S Silver Dollar		18.00
1989W $5.00 Gold	235.00	235.00

EISENHOWER

Issued to commemorate the 100th anniversary of Dwight Eisenhower's birth. The obverse is a doubled portrait of Eisenhower as Commander of the Allied Forces and as President. The reverse shows the Eisenhower home.

	MS60	Proof
1990W Silver Dollar	18.00	
1990P Silver Dollar		18.00

Mount Rushmore

Issued to commemorate the golden anniversary of Mount Rushmore. The half dollar shows the memorial on the obverse. On the reverse is a standing bison. The dollar coin again has a full-faced view of the mountain's carvings on the obverse; the reverse has the Presidential Seal superimposed on a map of the United States. The $5 coin's obverse shows an eagle over the memorial. On the reverse is found the inscription, "Mount Rushmore National Memorial."

	MS60	Proof
1991D Half Dollar	19.00	
1991S Half Dollar		18.00
1991P Silver Dollar	30.00	
1991S Silver Dollar		33.00
1991W $5.00 Gold	235.00	235.00

Korean War

Issued to commemorate the 50th anniversary of the Korean War. The obverse shows a soldier fighting up a hill; the reverse displays a map of Korea.

	MS60	Proof
1991D Silver Dollar	18.00	
1990S Silver Dollar		18.00

USO Commemorative

Commemorating the 50th anniversary of the USO, the obverse of this coin shows the flag of the USO; the reverse displays an eagle perched on the globe.

	MS60	Proof
1991D Silver Dollar	18.00	
1991S Silver Dollar		19.00

1992 Olympic

Three U.S. coins were minted to commemorate the 1992 Olympics. The half dollar displays a gymnast on the obverse, and torch and olive branch on the reverse. The silver $1 coin's obverse depicts a baseball pitcher, while an original flag of the U.S. topped by the Olympic rings is found on the reverse. The obverse of the $5 gold coin portrays a track athlete and the reverse displays the five Olympic rings above an eagle.

	MS60	Proof
1992P Half Dollar	8.00	
1992S Half Dollar		8.00
1992D Silver Dollar	22.00	
1992S Silver Dollar		22.00
1992W $5.00 Gold	290.00	240.00

White House

Issued to commemorate the 200th anniversary of the White House, the obverse of this silver dollar shows a frontal view of the building; the reverse portrays a bust of James Hoban, its architect.

	MS60	Proof
1992D Silver Dollar	30.00	
1992W Silver Dollar		36.00

Columbus Quincentenary

Issued to commemorate the 500th anniversary of Columbus' first voyage. The obverse of the half dollar shows Columbus coming ashore; the reverse is a portrait of his ship. The one dollar coin shows Columbus standing with the flag of Spain on the obverse. The reverse again shows his sailing vessel. The five-dollar coin has a portrait of Columbus facing the New World on the obverse. The reverse shows an early map.

	MS60	Proof
1992D Half Dollar	11.00	
1992S Half Dollar	11.00	
1992D Silver Dollar	27.00	
1992P Silver Dollar	38.00	
1992W $5.00 Gold	300.00	235.00

Bill of Rights/Madison

Issued to commemorate the 200th anniversary of the Bill of Rights. The half dollar shows James Madison on the obverse; a torch on the re-verse. The dollar coin shows a bust of Madison on the obverse; his Montpelier home on the reverse. The $5 gold piece has Madison reading over the Rights on the obverse; the reverse is inscribed "Equal Laws Protecting Equal Rights Are The Best Guarantee Of Loyalty And Love Of Country."

	MS60	Proof
1993W Half Dollar	18.00	
1993S Half Dollar		15.00
1993D Silver Dollar	18.00	
1993S Silver Dollar		19.00
1993W $5.00 Gold	300.00	245.00

World War II

Issued to honor America's contribution to the Allied victory in World War II. The half dollar shows soldiers of three service branches superimposed over the victory "V." The reverse shows a soldier ashore on a Pacific island. The dollar coin displays the Normandy Invasion of June 6th, 1944 on the obverse. The reverse displays a quotation by Dwight D. Eisenhower. On the $5 gold coin's obverse is a triumphant soldier. The reverse again depicts the "V" of the allied victory. Surcharges from the sale of these commemoratives helped fund two World War II memorials—one in Washington, D.C.; the other in Normandy, France.

	MS60	Proof
1993P Half Dollar	25.00	
1993P Half Dollar		28.00
1993D Silver Dollar	30.00	
1993W Silver Dollar		35.00
1993W $5.00 Gold	360.00	300.00

World Cup Soccer

Issued to honor the hosting by the United States of the World Cup Soccer matches during the summer of 1994.

	MS60	Proof
1994D Half Dollar	9.00	
1994P Half Dollar		8.00
1994D Silver Dollar	24.00	
1994S Silver Dollar		27.00
1993W $5.00 Gold	350.00	300.00

JEFFERSON 200TH ANNIVERSARY

Issued on the 200th anniversary of Jefferson's presidency.

	MS60	Proof
1994P Silver Dollar	23.00	
1994S Silver Dollar		28.00

PRISONERS OF WAR MUSEUM

Issued to commemorate the opening of the Prisoners of War Museum.

	MS60	Proof
1994W Silver Dollar	80.00	
1994P Silver Dollar		40.00

VIETNAM VETERANS MEMORIAL

Issued to commemorate the Vietnam Veterans. The obverse shows the Memorial Wall placed between the Lincoln and Washington monuments. The reverse shows various medals awarded to veterans during the Vietnam era.

	MS60	Proof
1994W Silver Dollar	75.00	
1994P Silver Dollar		65.00

WOMEN IN THE MILITARY

Issued to commemorate the women who have served in each of the military branches.

	MS60	Proof
1994W Silver Dollar	75.00	
1994P Silver Dollar		65.00

CAPITOL BICENTENNIAL DOLLAR

Issued for the 200th anniversary of the Capitol building.

	MS60	Proof
1994D Silver Dollar	20.00	
1994S Silver Dollar		23.00

CIVIL WAR BATTLEFIELDS

A portion of the monies raised for this issue was used to refurbish various Civil War battlefields.

	MS60	Proof
1995D Half Dollar	40.00	
1995S Half Dollar		37.00
1995P Silver Dollar	65.00	
1995S Silver Dollar		75.00
1995W $5 Gold	750.00	400.00

SPECIAL OLYMPICS

Issued to commemorate the Special Olympics World Games.

	MS60	Proof
1995D Dollar	24.00	
1995S Dollar		25.00

1996 OLYMPICS [ISSUED IN 1995 AND 1996]

Issued to commemorate the 1996 Summer Olympics. The XXVI Olympiad was held in Atlanta.

	MS60	Proof
1995S Basketball Half Dollar	20.00	15.00
1995S Baseball Half Dollar	21.00	16.00
1995D Gymnastics Silver Dollar	65.00	
1995P Gymnastics Silver Dollar		50.00
1995D Cycling Silver Dollar	130.00	
1995P Cycling Silver Dollar		40.00
1995D Track & Field Silver Dollar	85.00	
1995P Track & Field Silver Dollar		45.00
1995D Blind Runner Silver Dollar	85.00	
1995P Blind Runner Silver Dollar		55.00
1995W Torch Runner $5 Gold	800.00	400.00
1995W Atlanta Stadium $5 Gold	1100.00	560.00
1996S Swimming Half Dollar	140.00	32.00
1996S Soccer Half Dollar	95.00	90.00
1996D Tennis Silver Dollar	275.00	
1996P Tennis Silver Dollar		80.00
1996D Rowing Silver Dollar	300.00	
1996P Rowing Silver Dollar		65.00
1996D High Jump Silver Dollar	340.00	
1996P High Jump Silver Dollar		52.00
1996D Wheelchair Athlete Silver Dollar	340.00	
1996P Wheelchair Athlete Silver Dollar		75.00
1996W Olympic Flame $5 Gold	950.00	520.00
1996W Flag bearer $5 Gold	950.00	525.00

SMITHSONIAN 150TH ANNIVERSARY

Issued to commemorate the Institution founded in 1846 for the "increase and question of knowledge."

	MS60	Proof
1996D and P Dollar	130.00	65.00
1996W $5 Gold	1200.00	600.00

NATIONAL COMMUNITY SERVICE

Issued to commemorate community service in the United States.

	MS60	Proof
1997D and S Dollar	240.00	80.00

BOTANICAL GARDENS

Issued to commemorate the U.S. Botanical Gardens pavilion.

	MS60	Proof
1997P Dollar	42.00	39.00

A Botanical Gardens Coin and Currency set was also issued. This set includes a matte proof Jefferson nickel, the $1 coin above and a 1997 Federal Reserve note.

The issue price for the set was $36. It is currently being sold for $225-$250 due to the limited mintage of only 25,000. In 1994 a similar set was issued with the Jefferson dollar. It included a 1994 matte proof Jefferson nickel and a 1976 $2 bill which portrays Thomas Jefferson on the obverse. This set currently sells for $120.

Jackie Robinson

Issued to commemorate the 50th anniversary of Robinson's debut in the major leagues.

	MS60	Proof
1997S Dollar	90.00	75.00
1997W $5 Gold	5000.00	700.00

Franklin Delano Roosevelt

Issued to commemorate the 100th anniversary of the birth of FDR. The irony of course is that it was Roosevelt who took us off the gold standard.

	MS60	Proof
1997 $5 Gold	750.00	475.00

Law Enforcement Officers

Issued to commemorate the memorial of those who "Serve and Protect."

	MS60	Proof
1997P Dollar	175.00	140.00

Robert F. Kennedy

Issued on the 30th anniversary of RFK's death.

	MS60	Proof
1998S Dollar	28.00	45.00

In addition, a set of two coins were issued containing a matte finished RFK dollar and a JFK half dollar. This set currently trades at around $125.

BLACK PATRIOTS

Minted to commemorate Black Revolutionary patriots. The obverse is a portrait of Crispus Attucks, the first patriot killed in the Boston Massacre of 1770.

	MS60	Proof
1998S Dollar	145.00	100.00

DOLLY MADISON

Minted to commemorate the important contributions of James Madison's wife in saving governmental artifacts as British troops were about to burn the White House.

	MS60	Proof
1999P Dollar	50.00	55.00

GEORGE WASHINGTON

Minted to celebrate the life and legacy of the "Father of His Country."

	MS60	Proof
1999W $5 Gold	400.00	390.00

YELLOWSTONE NATIONAL PARK

Issued to commemorate our most famous National Park.

	MS60	Proof
2000 Dollar	48.00	50.00

Library of Congress

Issued to commemorate the 200th anniversary of the Library of Congress.

	MS60	Proof
2000 Dollar	37.50	37.50

Leif Erickson Millennium

Issued to commemorate the "Founder of the New World."

	MS60	Proof
2000 Dollar	80.00	60.00

U.S. Capitol Visitor Center

Issued to celebrate the first meeting of Congress in the U.S. Capitol and to help build the first ever Visitor Center for the U.S. Capitol.

	MS60	Proof
2001 Half Dollar	2.00	15.00
2001 Dollar	35.00	35.00
2001 $5 Gold	1800.00	400.00

American Buffalo

A reproduction of one of this country's favorite coin designs—the Buffalo nickel.

	MS60	Proof
2001 Dollar	180.00	200.00
Coin & Currency Set	375.00	

2002 Olympic Winter Games

	MS60	Proof
2002 Silver Dollar	30.00	31.00

	MS60	Proof
2002 $5 Gold Coin	500.00	375.00

West Point

Issued for the 200th anniversary of West Point.

	MS60	Proof
2002 Dollar (W)	19.00	20.00

Lewis and Clark Bicentennial

Issued for the 200th anniversary of the exploration of the Louisiana Purchase.

	MS60	Proof
2004 Dollar	34.00	35.00
2005 Marines	38.00	39.00
2005 Justice Marshall	35.00	35.00
2006 Franklin Scientist	35.00	45.00
2006 Franklin Father	35.00	44.00
2006 San Francisco Mint	40.00	40.00

	MS60	Proof
2007 Little Rock HS	35.00	40.00
2007 Jamestown	35.00	35.00
2008 Bald Eagle Half Dollar	12.00	15.00
2008 Bald Eagle Dollar	35.00	40.00
2009 Abraham Lincoln	50.00	50.00
2009 Louis Braille	50.00	50.00

CHAPTER 7

OTHER SPECIAL ISSUES

Throughout the history of the U.S. coinage, the Mint has seen fit to issue, for a variety of special purposes, coins that exhibit the highest achievement of the minting process. Until 1936 these "proof" coins, as they were called, were issued sporadically and usually for the purposes of souvenir presentations and the like. Since 1936, proof sets have been made available for the general public with the exceptions of the years 1943-1949 and 1965-1967. Until 1964 these sets were issued by the Philadelphia Mint. Since 1968 they bear the San Francisco Mint mark. These recent sets have generally contained only regular issue coins. Special "prestige" sets in 1983-1984 and 1986-1997 have included appropriate commemorative coins. Each year from 1992-1998, four separate kinds of sets have been issued—the regular set, the prestige, the silver and the silver premier.

Proof coins are stuck under a process whereby a great deal of care is taken so that each coin is sharply struck with virtually no imperfections or flaws. Each planchant is struck and restruck by highly polished dies so as to guarantee a sharp impression. Proof coins, unless mishandled, often evidence a mirror-like field with frosty surfaces. However, as is the case with regularly issued coins, differences in condition can be found depending on die wear, care in packaging, etc.

Proof Sets

Prices for early proof coins are considerable, most often in excess of even the highest uncirculated grades. The sets issued since 1936 undergo periodic large price fluctuations. Currently, they are priced as follows:

Year	Price			
		1942		$1,200.00
1936	$6,500.00	1942	w/type 2 5c	$1,250.00
1937	$3,600.00	1950		$650.00
1938	$1,600.00	1951		$550.00
1939	$1,600.00	1952		$325.00
1940	$1,300.00	1953		$300.00
1941	$1,300.00	1954		$150.00

Year		Price	Year		Price
1955		$125.00	1985S		$6.00
1955	Flat	$150.00	1986S		$10.00
1956		$65.00	1986S	Prestige	$30.00
1957		$30.00	1987S		$5.00
1958		$55.00	1987S	Prestige	$25.00
1959		$28.00	1988S		$6.00
1960		$20.00	1988S	Prestige	$30.00
1960	SM date	$35.00	1989S		$7.00
1961		$14.00	1989S	Prestige	$35.00
1962		$14.00	1990S		$8.00
1963		$15.00	1990S	Prestige	$25.00
1964		$15.00	1991S		$12.00
1968S		$7.00	1991S	Prestige	$70.00
1969S		$7.00	1992S		$7.00
1970S		$10.00	1992S	Prestige	$75.00
1970S	SM Date	$100.00	1992S	Silver	$15.00
1971S		$6.00	1992S	Premier Silver	$15.00
1972S		$5.00	1993S		$12.00
1973S		$10.00	1993S	Prestige	$35.00
1974S		$10.00	1993S	Silver	$34.00
1975S		$13.00	1993S	Premier Silver	$34.00
1976S		$11.00	1994S		$12.00
1976S	3 pc. Silver	$16.00	1994S	Prestige	$45.00
1977S		$8.00	1994S	Silver	$40.00
1978S		$9.00	1994S	Premier Silver	$40.00
1979S		$8.00	1995S		$45.00
1980S		$8.00	1995S	Prestige	$150.00
1981S		$8.00	1995S	Silver	$90.00
1982S		$5.00	1995S	Premier Silver	$90.00
1983S		$7.00	1996S		$16.00
1983S	Prestige	$100.00	1996S	Prestige	$500.00
1984S		$8.00	1996S	Silver	$50.00
1984S	Prestige	$25.00	1996S	Premier Silver	$50.00

Year		Price	Year		Price
1997S		$40.00	2004S	Silver 5 quarter	$20.00
1997S	Prestige	$200.00	2005S	11-pc. set	$18.00
1997S	Silver	$75.00	2005S	5-quarter set	$15.00
1997S	Premier Silver	$75.00	2005S	Sil. 11-pc. Set	$35.00
1998S		$18.00	2005S	Silver 5 quarter	$25.00
1998S	Silver	$25.00	2006S	11-pc. set	$25.00
1998S	Premier Silver	$25.00	2006S	5-quarter set	$16.00
1999S	9-pc. Set	$70.00	2006S	Sil. 11-pc. Set	$35.00
1999S	5-quarter set	$65.00	2006S	Silver 5 quarter	$22.00
1999S	Sil. 9-pc. Set	$375.00	2007s	15-pc. set	$30.00
2000S	10-pc. set	$18.00	2007s	5-quarter set	$15.00
2000S	5-quarter set	$12.00	2007s	Sil. 11-pc. Set	$45.00
2000S	Sil. 10-pc. Set	$32.00	2007s	Silver 5 quarter	$20.00
2001S	10-pc. set	$120.00	2007s	Presidential Set	$20.00
2001S	5-quarter set	$55.00	2008s	15-pc. set	$60.00
2001S	Sil. 10-pc. Set	$155.00	2008s	5-quarter set	$60.00
2002S	10-pc. set	$30.00	2008s	Sil. 11-pc. Set	$20.00
2002S	5-quarter set	$22.00	2008s	Silver 5 quarter	$30.00
2002S	Sil. 10-pc. Set	$55.00	2008s	Presidential Set	$20.00
2003S	10-pc. set	$24.00	2009s	20-pc. set	$50.00
2003S	5-quarter set	$19.00	2009s	DC/Terr Quarters	$18.00
2003S	Sil. 10-pc. Set	$30.00	2009s	Sil. 11-pc. Set	$75.00
2004S	11-pc. set	$35.00	2009s	Silver quarters	$25.00
2004S	5-quarter set	$22.00	2009s	Presidential Set	$20.00
2004S	Sil. 11-pc. Set	$35.00			

MINT SETS

Since 1947 official uncirculated sets of coins from each mint have been packaged for sale to collectors. Until 1959 each set contained two examples of each regularly issued coin, placed in small cardboard holders. This original packaging is important since the "official" mint sets sell for a bit more than privately assembled sets.

Beginning in 1959 uncirculated coin sets come sealed in plastic envelopes and contain only one example of each date and mint mark.

Only in the years 1965 through 1967 has any special care been taken by the mint to insure that better quality coins were used to make up the sets. This was likely done in lieu of proof sets which were not produced in those years.

Year	Price	Year		Price
1947	$1,250.00	1972		$7.00
1948	$675.00	1973		$20.00
1949	$850.00	1974		$7.00
1951	$850.00	1975		$10.00
1952	$800.00	1976		$9.00
1953	$500.00	1976	3pc. Silver	$15.00
1954	$250.00	1977		$8.00
1955	$175.00	1978		$8.00
1956	$175.00	1979		$7.00
1957	$250.00	1980		$7.00
1958	$160.00	1981		$15.00
1959	$55.00	1984		$6.25
1960	$30.00	1985		$6.50
1961	$50.00	1986		$17.00
1962	$28.00	1987		$8.00
1963	$28.00	1988		$8.00
1964	$28.00	1989		$6.00
1965	$11.00	1990		$7.00
1966	$11.00	1991		$9.00
1967	$18.00	1992		$6.00
1968	$5.50	1993		$8.00
1969	$8.00	1994		$8.00
1970	$20.00	1995		$18.00
1970	SM Date	$50.00	1996	$25.00
1971	$6.00	1997		$28.00

1998	$10.00	2004	$55.00
1999	$25.00	2005	$15.00
2000	$11.00	2006	$20.00
2001	$15.00	2007	$30.00
2002	$13.00	2008	$30.00
2003	$22.00	2009	

U.S. BULLION COINS

Silver Eagles

The one-ounce silver bullion coin is denominated "One Dollar." The obverse is a design virtually identical to the Liberty Walking half dollar last issued in 1947. The reverse displays the eagle with shield. Thus the coin is nicknamed the "silver eagle."

Silver Eagles (Silver at $17.50/ounce)

Year	Denomination	MS60	Proof
1986	$1	$20.00	$35.00
1987	$1	$20.00	$35.00
1988	$1	$20.00	$42.00
1989	$1	$20.00	$35.00
1990	$1	$22.00	$35.00
1991	$1	$22.00	$50.00
1992	$1	$22.00	$40.00
1993	$1	$22.00	$175.00
1994	$1	$20.00	$200.00
1995	$1	$22.00	$180.00
1995W	$1		$4,500.00
1996	$1	$55.00	$125.00
1997	$1	$22.00	$125.00

1998	$1	$22.00	$40.00
1999	$1	$20.00	$45.00
2000	$1	$21.00	$40.00
2001	$1	$20.00	$35.00
2002	$1	$20.00	$35.00
2003	$1	$20.00	$35.00
2004	$1	$20.00	$35.00
2005	$1	$20.00	$35.00
2006	$1	$20.00	$35.00
2006 w	$1	$75.00	
2006 Reverse Proof	$1		$250.00
2007	$1	$20.00	$35.00
2007 w	$1	$25.00	$50.00
2008	$1	$22.00	$30.00
2008 w	$1	$30.00	$80.00
2009	$1	$20.00	
2009 w	$1		

AMERICAN EAGLE GOLD COIN
1986 - PRESENT

GOLD COINS

S ince 1986 the United States has minted gold pieces in various denominations called Eagles to compete with similar bullion coins issued by other countries such as South Africa (Krugerrand) and Canada (Maple Leaf). These pieces have not been minted in order to circulate but rather to provide convenient units of value for the possession of the precious metal. However, the coins are denominated and, presumably, are legal tender. The obverse of all four denominations is reminiscent of the $20 Saint-Gaudens gold piece issued until 1933. The reverse shows an eagle landing on a nest.

Gold Coins   (Chapter 10)   (Gold at $900/ounce)

Year	Denomination	Size	MS60	Proof
1986	$5.00	1/10 oz.	$100.00	None made
1986	$10.00	1/4 oz.	$230.00	None made
1986	$25.00	1/2 oz.	$450.00	None made
1986	$50.00	1 oz.	$900.00	$1,010.00
1987	$5.00	1/10 oz.	$100.00	None made
1987	$10.00	1/4 oz.	$230.00	None made
1987	$25.00	1/2 oz.	$450.00	$525.00
1987	$50.00	1 oz.	$900.00	$1,010.00
1988	$5.00	1/10 oz.	$200.00	$130.00
1988	$10.00	1/4 oz.	$230.00	$275.00
1988	$25.00	1/2 oz.	$540.00	$525.00
1988	$50.00	1 oz.	$925.00	$1,010.00
1989	$5.00	1/10 oz.	$95.00	$105.00
1989	$10.00	1/4 oz.	$235.00	$275.00
1989	$25.00	1/2 oz.	$650.00	$750.00
1989	$50.00	1 oz.	$900.00	$1,010.00
1990	$5.00	1/10 oz.	$95.00	$105.00
1990	$10.00	1/4 oz.	$235.00	$275.00
1990	$25.00	1/2 oz.	$775.00	$525.00
1990	$50.00	1 oz.	$900.00	$1,010.00

Year	Denomination	Size	MS60	Proof
1991	$5.00	1/10 oz.	$125.00	$105.00
1991	$10.00	1/4 oz.	$325.00	$275.00
1991	$25.00	1/2 oz.	$1,300.00	$525.00
1991	$50.00	1 oz.	$900.00	$1,010.00
1992	$5.00	1/10 oz.	$95.00	$105.00
1992	$10.00	1/4 oz.	$235.00	$275.00
1992	$25.00	1/2 oz.	$525.00	$525.00
1992	$50.00	1 oz.	$900.00	$1,010.00
1993	$5.00	1/10 oz.,	$95.00	$105.00
1993	$10.00	1/4 oz.	$235.00	$275.00
1993	$25.00	1/2 oz.	$460.00	$525.00
1993	$50.00	1 oz.	$900.00	$1,010.00
1994	$5.00	1/10 oz.	$95.00	$105.00
1994	$10.00	1/4 oz.	$235.00	$275.00
1994	$25.00	1/2 oz.	$460.00	$525.00
1994	$50.00	1 oz.	$900.00	$1,010.00
1995	$5.00	1/10 oz.	$95.00	$105.00
1995	$10.00	1/4 oz.	$235.00	$275.00
1995	$25.00	1/2 oz.	$460.00	$525.00
1995	$50.00	1 oz.	$900.00	$1,010.00
1995	10th Anniversary Set			$6,500.00
1996	$5.00	1/10 oz.	$95.00	$105.00
1996	$10.00	1/4 oz.	$235.00	$275.00
1996	$25.00	1/2 oz.	$460.00	$525.00
1996	$50.00	1 oz.	$900.00	$1,010.00
1997	$5.00	1/10 oz.	$95.00	$105.00
1997	$10.00	1/4 oz.	$235.00	$275.00
1997	$25.00	1/2 oz.	$460.00	$525.00
1997	$50.00	1 oz.	$900.00	$1,010.00

Year	Denomination	Size	MS60	Proof
1998	$5.00	1/10 oz.	$95.00	$105.00
1998	$10.00	1/4 oz.	$235.00	$275.00
1998	$25.00	1/2 oz.	$460.00	$525.00
1998	$50.00	1 oz.	$900.00	$1,010.00
1999	$5.00	1/10 oz.	$95.00	$105.00
1999	$10.00	1/4 oz.	$235.00	$275.00
1999	$25.00	1/2 oz.	$465.00	$525.00
1999	$50.00	1 oz.	$900.00	$1,010.00
2000	$5.00	1/10 oz.	$95.00	$105.00
2000	$10.00	1/4 oz.	$235.00	$275.00
2000	$25.00	1/2 oz.	$460.00	$525.00
2000	$50.00	1 oz.	$900.00	$1,010.00
2001	$5.00	1/10 oz.	$95.00	$105.00
2001	$10.00	1/4 oz.	$235.00	$275.00
2001	$25.00	1/2 oz.	$460.00	$525.00
2001	$50.00	1 oz.	$900.00	$1,010.00
2002	$5.00	1/10 oz.	$95.00	$105.00
2002	$10.00	1/4 oz.	$235.00	$275.00
2002	$25.00	1/2 oz.	$460.00	$525.00
2002	$50.00	1 oz.	$900.00	$1,010.00
2003	$5.00	1/10 oz.	$95.00	$105.00
2003	$10.00	1/4 oz.	$235.00	$275.00
2003	$25.00	1/2 oz.	$460.00	$525.00
2003	$50.00	1 oz.	$900.00	$1,010.00
2004	$5.00	1/10 oz.	$95.00	$105.00
2004	$10.00	1/4 oz.	$235.00	$275.00
2004	$25.00	1/2 oz.	$460.00	$525.00
2004	$50.00	1 oz.	$900.00	$1,010.00

Year	Denomination	Size	MS60	Proof
2005	$5.00	1/10 oz.	$95.00	$105.00
2005	$10.00	1/4 oz.	$235.00	$275.00
2005	$25.00	1/2 oz.	$460.00	$525.00
2005	$50.00	1 oz.	$900.00	$1,010.00
2006	$5.00	1/10 oz.	$95.00	$105.00
2006	$10.00	1/4 oz.	$235.00	$275.00
2006	$25.00	1/2 oz.	$460.00	$525.00
2006	$50.00	1 oz.	$900.00	$1,010.00
2007	$5.00	1/10 oz.	$95.00	$105.00
2007	$10.00	1/4 oz.	$235.00	$275.00
2007	$25.00	1/2 oz.	$460.00	$525.00
2007	$50.00	1 oz.	$900.00	$1,010.00
2008	$5.00	1/10 oz.	$95.00	$105.00
2008	$10.00	1/4 oz.	$235.00	$275.00
2008	$25.00	1/2 oz.	$460.00	$525.00
2008	$50.00	1 oz.	$900.00	$1,010.00
2009	$5.00	1/10 oz.		
2009	$10.00	1/4 oz.		
2009	$25.00	1/2 oz.		
2009	$50.00	1 oz.		
Gold Buffalo 1oz				
2006w	Buffalo	1 oz.	$1,010.00	$1,200.00
2007w	Buffalo	1 oz.	$1,010.00	$1,200.00
2008w	Buffalo	1 oz.	$1,010.00	$1,200.00
2009 w	Buffalo	1 oz.		

United States Gold Bison
1oz. Coin

AMERICAN EAGLE PLATINUM COINS

Platinum Coins—Platinum at $1250/ounce

The year 1997 marked the inaugural issue of the American Eagle Platinum coins. issues are mint and proof.

Year	Denomination	MS65	Proof
1997	$10.00	$205.00	$210.00
1997	$25.00	$515.00	$525.00
1997	$50.00	$1,025.00	$1,040.00
1997	$100.00	$2,050.00	$2,075.00
1998	$10.00	$205.00	$210.00
1998	$25.00	$515.00	$525.00
1998	$50.00	$1,025.00	$1,040.00
1998	$100.00	$2,050.00	$2,075.00
1999	$10.00	$205.00	$210.00
1999	$25.00	$515.00	$525.00
1999	$50.00	$1,025.00	$1,040.00
1999	$100.00	$2,050.00	$2,075.00
2000	$10.00	$205.00	$210.00
2000	$25.00	$515.00	$525.00
2000	$50.00	$1,025.00	$1,040.00
2000	$100.00	$2,050.00	$2,075.00
2001	$10.00	$205.00	$210.00
2001	$25.00	$515.00	$525.00
2001	$50.00	$1,025.00	$1,040.00
2001	$100.00	$2,050.00	$2,075.00
2002	$10.00	$205.00	$210.00
2002	$25.00	$515.00	$525.00

2002	$50.00	$1,025.00	$1,040.00
2002	$100.00	$2,050.00	$2,075.00
2003	$10.00	$205.00	$210.00
2003	$25.00	$515.00	$525.00
2003	$50.00	$1,025.00	$1,040.00
2003	$100.00	$2,050.00	$2,075.00
2004	$10.00	$205.00	$825.00
2004	$25.00	$500.00	$1,500.00
2004	$50.00	$1,000.00	$2,500.00
2004	$100.00	$2,050.00	$2,750.00
2005	$10.00	$205.00	$210.00
2005	$25.00	$515.00	$525.00
2005	$50.00	$1,025.00	$1,040.00
2005	$100.00	$2,050.00	$2,075.00
2006	$10.00	$205.00	$210.00
2006	$25.00	$515.00	$525.00
2006	$50.00	$1,025.00	$1,040.00
2006	$100.00	$2,050.00	$2,075.00
2007	$10.00	$205.00	$210.00
2007	$25.00	$515.00	$525.00
2007	$50.00	$1,025.00	$1,040.00
2007	$100.00	$2,050.00	$2,075.00
2008	$10.00	$205.00	$210.00
2008	$25.00	$515.00	$525.00
2008	$50.00	$1,025.00	$1,040.00
2008	$100.00	$2,050.00	$2,075.00
2009	$10.00		
2009	$25.00		
2009	$50.00		
2009	$100.00		

Bullion coins cannot be ordered directly from the mint. Over 1,000 outlets are listed in a special mint publication entitled, "American Eagle Buyer's Guide." This brochure can be acquired by calling 1-800-USA-GOLD. Also, the order form for U.S. Mint Sets mentioned above has a section for requesting the brochure by mail. Recent provisions in federal tax law allow for the inclusion of American Eagle bullion coins in a qualified Individual Retirement Account — the only tangible asset permitted by law in an IRA.

U.S. Gold Bullion Medal/Coins

The original attempt by the U.S. Government to compete for the millions of dollars that were being used to purchase foreign bullion gold coins was to issue the American Arts Gold Medallion. Complicated ordering procedures, medal-like appearance and the lack of legal tender status doomed the project almost from the start.

The medallions honored various persons from the arts, writers, etc. Issued in one-ounce and half-ounce sizes, the series lasted from 1980-1984.

Year	Size	Obverse Portrait	Mint State
1980	1/2 oz.	Marian Anderson	550.00
1981	1/2 oz.	Willa Cather	550.00
1982	1/2 oz.	Frank Lloyd Wright	550.00
1983	1/2 oz.	Alexander Calder	550.00
1984	1/2 oz.	John Steinbeck	550.00
1980	1 oz.	Grant Wood	1100.00
1981	1 oz.	Mark Twain	1100.00
1982	1 oz.	Louis Armstrong	1100.00
1983	1 oz.	Robert Frost	1100.00
1984	1 oz.	Helen Hayes	1100.00

The price of medallions is, of course, bullion sensitive.

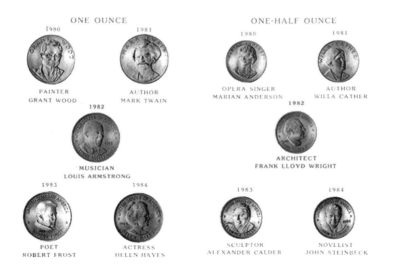

ONE OUNCE

1980 — PAINTER GRANT WOOD
1981 — AUTHOR MARK TWAIN
1982 — MUSICIAN LOUIS ARMSTRONG
1983 — POET ROBERT FROST
1984 — ACTRESS HELEN HAYES

ONE-HALF OUNCE

1980 — OPERA SINGER MARIAN ANDERSON
1981 — AUTHOR WILLA CATHER
1982 — ARCHITECT FRANK LLOYD WRIGHT
1983 — SCULPTOR ALEXANDER CALDER
1984 — NOVELIST JOHN STEINBECK

CHAPTER 8

WHERE TO FIND COINS

Was it easier to find interesting coins in circulation years ago? The answer is most certainly yes. Back in the early 1960's, when I first began collecting coins, you could find many more types of coins in pocket change and a much wider selection of dates on the coins received in change. One could still find an occasional Indian Head cent, Liberty V Nickel, or Barber dime from the 1800's. Living in a small city in Wisconsin, I was able to find a considerable variety of coins through my paper route. Everyone paid in change, and it was very common for me to have shiny, full-date Walking Liberty Half Dollars or Standing Liberty Quarters handed to me as payment each week. One customer of mine, who knew I was interested in coins allowed to reach into a big jar of old coins she had saved and pull out a few pennies or a nickel as a tip each week. It did not take long for me to put together a complete date set of Indian Head Pennies and Liberty V Nickels. Early Lincoln cents and Buffalo nickels were so common that they were almost not worth saving. It was not until I bought my first Red Book (a used one at that) that I began to notice the premium values that many of these coins brought!

When my paper route no longer provided me with enough change to search for that elusive complete set, I would go to my local coin shop and try to trade in a few of the more valuable extra Indian Head Cents or Nickels I had put aside, in order to fill those last few holes in my penny, nickel and dime collections. Back in those days, one only needed about 100 different Lincoln cents to complete the set. Quarters and Halves were interesting, but way out of my league. I can also remember riding my bicycle to the bank downtown to obtain a few rolls of coins to search through. I could always find a couple of "good dates" in nearly every roll.

The 1922 no D Lincoln Penny and 1916 D Mercury Dime were the highlights of these early years. Amazed, as I think back, must have been my parents when their son would be found occasionally searching through a bag of fifty-cent pieces. One thousand dollars would have been transported without benefit of an armed guard to the family kitchen table. There is something to be said for having one's entire fortune within one's immediate grasp.

Those days are gone. Virtually every coin I touched then now sells for a premium over face, albeit in most cases a small one.

Are there finds that can be made today from pocket change or an occasional trip to the bank? Probably not. There are reports from lucky collectors who have been fortunate enough to have found a coin or two probably spent by a child from a parent's collection. Then, too, sometimes some silver coins get rolled up and deposited by someone unaware of their value. But I have to think such occurrences are extremely rare these days.

Coins in circulation, however, still provide a place to start. Try this experiment. Save your pocket change for several months. Then some evening take out all the coins you have saved to see what might be there. You can probably find most cents minted for circulation since 1959. You will find an array of Jefferson nickels from the 1950s through the 1980s, dimes and quarters from 1965 to 1993. No halves or dollar coins, although the bank may have a few. No Lincoln wheat pennies (before 1958), and, alas, no silver!

An error coin or two may come your way. A slightly double-struck coin or one with a minute die crack may pique your interest along the lines of errors, freaks, and other oddities.

But at least you now have some idea of what is available from this source and what is not. That's the bad news. The good news is that many other coins can be obtained for a minimal amount over face. Their cost is so reasonable that it would have hardly made sense to search the coins in circulation for them.

Other more fruitful places to continue your search might be desks or bureau drawers and jewelry boxes. Almost everyone during their lifetime has set aside an interesting coin or two, received as a gift or kept as a little memento of an event now long forgotten. You will do well to ask other family members or friends concerning such small keepsakes. In most cases there will be an emotional attachment to the item, but at least you might persuade the owner to let you find out about the coin. In some cases since the value will be

Minimal, the owner may well decide that your new-found appreciation deserves to be encouraged.

Metal detecting is undoubtedly a hobby in its own right. But the obvious connection to coin collecting is evident with that initial find of a coin that is apparently one not currently found in circulation. Hobbyists of this ilk may soon find themselves researching county records that provide clues as to the sites of previous schools, businesses, and industries. The grounds of such places provide the opportunity to unearth coins that may be quite old, lost by playing children or customers and employees in a rush.

These more solitary pursuits, while rewarding, can take you only so far. Your next source might be other collectors. Contact a family member whom you know is a collector or attends the next meeting of your local coin club. Become price savvy — try to have a basic range of what coins are worth (What is the silver value of a Mercury Dime? At 12 times face, you know that it would cost at least $1.20 but what about the upper end?)

Nothing discourages the desire to collect coins more than overpaying for the first few of them. You may want to subscribe to a numismatic paper or magazine. Get an idea of what is available, prices, condition, terms, etc., from the many ads that appear there.

Every collector has more duplicates than he or she will ever need. You may begin by buying a few wheat pennies or a circulated silver dollar or two. Your accumulation will grow surprisingly fast. But don't let it run too far ahead of your accumulation of information. Research your purchases. Find out everything you can about the peculiarities of each coin. Learn about where and how and why it was minted. Develop a consciousness with regard to its value.

Other collectors cannot always provide the specific coins that you may wish to acquire. At that time you may wish to enlist the services of a dealer. There are thousands out there to help you. Some are willing to educate you as you make purchases, some are not. And, of course, as is possible in any business dealing, the opportunity to make a really poor purchase is forever lurking out there. In Chapter 13, I shall discuss in more detail suggestions for buying coins. There are some obvious things to do and avoid.

One last source, more for the acquisition of newly minted and specially struck coins, is the U.S. Mint itself.

Over the last two decades the Mint has struck coins commemorating the 250th anniversary of Washington's birth (a half dollar in 1982), the 1984 Olympic Games ($1 and $10 gold coin), the 200th anniversary of the Statue of Liberty (a half dollar, $1, and $5 gold coin in 1986), and the 200th anniversary of the Constitution ($1 and $5 gold coin in 1987).

The 1988 U.S. Olympic coins, to commemorate the Summer Games in Korea, were available (a silver dollar and $5 gold coin). The Bill of Rights and World War II commemoratives could be ordered from the Mint just last year. More commemoratives have been issued through 2002.

In addition, each year the Mint issues proof and mint sets along the lines of coins placed in general circulation for that year (some with special mint marks), various dated bullion coins, and even a number of medals (See Chapter 10).

Proof sets and special commemoratives are easily acquired and are beautifully struck. As I mention elsewhere, recent issues have not always held their value very well, but for a beginning collector the thrill of receiving these official coins directly from the Mint cannot be discounted.

Modern coins are finally getting their "due". Tracking the regular mint issue each year is nearly enough to keep the new collector busy with their numismatic interests. The 2009 US Mint Set could easily be 38 coins (19 each from Philadelphia and Denver). Add in the President's wives, the Gold, Silver, and Platinum Eagles, the Buffalo Gold coin, the St. Gaudien's high relief issue, - and then do it all again in Proof strikes. The US Mint is a treasure house for the new collector.

CHAPTER 9

STARTING A COLLECTION

Many people who refer to themselves as "coin collectors" are really coin accumulators. I suppose this happens to most of us simply because we have no clear plan for the direction we want our collecting to take. We change our mind concerning what interests us. We tend to buy what is available or offered without much thought as to the scope of what we want to achieve.

A collection presumes order and direction toward a certain degree of completeness. Collecting by date and mint mark has traditionally been a way to assemble 19th and 20th century series.

For example, a Jefferson nickel set is composed of 194 pieces dated from 1938 to 2009 The "S" mintmarked coins from 1968 to the present exist only in proof and, therefore, must come from the proof sets of those years. They are not expensive but since they were not struck for circulation, acquiring them demands a purchase.

Throughout the rest of the set, there are just a few key dates. However, no coin retails for more than $6 in circulated condition. The entire set retails for about $50 although such a purchase would short-circuit the pleasure of assembling the set piece by piece. Also lost would be the knowledge acquired as an accidental feature of checking mintages and seeing the variety of conditions and pricing available.

More often today, collectors are more interested in acquiring coins by type, if for no other reason than the high cost of assembling every date and/or mint mark of some series. Essentially, this means picking a representative coin from each of the various series minted. Some series have fairly substantial design changes within them, so some decisions have to be made concerning how major such a change must be in order for the coin to be considered a different type. Changes in alloy complicate the matter also. The definition of the "type" might have broadened to include such changes.

A complete set of 20th century type coins (excluding gold coins) would make an interesting and fairly challenging "starter" type set. Such a set would include:

    $ .01 Indian (dated after 1899)
    $ .01 Lincoln (wheat reverse before 1959)
    $ .01 Lincoln (zinc-coated steel, 1943)
    $ .01 Lincoln (cartridge case alloy, 1944-46)
    $ .01 Lincoln (Memorial reverse after 1958)
    $ .01 Lincoln (copper-plated zinc, 1982-87)
    $ .05 Liberty (dated after 1899)
    $ .05 Buffalo (raised ground, 1913)
    $ .05 Buffalo (non-raised ground, 1913-1938)
    $ .05 Jefferson (copper-nickel alloy)
    $ .05 Jefferson (copper-silver alloy, 1942-45)
    $ .10 Barber (dated after 1899)
    $ .10 Mercury (1916-1945)
    $ .10 Roosevelt (90% silver, 1946-1964)
    $ .10 Roosevelt (clad 1965-date)
    $ .25 Barber (dated after 1899)
    $ .25 Standing Liberty (1916-1917)
    $ .25 Standing Liberty (redesigned, 1917-1930)
    $ .25 Washington (90% silver 1932-1964)
    $ .25 Washington (clad 1965-date)
    $ .25 Washington
      (Bicentennial design dated 1776-1976, clad, 40% silver)
    $ .50 Barber (dated after 1899)
    $ .50 Walking Liberty (1916-1947)
    $ .50 Franklin (1948-1963)
    $ .50 Kennedy (90% silver, 1964)
    $ .50 Kennedy (40% silver, 1965-1970)
    $ .50 Kennedy (clad, 1971-date)
    $ .50 Kennedy
      (Bicentennial design dated 1776-1976, clad and 40% silver)
    $1.00 Morgan (dated after 1899)
    $1.00 Peace (1921-1935)
    $1.00 Eisenhower (1971-1978)
    $1.00 Eisenhower (1971-1978, 40% silver)
    $1.00 Eisenhower
      (Bicentennial design dated 1776-1976, clad and 40% silver)
    $1.00 Anthony (1979-1999)
    $1.00 Sacagewa (2000-date)

The alloy differences might well be ignored making for complete sets of considerably fewer coins. A much more expensive, although not difficult, challenge would involve collecting an example of each denomination of coin that has been minted—half cent to $20 gold. (15 coins in all).

Basic Coin Knowledge

However, no matter what directions your collecting interests take you, the most important thing you can do is to keep your knowledge of coins a pace with the monies spent on the coins themselves. Put together a small library as you go. Essential are the following:

A book on grading coins.
A comprehensive catalog.
A comprehensive almanac and history of U.S. coinage.
A weekly or monthly paper or magazine.
A volume on the aesthetic considerations of U.S. coins.
A volume on coin investing.

The following is a list of sources that would be suitable for such a beginning library: One item in each category.

1. Coins 2010. Steve Nolte. Frederick Fell Publishers, Inc., Hollywood, FL (2009) Price $18.95 Published since 1943, Fells is the Definitive US Coin Guide. www.Fellpub.com

2. A Guidebook of United States Coins. R.S. Yeoman, Whitman Publishing, LLC, Atlanta, GA Price $14.95. Commonly referred to as the "Redbook" published every year since 1947 www.whitmanbooks.com

3. Official American Numismatic Association Grading Standards for United States Coins (Sixth Edition) Kenneth Bressett. Whitman Publishing, LLC, Atlanta, GA Price $16.95. (2005) www,whitmanbooks.com

4. Walter Breen's Complete Encyclopedia of US and Colonial Coins. Walter Breen, Doubleday, New York 1988 Price $125.00

5. Coin World Weekly newsmagazine published by Amos Press, Sidney, Ohio 1 (800) 253-4555 Price $49.95 for 52 issues.

6. Numismatic News Weekly newsmagazine published by Krause Publications, Iola, WI www.numismaticnews.net. Price $35.99 for 52 issues

A more extensive list of sources will be found in Chapter 13.

BASIC COIN SUPPLIES AND ACCESSORIES

The coin board is an ingenious and inexpensive device for helping you bring some order to your ever growing collection. The task of filling the holes is at once finite and seductive. The most basic kind of coin board or folder costs about $1.95. Prices for more elaborate ones, usually purchased for better grade coins, can range up to $10 and even $50 for some of the fancy plastic holders.

Keeping track of duplicates and other coins you want to save can be done in a variety of ways. Small 2" x 2" coin envelopes and several styles of transparent holders are available. The most recent of these is called a "vinyl flip," actually two adjoining clear pockets, one for the coin another for inserting a small sheet for descriptions and pricing information. Retail they cost from $40-$45/1,000. Any of the above can be placed in specially made vinyl sheets or coin boxes.

Plastic tubes can be purchased to hold rolls or part rolls of coins of current denominations. These are priced at $.20 to $.25 each.

A good 10 or 20 power magnifying glass is a must for any sort of precise grading.

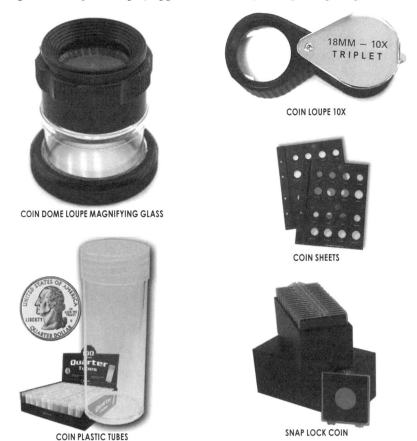

COIN LOUPE 10X

COIN DOME LOUPE MAGNIFYING GLASS

COIN SHEETS

COIN PLASTIC TUBES

SNAP LOCK COIN

CHAPTER 10

HOW TO BUY COINS
Coin Shops and Coin Shows

A collector's first exposure to someone from whom he will buy coins in any systematic way used to be the traditional neighborhood coin dealer. Most coin shops these days have diversified into other collectibles including stamps, baseball cards, political buttons, and almost anything else you can think of. Some may even remind you more of precious metal and money exchanges. A few do considerable business in gold and silver jewelry. But many still exist.

With all this in mind, it is no wonder that a first experience with a coin dealer can be somewhat disappointing. If he or she is busy selling 10-ounce silver bars he may have little patience with a collector who wishes to pursue his stock of late date Lincolns. Don't be discouraged. Visit several shops. You will eventually find a dealer who is interested in bringing you along as a collector and customer.

Plan to educate yourself as you proceed to buy coins in his shop. Ask questions about grading standards. Compare prices.

If a dealer does not have the coin you are looking for in stock, suggest that he attempt to find one for you. Once you are reasonably comfortable with a particular dealer, you might even supply him with a small want list of coins you are very interested in buying. Good etiquette demands that you give such a list to only one dealer at a time, since he will presume that if the coin meets your standards you will very likely purchase it. Obviously, you would not likely intend to purchase the same coin from several dealers.

Other collectors will also likely be willing to sell coins to you from time to time. And clearly you should be able to get a somewhat better price from a collector since he does not incur a dealer's usual costs of doing business.

Paying that lesser price, however, is a double-edged sword. Most collectors will be less willing than a dealer to allow you to return purchases. Also, you will not have near the leverage to satisfactorily clear up any dispute that may arise concerning a purchase. The law looks differently at private party transactions. You will do well to make very clear the conditions for the return of any coins sold to you.

Once you become a bonafide member of your local coin club, the club itself will open to you a variety of ways to purchase coins.

Other members can offer you duplicate coins from their particular specialty that even many dealers would have in stock on only a sporadic basis.

Some members will, in fact, be part-time dealers, sometimes called "vest-pocket" dealers. They will have no shop, maybe any business cards or pricelists. Seldom will they have a retail sales license.

The commodity they are selling is price. Often coins can be purchased from an entrepreneur of this sort at or near the prevailing dealer "buy prices" (See Chapter 2 for a discussion and explanation of prices).

Making deals in such circles is probably best conducted by an experienced collector. A vest-pocket dealer, given his small markups, is considerably less inclined to spend a great deal of time educating his customer. At the prices he charges he can just as easily sell to a dealer and minimize any problems that arise due to the ignorance of the prospective buyer.

Coin clubs will also sponsor courses, where several, and sometimes up to hundreds of dealers are invited to set up tables and display their coins for sale.

Regular lists of the dates of these events are published in most coin papers. The benefits to the collector are obvious. Having so many dealers available makes for a much more efficient way to search for coins and coin knowledge.

Your first visit to a large "coin show," as they are sometimes called, will likely be an overwhelming experience. Millions of dollars worth of coins piled in display trays, bags of coins on the floor behind dealer tables, the unusual racket made by a machine counting junk silver, and armed guards everywhere are just some of the things you will see and hear. And here you will be looking for a 1950D nickel!

But don't return to your car in embarrassment. There will be someone on the floor to help you. Take your time. Get acquainted with a few dealers from your area. You may want to visit their shops at a later date, since in this environment it may be difficult to ask all the questions you want. Also, these dealers may very well have other things to show you that they did not bring along.

Peruse the tables to get a sense of grading and pricing by the various dealers. You will undoubtedly be startled by huge discrepancies on both counts.

BUYING BY MAIL

For collectors who live in areas where there are no local dealers, and coin shows are quite difficult to attend, buying coins online or by mail is a relatively painless alternative.

Coin magazines and newspapers are filled with ads for every conceivable coin. Read them carefully and compare. Be aware of the terms. These will include costs for postage and handling, appropriate sales taxes, return privileges, the manner in which payment should be made, etc. Often a toll-free number will be listed for convenience in ordering.

Since there can be a considerable delay between the time an ad is placed and the time it actually appears in print, it usually does not hurt to confirm the prices of coins that may be of interest. This would be especially true of coins whose prices are bullion sensitive.

You may also wish to take notice of the professional organizations to which a dealer belongs. Membership is often prominently displayed in an ad. And such may well provide a safety net for any disputes that may arise concerning transactions. A significant drawback to buying by mail has to buy sight unseen. This problem is magnified with an initial purchase since grading standards vary so. Showing a coin around to collector friends for other opinions makes sense. Trial and error adds to the expense of buying. But there is no real substitute for it.

Asking another dealer for an opinion concerning a coin you have bought by mail is somewhat more problematic. I think it puts a dealer on the spot and I do not recommend it for that reason. Any negative remark could be construed as sour grapes, as in, "Why not buy this coin from me?" On the other hand, positive comments could well be interpreted as encouragement to continue dealing with the other firm. What dealer wants to be put in such a dilemma?

Returning coins purchased by mail is not an inexpensive proposition, although the costs would certainly be less than a drive to the local coin shop.

The U.S. Postal Service offers two ways to protect you in mailing shipments of value. Postal "insurance" can be purchased in various increments to $5000. An amount of $500 costs around $8 plus postage. Registered mail runs around $8 plus postage for $500 and shipments of considerable value (up to $25,000) can be fully covered.

Registered mail is the preferred method for valuable coins that you may not want to get lost or tampered with. Both services insure the items and will cover the dollars lost. I've only had one package lost by the post office and insurance reimbursed me efficiently and fully. Both services are very reliable.

Returning or sending coins via certified mail makes no sense, although I know it is occasionally done. No insurance claim can be made for such delivery. "Certified" merely means that the delivery will be signed for. If it is damaged or lost, the sender has little or no recourse. Most use delivery confirmation any more. It is inexpensive, and lets you know that the package arrived at its destination.

Other carriers, Federal Express, DHL Courier, etc. will carry numismatic packages, but the insured limits are quite low, ranging from $50 to $500.

UPS says that it will not be liable for shipments of numismatic items (rare coins) or gold and silver bullion. These terms seem to permit the insured shipment of pennies and nickels having no numismatic value. Presumably, one could ship a bag of wheat pennies and recover at least the $50 face value should they be lost. However, the few times that I have put in a claim for a lost package, payment has been made with no regard to the fact that the contents were coins.

The Internet as a Buying Tool

The local coin shop is most likely now an online coin store too. Many dealers report that the greatest share of their business is through EBay, Online Stores, or websites that allow individuals to purchase coins directly on line from them. Perusing the remaining chapters and text of this resource guide, one will quickly notice that the URL or web address or most companies, clubs, dealers, or numismatic resource areas is now a crucial contact point along with phone numbers and mailing address.

EBay is one of the most exciting options. Direct your web browser to www.ebay.com and either sign up or survey the items for sale. (You'll need to be a formal member to buy or to sell, however). At any one point in time, there may be 250,000 coins up for sale - to the highest bidder. With that many auctions occurring, however, a few cautions are necessary. Most individual coins are described in fairly good detail, and almost everyone includes a picture of the coin, or sets of pictures of the coin showing the mint mark, date, or other areas that could lead the potential buyer to make a decision to bid on the coin. Each seller's reputation is shown along side the coin as a feedback rating. And with this many coins available, there are certainly bargains to be found. Cautions include:

Study the pictures closely, they are almost always photographs of the coin up for sale, but they do not always catch the nuances that could change its value: rim nicks, harsh cleaning, artificial toning, and just plain low resolution photographs. If you have any doubts, talk to the seller before bidding or purchasing a coin. Frequently they will provide additional photographs or details to anyone who requests more information.

Check out the seller's reputation. You can look up basic information about the seller — including feedback — right from the eBay screen. Each seller receives positive or negative feedback after each transaction. A seller with a low number of total feedback scores is most likely a relatively new seller. The seller's profile will tell you when they first signed up to buy or sell on eBay, and display the most recent bits of feedback submitted by people who have either bought items from this person, or sold items to the person. Some people steer clear of sellers with feedback totals under 100. Some will not do business with anyone who has a feedback rating of 98 or less, or who has had more than one negative strikes in the past few months.

Make sure that the seller supports both the return of an item purchased and refunding your money if the coin is not satisfactory. Most sellers list their return policy right on the site where the coin is being sold.

Buying Directly from the Mint

The U.S. Government has become the biggest dealer in the country. So, I suppose, no discussion of how and where to buy coins would be complete unless mention was made of this source.

Should you wish to purchase current mint or proof sets, bullion coins, medals, etc., you will find below an address where you can write to obtain the latest information on products available from the mint. Write to:

U.S. Mint
Customer Care Center
2799 Reeves Rd
Plainfield, IN 46168

CHAPTER 11

HOW TO SELL COINS
A Day in the Life of a Dealer

To understand some of the dimensions of selling the coins we may have lovingly amassed over a lifetime, let us sit with a dealer through a typical day. Such knowledge may also have an impact on how we go about assembling our collection from the start.

Unlike you, a dealer need not be in love with the coins he buys. This gives him or her an entirely different attitude in any transaction. When he looks at the "deal," he wants to be virtually assured that a profit can be made. He must "feed" every coin until the day it is sold. Since his living is based on his judgments, he must "live" with his mistakes in a different way than a collector does.

For some dealers this means making the absolutely lowest offer for a collection that he thinks the seller might accept. Ethics aside, this works sometimes and indeed there are at least some positive things that can be said about such a strategy. I am not recommending this approach and I shall say more about it later.

Well what can a collector expect? The person on the other side of the counter has been in the office since 9 a.m. In the next few hours several calls will be received that are seemingly price inquiries.

"How much will you pay for a 1964 Proof Set?"

"Do you sell silver bars? How much are they?"

"I have a coin the size of a half dollar with a horse on it. What's it worth?"

These are typical. But care must be taken in answering them. Later the proof set is brought in but the coins have been neatly placed in a metal container. Silver has shot up 13 cents an ounce since the inquiry concerning the bars. The owner of the "horse coin" refuses to bring it in, declaring he "does not have the time."

Since it is so often a mistake to answer questions over the phone, especially those concerning price, most any dealer will invite you to come into his shop. There can be slight differences in the condition of even a 1964 Proof Set. There is nothing gained in explaining later that the coins in the set are scratched and, therefore, worth far less than the $10 originally offered.

The silver bullion customer might better have the dynamics of the metals markets explained to her so as not to be disappointed by daily or even hourly price changes.

"Horse coin" questions may be well-intentioned, but are often insensitive to even the barest concerns of etiquette.

Don't blame the dealer who is emphatic about wanting to "see it." It's his only defense. A mark of a genuine offer to sell a coin is to have brought it in. The one person every dealer appreciates is someone who makes it clear that he realizes the dealer's time is at least as important as his own. So if you have decided to dispose of those duplicates, how should you handle it? First call and make an appointment. Put together an inventory of what you wish to sell. A dealer may have no particular interest in what you have for sale. A glance at the inventory can save everyone's time.

Further, unless your intention is to sell the group of coins piecemeal, the question may arise as to what you want for the lot. If you have put together a total of the average retail prices of the coins then at least both buyer and seller have a place to start.

But now here is where things may get difficult. Whether you are paying for an appraisal or not, any offer made by the dealer has a value. It is worth something. For example, in negotiating a price with another buyer, it provides a degree of knowledge that would not otherwise be there. The seller can now deal from somewhat more a position of strength.

Consequently, many dealers are loathing to make an outright offer. Dealers rightly believe that should the seller decline this offer and then seek another; the chance to buy the collection will be lost. The next offer may top the original by some negligible amount. Some dealers respond to this by asking the seller to get several offers and then return. Sometimes it is to the dealer's advantage to make the last offer or at least have the opportunity to top any offers.

Another response on the part of the dealer may be to inquire as to what "ballpark" figure the collector has in mind. This can be a specific amount or percentage of retail. At least now the buyer will have an idea as to whether further discussion is worthwhile. Then too if the two parties are far apart, the dealer has not had to make an offer that proved offensive or ridiculous to the seller.

The situation is complicated when, as often happens, the seller is quite ignorant about the coins he wishes to sell. My advice here is two- part: (1) Ask a disinterested coin collecting party whether the collection or accumulation is worth an appraisal. (2) Assuming the answer is "yes," inquire as to respected dealers in the area and arrange for an appraisal only, as opposed to an offer.

APPRAISED VALUE AND WORTH

An appraisal can be done on an hourly basis or as a percentage of the appraised price. I would expect to pay $20+/hour or anywhere from 2%-5% of the appraised value. Make it clear that you wish to know realistic retail prices. Sometimes an appraisal for insurance purposes can be substantially inflated since in such a case the intention will be to cover all possible replacement costs in full.

Now armed with an appraisal, the seller is not as quite at the mercy of any potential buyer. The "ballpark" figure can be given with some confidence.

And here the seller might expect to receive something around 40-60% for an accumulation of common coins, 65-75% of retail for an intermediate level collection, somewhat more for a specialty collection, up to 90%+ of retail if the group consists mainly of bullion coins. Damaged coins, of course, may sell for only a small fraction of their retail price, if at all.

Selling at Auction

Another avenue for disposing of a collection is through an auction. This method does not, however, shift all decision-making away from the seller. Most auction houses want lots that cannot easily be purchased anywhere else. Of course, these are just the sorts of items that usually make up only a small part of most collections. Run-of-the-mill items will be lumped together in "wholesale" lots, provided the auction house wants them at all.

On the other hand, truly rare items or coins in extraordinarily high grades should probably not be sold anywhere else but at an auction, especially where the seller is ignorant of the market. In such an arena the seller can be virtually guaranteed that the prices realized will be competitive. This is extremely important when condition is so critical in determining price. One "nice" uncirculated Standing Liberty quarter can be worth $150; another $2,500. The uneducated eye certainly cannot see the difference. Now the auctioneer and all those potential bidders make independent assessments. Their joint decision cannot help but be very close to the true condition/value of the coin.

As a seller at an auction, you can expect to receive the price realized on any lot less a 10 or 15% commission to the auction house. On very large groups or expensive rarities the commission can be negotiated. I have even seen consignments accepted for 0% commission. In these cases the firm conducting the auction is willing to forego the commission from the seller because that received from the buyer alone makes selling the coin worthwhile.

It is also not uncommon for an auction house to advance the seller a portion of the estimated value of the coins consigned. Then again, months can often go by between the time the coins are sent and the time when a final settlement is made.

The consignor should make himself very aware of the specific terms of the auction house, and there are considerable differences among them. Also, this may not be the preferred method of selling if quick payment is needed.

Buy Ads

A somewhat trickier method by which to sell coins is through the buy ads in collector papers and magazines. In some cases these ads are extensive and list prices and conditions wanted on a variety of different coins. At the very least, familiarizing oneself with these prices will give a seller a good idea about what coins are being sought and the range of prices offered.

Such sources provide an outlet for quantities of similar coins that often make up an accumulation. A local dealer cannot always use multiples of the same issue.

Dealing by mail is however associated with a bit of apprehension. I do not recommend large initial shipments to buyers working out of a post office box. Better to gradually get a feel for the grading standards and dollar limits of the person at the other end. Many ads reserve the right to limit quantities. Others state that "over graded coins will be returned at the sender's expense."

As a matter of practice, buyers of this sort are not always happy to receive lists of inventories to evaluate. Nor do they take kindly to a sender's demand to buy all or nothing from a shipment.

Do not be surprised should part of the shipment be returned and only a few of the invoiced coins have been purchased. In such a case you must decide if the buyer is engaging in a practice called "cherry picking," where only the coins at the high end of a grading range have been selected; or whether it is truly the case that those returned were over graded and/or the buyer received too great a response from the ad and is now overstocked on some issues.

Only after dealing for a time in this way will you get a feel for the integrity or idiosyncrasies of the buyer. This method of selling coins would be more appropriate for a collector who intends to sell over a number of transactions. The one-time seller will be "shooting in the dark" with unhappy results.

Buy prices must be regarded by the collector as ephemeral. They represent a price that a buyer is willing to pay at some given period of time. Weeks pass before the ad appears in print. Financial positions change.

I think it always makes sense to give the advertiser a preliminary call. Ask questions about when payment can be expected, what quantities are being sought, what other items are needed. A $2 call can go a long way toward preventing the inevitable anxiety that arises when you've heard nothing three weeks after making a shipment.

Also, follow the normal good practices of securely wrapping the package. Remember coins are heavy and extra precautions should be taken. Include a copy of an invoice. Fully insure or register the package. (See our earlier discussion in Chapter 10 for mailing costs).

Undoubtedly it is aggravating to send coins in the mail and then weeks later receive most of them back with counteroffers. But the same sort of things can happen face to face with a dealer. I believe the best attitude to have is that if you think coin "X" is really worth $8 then there is no reason to take less for it. A buyer will certainly be discovered.

Advertised buy offers do tend to raise expectations since something like an actual price is being quoted. Maybe that is why a mail deal gone sour can be so upsetting.

OTHER COLLECTORS

Some success is achievable by offering coins to collector friends, relatives, and club members. However, they may be willing to purchase only coins within their collecting interests. And, too, they are less likely to be in a cash position necessary for the purchase of a large collection or individual rarities.

CHAPTER 12

HOBBY OR INVESTMENT
History and Aesthetics

Some suggest that sooner or later every serious collector has to face up to the fact that his collection represents some considerable wealth. As the years go by, a casual inventory of a collection or accumulation can produce surprising results. Even if the coins purchased are able to be sold at only 65% of the price paid, putting aside any modest appreciation, your collection may be worth something in the thousands of dollars.

Although there is a tendency to ignore this accumulated wealth, it is nevertheless clear that the time can soon come when the collection must be understood as some sort of investment. Such a realization need not diminish the enjoyment that coin collecting brings. However, coin collecting is unlike other hobbies where the monies paid out are rarely recovered.

A photography enthusiast usually has no expectation of selling his photos, and, therefore, is even less concerned about any possible appreciation in the value of his productions. People who build and fly radio-controlled airplanes probably never sell at a profit. A more realistic expectation is that their work of several months will be destroyed on the runway someday.

Coins are different. The supply is fixed or diminishing. And the presumption is that with new collectors the demand for many coins will increase.

Different series can be popular for years and then it seems almost as if no one is interested in them. Lincoln pennies, silver dollars, and gold coins have all experienced times when they were "hot" and times when they were "not."

The average collector may well pay little attention to such trends. And if one's collecting interests do not extend to uncirculated coins or coins costing over $50 or so, probably no great price is paid for being oblivious to the possible investment angle to coin collecting.

But, then, too, part of the joy of collecting can be found in selling coins at a profit. Since the 1960s, pressure has come from a variety of sources to treat coin investing as somehow analogous to the stock market. Coin World and many other publications and newsletters now have quite extensive coin "trends" sections. Some endeavors are made to plot individual price increases and decreases over as short a period as a week. Excellent books now exist on treating coins as long term investments much as one would buy real estate (See, for example, the Q. David Bowers book mentioned in Chapter 9).

Investment fever is not an uncommon phenomenon. Buying an extra roll or two of an item that is perceived as "under priced" in the market is one response. And should the retail price of these items shoot up, the effect is seductive. Price appreciation can easily become the entire goal of one's collecting interests.

To avoid reducing coin collecting to nothing but dollars and cents, an effort should be made to see the coins in one's collection for their historical and aesthetic significance.

Interesting historical questions might include researching the various changes in the metal content of certain denominations. Why was the alloy for the Lincoln cent and Jefferson nickel changed during World War II? Was it a necessary change? Why did the Trade Dollar contain more silver than a regular silver dollar? Why are little chop marks often found on these coins?

Why do some coins have arrows next to the date? Why were weird denominations like three-cent and twenty-cent pieces minted? Why were no gold coins minted for circulation after 1933?

Coins can be viewed as miniature sculptures in limited editions. The sheer beauty of a lightly toned uncirculated Liberty Standing quarter can be breath-taking.

Studying a coin closely can bring to one's attention design features never really noticed. Studying the different patterns considered can give one an insight into the reasons for the design that an engraver finally selected.

An even closer inspection of a coin can often give clues concerning the conditions under which it was struck. Had the die cracked or been damaged in some other way? Had it been re-engraved as a shortcut in the striking process? Many coins have one date engraved over another.

Again certain metals seem to function as better mediums for the striking of the details of an engraving. Our recent clad coins appear dull and flat even before they can be circulated. They pale in comparison to high grade Barber coins. They make even a Franklin half dollar look like Michelangelo's David.

An appreciation of these sorts of considerations provides a depth to one's collecting interests. The question, "How much is it worth?" can be considered superfluous.

A Peek at the History of Coin Price Appreciation

As I look back, many coins, especially the most easily acquired the ones that probably form the nucleus of most accumulations, have not done particularly well over the years. Unless one is able to anticipate significant commodity price changes, the prospect of making money in ordinary obsolete coinage is remote.

On the other hand, assuming the ability to grade uncirculated coins and an access to coins that are truly rare, we may well have another matter.

The charts found below attempt to plot price changes of several typical coins over the years.

1. Large Cent F (Coronet type coin)
2. 1909S Lincoln Cent F
3. Liberty Nickel BU (Type coin)
4. 1950D Nickel BU
5. 1916D Dime G
6. 1796 Quarter G (Type coin)
7. Bust Half F (Type coin)
8. Trade Dollar XF (Type coin)
9. 1895P Morgan Dollar PR
10. $1 Gold VF (Type 1)
11. $20 Saint-Gaudens XF-AU (Type coin)
12. Isabella Quarter MS60
13. 1950 Proof Set PR60

The chart below sets out the value of each of these coins for the years 1962, 1975, 1988 and 2008. These years were within relatively stable periods for the coin market and give us, therefore, a reasonably accurate picture of how an investment might have performed over the past 40 years. The above coins were selected as a representative selection, with the exception of the 1895P Morgan dollar and the 1796 quarter, that would turn up in the average person's collection. This comparison also shows that the dramatic price changes occurred in more expensive coins.

Coin	1962	1975	1988	2008
Large Cent F	$2.00	$5.00	$7.00	$35.00
1909S Lincoln Cent F	12.00	20.00	50.00	115.00
Liberty Nickel MS60	10.00	45.00	125.00	80.00
1950D Nickel MS60	5.00	9.00	8.00	20.00
1916D Dime G	40.00	80.00	325.00	900.00
1796 Quarter G	300.00	750.00	3100.00	10000.00
Bust Half F	4.00	20.00	35.00	75.00
Trade Dollar XF	12.00	70.00	150.00	155.00
1895P Morgan Dollar PR60	850.00	6000.00	15000.00	35500.00
$1 Gold VF	25.00	100.00	150.00	175.00
$20 Saint-Gaudens XF-AU	50.00	300.00	550.00	925.00
Isabella Quarter MS60	40.00	175.00	500.00	600.00
1950 Proof Set PR60	55.00	115.00	525.00	650.00
Totals	1405.00	7689.00	20525.00	49,230.00

Even if one were to assume a return of 75% of the above amount after commissions, etc., the original investment would have increased by roughly 20 times. If one were to remove the two most expensive items the investment would still have increased by 6 times. What other investments have performed so well?!

The promise of fantastic profits can always be established by looking selectively at the past. Indeed, some coins have done very well over the years. Logically, there is nothing that necessitates that this will continue to happen. The forces are largely psychological and, consequently, quite unpredictable.

One need only look at what happened to coin and metal prices in the wake of the stock market "crash" on October 19, 1987. Historically, hard assets have often leaped in value given uncertainty in financial assets. But, six months later, the drop in the market had not appreciably affected coin or bullion prices. If anything, both were somewhat lower.

My experience has been that those who come to coin collecting primarily as an investment vehicle soon leave greatly disappointed. They are preyed upon by investment promoters, take shortcuts instead of learning how to grade coins, and in virtually every case, leave the hobby in disgust.

Even for the proficient and wary, investing in coins is full of minefields. A number of years ago, the American Numismatic Association Certification Service drastically revised its grading standards, especially for uncirculated grades. And, of course, the standards were toughened, leaving many who had purchased supposedly MS65 coins holding very expensive MS63s.

Even now, when a coin is purchased which is certified as to its grade, the purchaser will do well to act with care. The year it was graded is a factor for deciding how it might currently be graded and priced. For example, some dealers advertise to buy 1982 ANA graded coins at 50% of what they will pay for those graded in 1986.

Such a change in direction does nothing if not shake the confidence of those who primarily hope to profit from the coins they have acquired. It also points up that grading is at its foundations and art not a science, and worse, an art dependent upon the supply and demand forces in the market.

When demand is high and the market is bullish the tendency is to push the limits of previous grading conventions. When a buyer's market returns, prices fall and standards rise.

One beneficial role that investors play in the market is setting aside rolls, even bags, of current coinage for future generations. Unless there had been someone with an eye toward investment it is doubtful that we now could enjoy the variety of well-preserved coins at today's reasonable prices. If anything, over the long run, investors probably keep the prices of coins down.

COIN INVESTMENT AS A HEDGE

During the period 1977-1980, at which time the country was experiencing significant inflation, a huge run up in the price of gold and silver took place, and many predictions were made concerning the total collapse of financial markets.

Some suggested that silver and gold in coin form should be made a part of any thinking person's portfolio as a hedge against disaster.

In this scenario, paper money would quickly become worthless. The image of wagons of Marks, circa 1923, was useful. Bartering, initially at least, would be difficult since communications would be poor or non-existent. Consequently, what was needed was a reliable, negotiable, small unit of real value. Presumably gold and silver bars would need assaying. Obsolete 90% silver coins would become the perfect vehicle. A hedge against disaster.

To some this plan made sense, although planning for such an eventuality would have, by now, over 30 years later, involved considerable cost.

Decision-making in this area is reminiscent of good science fiction. I suppose the best one could do, would be to make a reasonable estimate of the probability of a disaster of this magnitude. Then apply that probability in percentage terms to one's own wealth and security quotient.

For example, if one thought the chances of financial collapse were something on the order of 5% over the next five years, then putting 5% of one's assets into disaster-oriented "hard" assets would seem appropriate. A one-year's food supply, a shotgun and shells, 100 cords of wood, and $500 face in Roosevelt dimes might be bought in for simple peace of mind.

But do coins make sense as a hedge in more normal times? My answer would be "yes," but only if I were speaking of a very astute buyer. This buyer would certainly have to know how to accurately grade coins. He or she would almost as certainly have to be able to make purchases at or near wholesale levels. Knowledge of the marketplace would be helpful but not an absolute necessity.

Coins, especially rare ones, can at times present a liquidity problem. They do not trade as easily as stocks and bonds due partly to their individual uniqueness. A buyer must be sought out. Even then prices are usually negotiated.

But for an investor willing to be patient and able to avoid any pressure for quick liquidation, coins provide an interesting but not easy alternative to more traditional and orthodox investments.

The easier path to coin investment, and a much more precarious one, is to turn over the decision-making process to a reputable coin dealer/investment advisor. The commissions charged with this approach are considerable. Breaking even, that is, price appreciation in an amount equal to the purchase charges, may take several years (Sales taxes present an additional hurdle to profit realization).

And remember all this is said within the context of reliance on a dealer's reputation. If one peruses the advertisers of 1963, very few names survive.

Further, most dealers are automatically in a conflict of interest situation. It is easier to tout coins that can be acquired relatively easily rather than attempt to buy for one's clients coins that are always in short supply.

And when you think of it, if any person, dealer or otherwise, really was convinced that a coin were going to perform extremely well over the next five to 10 years, why would he sell it? That unwillingness to take anything like the risk that the client is asked to take makes any advice rather suspect.

CHAPTER 13

WEB SITES

ollowing are listings of Retail Coin Collector and Coin Auction Web Sites, Coin Organization and Convention Information Sites, Coin Certification Sites, Hobby Publications and Numismatic News Groups which might prove informative and useful for both the beginning and advanced numismatist.

Retail Coin Collector & Coin Auction Sites

ANA Dealership A Listing: American Numismatic Association Member, Professional Coin Collectors and Dealers. This site contains an extensive listing of coin dealers in alphabetical order by state. All are members of the association. This provides some degree of safety in coin transactions.
SITE: http://anamarket.money.org/index_a.html

Bowers and Merena
SITE: http://web.coin-universe.com/bowers/Have_a_Great_Time.html

Coin World Online
This site provides thousands of online classified ads for numismatic purchases.
SITE: http://www.coinworld.com/

Coin Universe
This site is an easy link to the home pages of many dealers.
SITE: http://www.coin-universe.com/

EBay Coins
Provides thousands of coin offerings and an online auction.
SITE: http://coins.ebay.com/

Heritage Rare Coins: Rare Coins and Numismatic Auctions
Heritage Rare Coin Gallery is the largest rare coin dealer in the world with $20 million inventory specializing in US rare coins, world gold coins, and buying and selling rare coins.
SITE: http://www.heritagecoin.com/

Jake's Marketplace, Inc.
SITE: http://www.jakesmp.com/

LEGACY—Rare Coins & Bullion
SITE: http://www.legacycoins.com/

Spectrum Numismatics
SITE: http://www.coincity.com/Spectrum/default.htm

Steinbergs Gold Coins
SITE: http://www.steinbergs.com/

The U.S. Mint
SITE: http://www.usmint.gov/

Coin Organization & Convention Information Sites

American Numismatic Association

The ANA, a non-profit, educational organization chartered by Congress is dedicated to the collection and study of coins, paper money, tokens and medals, and was created for the benefit of its members and the numismatic community. The organization provides a number of conventions with courses throughout the year. Check the site for dates and places.
SITE: http://www.money.org

PNG

Professional Numismatists Guild 3950 Concordia Lane Fallbrook, CA 92028 (760) 728-1300 FAX (760) 728-8507 E-mail: info@pngdealers.com. This organization has strict requirements for dealer members and includes a listing of these dealers.
SITE: http://www.pngdealers.com

Coin Clubs

Lists coin clubs and shows by locality.
SITE: http://www.money.org/ana_custom/club_search/club_search.cfm

Coin Certification Sites

ANACS

P.O. Box 182141 Columbus, Ohio, 43218-2141, (800) 888-1861.
SITE: http://www.anacs.com

Professional Coin Grading Service, Inc.
SITE: http://www.pcgs.com

Independent Coin Grading Company
(ICG), 7901 East Belleview Ave.,
SITE: http://www.icgcoin.com/index.htm

Numismatic Guaranty Corporation of America (NGC)
SITE: http://www.ngccoin.com/census_report.cfm

HOBBY PUBLICATIONS

Coin Dealer Newsletter
A serious resource for wholesale rare coin prices, bullion values and industry news, CDN publishes the Certified Coin Dealer newsletter, Bluesheet; the Currency Dealer newsletter, Greensheet; and the Numismatic Dealer Directory, Greysheet.
SITE: http://www.greysheet.com

Coin World Weekly
Weekly numismatic magazine and marketplace for young and old coin collectors. Besides industry news, the site features forums, club links, convention and bourse dates, numismatic trivia and games.
SITE: http://www.coinworld.com

Numismatic News
Weekly numismatic newspaper includes coin ads and articles with an extensive classified section.
Site: http://www.numismaticnews.net

CHAPTER 14

SOURCES REFERENCE

This chapter provides the reader easy access to the acquisition of numismatic information.

1. COIN PAPERS AND MAGAZINES

COINage Magazine
www.coinagemag.com
290 Maple Ct. #232
Ventura, CA 93003

Coins Magazine
www.coinsmagazine.net
700 E. State Street
Iola, WI 54990

Numismatic News Weekly
www.numismaticnews.com
700 E. State Street
Iola, WI 54990

Coin World
 www.coinworld.com
P.O. Box 926
Sidney, OH 45365

The Numismatist
www.money.org
818 N. Cascade Ave.
Colorado Springs, CO 80903

2. BOOKS—GENERAL

American Guide to U.S. Coins. Charles F. French. Simon & Schuster, Inc., New York (1988).

Annual Report of the Director of the Mint. United States Mint, Department of the Treasury, Washington, DC 20220.

Coin Collecting Made Easy: Basic Knowledge for the Coin Collector and Investor. Staff of Coin World. Amos Press Inc., Sidney, OH (Fourth printing 1987).

Coin World Almanac. Staff of Coin World. Amos Press Inc., Sidney, OH (sixth edition 1990). The Catalogue and Encyclopedia of U.S. Coins. Don Taxey. Scott Publishing Co., New York (1976).

A Guide Book of U.S. Coins. R.S. Yeoman. Western Publishing Co., Racine, WI (1988).

The Macmillan Encyclopedic Dictionary of Numismatics. Richard C. Doty. Macmillan Publishing Co., New York (1982).

Numismatic Art in America. Cornelius Vermeule. Belknap Press, Cambridge, MA (1971). U.S. Coins of Value. Norman Stack. Dell Books, New York (1988).

U.S. Mint and Coinage. Don Taxey. Durst Numismatic Publications, New York (1983).

3. Books—Grading

Grading Coins: A Collection of Readings. Edited by Richard Bagg and James Jelinski. J. Essex Publications, Portsmouth, NH (1977).

A Guide to Grading United States Coins. Martin R. Brown and John W. Dunn. General Distributors Inc., Denison TX (1980).

NCI Grading Guide. James L. Halperin. Ivy Press, Dallas, TX (1986).

Photograde19th Edition. James F. Ruddy. Bowers and Ruddy Galleries, Irvine, CA (2005).

Official American Numismatic Association Grading Standards for United States Coins. 6th Edition ANA and Western Publishing Co., Atlanta, GAI (2006).

4. Books—Specialized

American Half Cents. Roger S. Cohen. Wigglesworth & Ghatt Co., Arlington, VA (1982).

America's Copper Coinage 1783-1857. American Numismatic Association (1985).

The Comprehensive Catalogue and Encyclopedia of U.S. Morgan and Peace Silver Dollars. Leroy C. Van Allen and George Mallis. Arco Publishing Co., New York (1976).

The Early Coins of America. Sylvester S. Crosby. Quarterman Publications, New York (1983, a reprint of a 1875 edition).

Early Half Dollar Varieties. Al C. Overton. Colorado Springs, CO (1970).

The Early Quarters of the United States. A.W. Browning. Sanford J. Durst Numismatic Publications, New York (1977, a reprint of a 1925 edition).

Early United States Dimes: 1796-1937. David J. Davis, and others. John Reich Collectors Society (1984).

The Encyclopedia of United States Silver & Gold Commemorative Coins. Walter Breen and Anthony Swiatek. Arco Publishing Inc. (1981).

Encyclopedia of United States Liberty Seated Dimes. Kamal M. Ahwash. Kamal Press (1977).

The Fantastic 1804 Dollar. Kenneth E. Bressett and Eric P. Newman. Whitman Publishing Co., Racine, WI (1962).

The Morgan and Peace Dollar Textbook. Wayne Miller. Adam Smith Publishing Co., Metairie, LA (1982).

Penny Whimsy. William H. Sheldon. Quarterman Publications Inc., Lawrence, MA (1983, reprint of a 1958 edition).

Standing Liberty Quarters. J.H. Cline. Cline's Rare Coins, Palm Harbor, FL (1986).

United States Copper Cents 1816-1857. Howard R. Newcomb. Quarterman Publications Inc., Lawrence, MA (1981, reprint of a 1944 edition).

United States Copper Coins—An Action Guide to Collectors and I nvestors. Q. David Bowers. Bowers and Merena Inc., Wolfeboro, NH (1984).

United States Gold Coins, an Illustrated History. Q. David Bowers. Bowers and Ruddy Galleries, Los Angeles (1982).

The United States Half Dimes. Daniel W. Valentine. Quarterman Publications, Lawrence, MA (1975, a reprint of a 1931 edition).

The United States Trade Dollar. John M. Willem. Sanford J. Durst Numismatic Publications, New York (1983, a reprint of a 1959 edition.

The Walking Liberty Half Dollar. Anthony Swiatek. Sanford J. Durst Numismatic Publications, New York (1983).

5. Books—Errors

The Encyclopedia of Double Dies, (2 Vols.). John A. Wexler. Robert C. Wilharm News Printing Co. Inc., Fort Worth, TX (1978 and 1981).

How Error Coins Are Made at the U.S. Mints. Arnold Margolis. Heigh Ho Printing Co., Newbury Park, CA (1981).

Modern Mint Mistakes. Philip Steiner and Michael Zimpfer. Whispering Pines Printing, Indiana (1974-60).

Official Price Guide to Mint Errors and Varieties. Mark Hudgeons. House of Collectibles Inc., Orlando, FL (1985).

The RPM Book. John A. Wexler and Tom Miller. Lonesome John Publishing Co., Newbury Park, CA (1983).

The Cherrypickers' Guide to Rare Die Varieties, Volume 1 Bill Fivaz and JT Stanton. Stanton Books and Supplies, Inc. Savannah GA 31416-2177 (2000)

The Cherrypickers' Guide to Rare Die Varieties, Volume I1 Bill Fivaz and JT Stanton. Whitman Publishing Company, Atlanta, GA 30329   (2006)

6. Books—Counterfeits

Counterfeit Detection. (2 Vols.) Staff of the American Numismatic Association Certification Service. American Numismatic Association, Colorado Springs, CO (1983 and 1987).

Counterfeits of U.S. Coins. Larry Spanbauer. Service Litho-Print Inc., Oshkosh, WI (1975).

Detecting Counterfeit Coins. (Book 1). John Devine. Heigh Ho Printing Co., Newbury Park, CA (1975).

Detecting Counterfeit Gold Coins. (Book 2). John Devine. Heigh Ho Printing Co., Newbury Park, CA (1977).

7. Books—Investing

The Big Silver Melt. Henry A. Merton. MacMillan Publishing Co., New York (1983).

The Coin Collector's Survival Manual. Scott A. Travers. Arco Publishing Co., New York (1987).

High Profits From Rare Coin Investment. Q. David Bowers. Bowers and Merena Galleries Inc., Wolfeboro, NH (1983).

Investing in Rare Coins. Dennis Steinmetz. Steinmetz Coins and Currency, Lancaster, PA (1981).

The Investor's Guide to United States Coins. Neil S. Berman and Hans M. F. Schulman. Coin & Currency Institute Inc., New York (1986).

The Official Investor's Guide To Gold Coins. Marc Hudgeons. House of Collectibles, New York (1985).

Survive and Win in the Inflationary '80's. Howard J. Ruff. Warner Books, New York (1982).

8. Newsletters

The Coin Dealer Newsletter
Box 11099
Torrance, CA 90510

The Certified Coin Dealer Newsletter
Box 11099
Torrance, CA 90510

There are scores of other newsletters on the market. Often, however, these are put together by firms with coins for sale.

9. Professional Organizations and Associations

The American Numismatic Association
818 N. Cascade Ave.
Colorado Springs, CO 80903

The American Numismatic Society
c/o Secretary of the Society
Broadway Between 155th and 156 Streets
New York, NY 10032
Central States Numismatic Society
P.O. Box 223
Hiawatha, IA 52233
Combined Organization of Numismatic
Error Collectors of America
Route 2, Box 6
Andover, SD 57422

Industry Council for Tangible Assets
25 E. St. N.W. Eighth Floor
Washington, DC 20001
Liberty Seated Collectors Club
5718 King Arthur Drive
Kettering, OH 45429

New England Numismatic Association
P.O. Box 99
West Roxbury, MA 02132

Numismatic Literary Guild
P.O. Box 970218
Miami, FL 33197

Pacific Coast Numismatic Society
610 Arlington Ave.
Berkeley, CA 94707

Professional Numismatists Guild, Inc.
P.O. Box 430
Van Nuys, CA 91408

Society of Philatelists and Numismatists
1929 Millis St.
Montebello, CA 90640

Society for U.S. Commemorative Coins
912 Bob Wallace Ave.
Huntsville, AL 35801

10. Grading and Authentication Services

Numismatic Guarantee Corporation of America
P.O. Box 4776
Sarasota, FL 34230

Professional Coin Grading Service
P.O. Box 9458
Newport Beach, CA 92658

ANACS
P.O. Box 6000
Englewood, CO 80155

ICG — Independent Coin Grading
P.O. Box 276000
Tampa, FL 33688
www.ICGCOIN.com

CHAPTER 15

COUNTERFEIT COINS

Collectors and dealers sooner or later encounter counterfeit coins. Two kinds exist. One is made for circulation and intended to cheat the public. Coins of this sort are very crudely made usually from base metals and will more likely be higher denomination coins. You can realize that it would hardly be worthwhile to go to the trouble of illegally reproducing coins of lesser value.

In 30 years of sorting through coins from circulation I have only encountered two or three pieces that were counterfeits of this sort. My view would be that such coins are so seldom seen that they probably have some value as curiosities. I would think it silly to spend them. Having several specimens as examples is worth more than any monetary loss one would suffer for having accepted them.

Both ways of producing counterfeits of this sort are readily detectable. One process is to cast the coin by taking an impression of the genuine one and using that as a mold. This counterfeit has a soapy feeling, and under a ten-power magnifying glass you can see pit marks made by air bubbles.

The second process is to produce an electrotype, made by taking an electrolytic impression of both sides of the coin. The counterfeiter then has two shells which are glued together with a base metal in the hollow center. The type of counterfeit is detectable by the false ring which the fake coin usually has. Unless the job is very skillfully done, you can also see a line around the edge of the coin where the two halves were joined.

The other kind of counterfeit is intended to cheat collectors. These usually involve altering genuine coins. For example, should one be able to successfully remove the "D" mint mark from a 1922D cent, the coin might be passable for the much rarer 1922 cent produced without a mint mark due to a defective die.

Other coins can be altered by adding a mint mark. The 1909S VDB is a notorious example. And any collector should be careful in purchasing one.

With sophisticated minting facilities, coins of even moderate numismatic value have in the past and are currently being produced in order to dupe collectors. Purchasing gold coins has become something of a nightmare. Such coins as the $5 Indian have an incused design making them relatively easy to reproduce. Many gold coins are found in finenesses matching the genuine article. Thus the whole idea is to cheat the person willing to pay above the gold content value of the coin. The face value of these counterfeits is, of course, well below the gold value. When these coins were circulating there was little incentive to counterfeit them. Rather, one was more likely then to encounter a gold-plated Liberty nickel dated 1883 without "Cents." A change was made that year to place "Cents" on the coin so as to preclude a gold-plated version being passed for a genuine $5.00 gold piece.

Only experience will give you the ability to detect counterfeits. I do not mind saying that I have been fooled. After all, the counterfeiter keeps up on the state of the art and in some ways has a greater incentive to keep his skills honed. In the near future it is not inconceivable that the quality of the product could surpass that of the genuine article if predatory foreign mints are permitted to operate with no restrictions. Such attempts have already been alleged.

CHAPTER 16

SLABS

Encapsulated coins (slabs) have become an integral part of the coin collecting world. There are some collectors who will only buy coins that have been authenticated and graded by a third party service. Recently I bought a complete Lincoln Cent collection from an estate I was asked to appraise and immediately sold this complete set of Lincoln Cents from 1909 to 1970 to one of my regular customers. My examination of the coins suggested that they were all nice, original coins. The woman who bought the collection brought the 1909 S VDB back to me, questioning the authenticity of the coin. The general rule of thumb in this situation is that the coin be sent to one of the grading services for authentication. If the coin turns out to be authentic, the person who contests the coin (in this case, the buyer) would pay for the certification fees. If the coin were not authentic, the seller (me) would bear the costs. Lo and behold, the coin came back as a 1909 S with an "added" VDB. Obviously a counterfeit/forgery coin. I purchased a replacement coin from a dealer friend of mine to replace the coin, but now the buyer was a little hesitant. So, of course, we sent this coin off to NGC and a few weeks later the coin came back as a 1909 VDB with an added S. URGHHHH. In the end, I purchased an ANACS certified 1909 S VDB coin that we could all agree was in the proper condition and authentic. I know that I will never try to sell a key date, high value coin such as this one unless it has been graded and encapsulated by a reputable third party grading service.

Here is how these services work: When a buyer and seller meet and try to agree on a price for a coin, authenticity and grade are often at issue. Experienced buyers and sellers may likely have no problems in this regard. But sometimes, it is critical to be able to tell, with certainty, whether a coin is a counterfeit or has been altered. Grading, especially of mint state coins, takes years of experience. Large amounts of money can be at stake. That altered 1909SVDB Cent you purchased raw (unslabbed) for $450 has little or no value. Since this coin is a common target for alteration, my advice would be to never purchase it unslabbed. A Liberty $20 gold piece is common in AU and commands a price of about $1000. In MS65 it can easily be sold for $3000+. The differences are subtle. Getting expert opinions makes good sense.

The process of submission to an authentication service is simple. Information on four services is found below. For PCGS and NGC, the coins must be submitted through an authorized dealer, unless one is a member of the American Numismatic Association. ANACS and PCI take coins directly.

When the coin reaches the service it is examined by several graders. The consensus opinion is the grade given to the coin. It is then sealed in a reasonably airtight plastic holder. The date, denomination, and grade are placed on the holder, as well as the logo of the grading service. I contend that the prices charged are very reasonable and range from $10.00 to $25. Express service can cost $70 or more. I further contend that the services have been a great boon to coin collecting, as it greatly reduces the possibility of fraud and overgrading.

That is not to say that there are not some disadvantages to slabs.

1. The grade is not a guarantee. Differences of opinion are still possible and I have seen coins in slabs that I believed to be overgraded. Knowledge of grading is still important, although probably less so. (Authenticity is another matter. Grading services will refund something approaching the dealer buy price for a coin later determined to be inauthentic.)

2. Copper coins especially are susceptible to changes such as spotting and corrosion even in a tightly sealed holder. My experience has been that the services will not guarantee the continued condition of such coins. This is important since the price difference between a red (brightly copper-colored) cent and a brown (chocolate-colored) one can be enormous.

3. Aesthetically, "entombing" a coin, as some refer to it, takes some of the fun out of collecting. An artificial barrier is created between owner and owned. Holding a gold piece in your hand is a different, and less satisfying, experience as compared to possessing it in a slab.

4. No albums currently exist that do aesthetic justice to slabbed coins. The enjoyment of seeing that entire set of Bust Half Dollars in a book is lost.

On balance, however, the advantages of slabbing outweigh these small disadvantages. Certainly, I would advise having any coin slabbed that may be worth $200 or more, should there be any question about genuineness or grade.

One last comment on slabbing: A common practice among dealers and some collectors involves resubmissions of slabbed coins if the grade received is less than expected. Where prices take huge leaps on only slight grading differences, the incentive is very high to "crack out" the coin and send it in again to the same or different grading service. The fee must be paid again and there is the additional downside risk that the new grade will be a lower one. Those risks usually pale against the upside potential.

NGC and PCGS keep population reports on the coins they grade. The presumption is that these figures can be checked to ascertain the relative scarcity of coins in each grade category. These reports are helpful, but these figures may be somewhat out of line due to resubmissions. If my 1855 O $1 gold coin gets sent in time and time again it may look as if there is a large number of these coins when there is only one.

Following are four services that I would recommend. Each of the following are further identified as the only grading services which eBay allows having their name identified in a coin listing. All other services are not allowed to identify their service and grades in an eBay listing.

ANACS
ANACS
6555 S. Kenton St, Suite 303
Englewood, CO 80111
www.ANACS.com
1-800-888-1861

Coins may be submitted directly to ANACS. Cost of encapsulation: Typically, $10-$21, plus shipping and insurance both ways. Turn around time (including shipping time): Typically 25 days.

Numismatic Guaranty Corporation of America (NGC)
www.ncgcoin.com
P.O. Box 4776
Sarasota, FL 34230

NGC does not accept direct submissions. For a listing of the 1200-plus authorized NGC dealers who can submit your important coins, call 1-800-NGC-COIN. The American Numismatic Association has a special relationship with NGC. Members of the American Numismatic Association can submit their coins to that organization. The ANA then sends the coins to NGC. Submission forms are found in every issue of the ANA journal, The Numismatist. Cost of encapsulation: Typically, $15-$25, plus shipping and insurance both ways. Turn around time (including shipping time): Typically 30 days. Advantage: One of the two most widely accepted grading services.

Professional Coin Grading Service (PCGS)
www.pcgs.com
Box 9458
Newport Beach, CA 92658
1-800-447-8848

PCGS does not accept direct submissions accept from members of the American Numismatic Association. For a list of authorized dealers call the number above. Cost of encapsulation: Typically, $25.00, plus shipping and insurance both ways. Turn around time (including shipping time): Typically 30 days. Advantage: One of the two most widely accepted grading services.

Independent Coin Grading (ICG)
www.pcgs.com
7901 East Belleview Ave. Suite 50
Englewood, Co. 80111 877-221-4424
303-221-4424
303-221-5524 (fax)

GLOSSARY

Base Metal
Metal other than precious metal (silver, gold, platinum) used to manufacture coins.

Blank
A planchantthat has been further prepared for the coining process.

Braided Hair Type
Middle 19th century type where hair of Liberty is worn up in braids.

Bullion Coin
A coin minted more for the exchange of units of precious metal than for the purposes of commerce.

Bust Type
Showing only the head and shoulder of a figure.

Cameo Proof
A proof coin where the contrast between the design and field is so remarkable that the design often appears to stand out as if on a black background.

Clad
Recent coinage, since 1965, composed of copper and nickel in a sandwich fashion such that the nickel gives the coin a silvery appearance somewhat like previous silver coinage it was meant to replace.

Classic Head Type
A style of the bust of Liberty used in the early 19th century.

Coin
A piece of metal, wood or plastic with a design and legend, intended for use as money.

Common Type
Refers to the least expensive date of a particular design.

Commemorative
A special coin, celebrating a person, place or event.

Condition
Usually refers to the amount of wear or absence of wear a coin has had. Also may take into account any damage or special eye appeal a coin may have.

Coronet Type
A style of bust of Liberty used in the early to mid 19th century.

Cull
Damaged or otherwise very low grade coin. May have bullion value or some numismatic value if it is rare.

Die
The form from which coins are struck.

Draped Bust Type
An early Liberty type where the bust is covered with a loosely fitting gown.

Field
The background behind the principal figure in a coin design.

Fineness
The proportion of precious metal to base metal in a coin.

Flowing Hair Type
An early Liberty type coin where the hair is not braided or covered.

Fractional Currency
Paper money issued in amounts less than one dollar.
Inscription
All lettering that appears on either the obverse or reverse of a coin.

Impaired
Referring to a proof coin that has seen wear.

Lettered Edge
Inscription on the edge of a coin. Found especially on our early coinage prior to the use of reeding.

Liberty Cap
A bust of Liberty wearing a distinctive cap.

Liberty Seated
An allegorical figure of Liberty seated, used on our coinage throughout the middle portions of the 19th century.

Liberty Standing
An allegorical figure of the Goddess of Liberty standing, found on the quarter dollar of 1916-1930.

Liberty Walking
An allegorical figure of the Goddess of Liberty walking, found on the half dollar of 1916-1947 and the silver $1 bullion coin 1986-date.

Medal
A metal piece with no legal tender status used to commemorate some person, place, or event.

Milled edge
Parallel vertical ridges around the edge of a coin called reeds.

Mintage
The number of coins produced in a specified period of time.

Mint Error
Any of a variety of mistakes made by the mint in the production of a coin. See Chapter 4 for types.

Mint mark
Small letters placed on a coin to show the place of mintage.

Mint Set
A group of coins of a given year specially packaged or struck for collectors by the Mint.

Numismatics
The science or study of coins and coin collecting.

Obverse
Front of a coin, the side having the principal design feature. Also referred to as the "heads" side of the coin.

Overdate
Coin made from an altered die, showing traces of a different date.

Pattern
Experimental coin struck to experiment with different metals or designs.

Plainchant
The blank piece of metal on which a coin design is stamped or struck.

Proof
Condition of a coin struck from a polished die, often giving the coin a mirror-like appearance.

Proof Set
A group of coins of a given year specially struck and packaged by the mint under the conditions mentioned above.

Relief
The relation of the design of the coin to the field. Bas-relief means the design features are raised with reference to the field. An incused design means the design features are below the field or recessed.

Reverse
The side opposite the principal design feature. Also referred to as the "tails" side of the coin.

Restrike
A coin made at a later date from an original die.

Symbols
Small additions to the design supplementing the main subject.

Token
A private coin-like piece made for advertising or propaganda purposes.

Type
The kind of coin as designated by the principal design.

Varieties
Minor variations in coins, such as size of letters, size of date, added dot, different metal content, etc.

Notes